Thanks to my wife for allowing this…

Thanks to the Cycling Oracle for facilitating this…

Thanks to Carlos for… just being Carlos.

Available in eBook or Paperback at Amazon.

Email: **steve.holly@outlook.com**

Twitter: **@UncensoredMAMIL**

Prologue: Grumpy

Becoming 40 turned out to be a rather crap experience. And with it, I found myself becoming really, really grouchy…

… I'd noticed a general sense of irritability for a while. But as the clock ticked past this major milestone in my life, and I officially became 'middle-age', the grumpiness morphed into general unhappiness, and then settled into full blown despair. I had initially put this dejection down to the physical changes I was going through such as the greyness rapidly enveloping what little hair I still had, or the frequency with which I needed to drain my bladder in the middle of the night. But deep down I knew it was more than this, more than the fact I looked like I'd just got out of bed regardless of the time of day. I knew it was something far less superficial and, more worryingly, something at my very core.

At first I tried to ignore the feeling and to pretend to be happy going through the motions of a life spent in the mundanity of a work-TV-sleep-repeat cycle. But I could never keep it up for too long before I was back drowning in my inner thoughts. I would find myself spending hours lying in bed, awake, wondering what the hell was wrong with me that I couldn't find happiness in a good job, a lovely home, and a beautiful and caring wife. I'd find myself looking at other people wondering if they were happy with their world and, if so, then why did they find it so easy to achieve? What made them so special to be allowed happiness when all I wanted to do was crawl into the foetal position, or if they were smaller than me, to punch them square in the face?

There was only one thing for it, I needed to find something to feel good about again. I didn't know what, but I needed to find anything that would break this downward spiral. I needed something that would again make me appreciate the many great things I knew I had in my life. I needed a proverbial slap in the face, kick up the arse and a bloody good talking to. I needed time to declutter my mind and to think clearly again. I needed to step out from work, from life, from the humdrum of monotonous living. What I needed, as it transpired, was to go on an epic adventure....

Chapter 1: From Grumpy to a Giddy

'Hey love.' I shouted upstairs in my super-nice tone after taking off my coat, and dumping my bags on the sofa. I was feeling knackered but I knew tonight there was something that needed to be done. During the flight home from Barcelona, after 3 days of drab meetings sat in a customer's unbearably warm offices, I'd finally made a decision about what I wanted to do to try to tackle this cycle of despair I'd been feeling recently, and I'd been spinning a monologue over in my mind ever since. I'd been practising the same opening line word for word, and calculating what the response might be to ensure I was armed and ready for the awkward conversation I knew lay ahead. I knew what to say, I just needed to deliver it before it was too late and I lost my nerve.

'Hey!' Sue shouted back sleepily. It was late and I was glad she was awake. I was also hopeful that she'd been asleep for a while and was therefore likely to be slightly subdued and less angry when I told her my plans. I practised the first line of my speech one last time, built myself up to a bullish yet wafer-thin confidence, and headed upstairs to our bedroom.

'Hey, how was the flight?' she asked, slightly muffled from being wrapped-up tight under the duvet.

'Errm, very good thanks.' I replied with a wobble. Shit, am I ready to do this? I didn't feel anywhere near prepared, but then I knew I never would. I knew it just needed to be done, it was time to man-up and to face the consequences. 'So I've been thinking…'

I could see one of her eyes slowly open under a furrowed brow, the other hidden in the pillow below her face. My wife had heard this conversation opener from me before…

3

I have threatened to do all sorts of weird and wonderful adventures over the years, some have come off, but most have sadly stayed as threats. I wanted to walk to the top of Kilimanjaro in Africa till I found out you need to have an experienced guide to support you due to altitude sickness and other issues you need to contend with. I reckon I could have made it, but having a guru telling me what time to get up, what time to eat, and when to sleep, kind of detracts from the very reason to do it. Not to mention the fact they carry all your gear and set you up in accommodation with more stars than most Blackpool B&B's.

I had also considered walking the length of France along the canals and rivers, from Calais in the north, to the Mediterranean Sea in the south. I was contemplating doing it with my mate Carl (a.k.a. Carlos, given he spent 3 years in Spain). However, spending 2 months on the path with Carlos would have been more of a challenge than the journey itself. It's fair to say Carlos likes a drink, so the thought of traipsing 10 km in the wrong direction just to go to an off-license he remembers passing 3 hours ago, was not something I wanted to do.

'What have you been thinking about?' Sue replied. Her voice sounding rightly apprehensive.

'I think I want to cycle to Gibraltar.'

And with that one line the mood of the moment changed. It was enough to bring her from the comfort of her bed, even given the coldness of the evening. She bolted upright to meet me face to face.

'Where the hell's Gibraltar?!' She was no longer subdued and now well on the way to becoming angry.

'It's a little bit of the UK at the southern tip of Spain. I'm thinking of going on a cycling adventure.'

'Christ! You want to cycle to… to Spain?'

'Gibraltar'

'You want to cycle to Gibraltar?'

'Yeah, I think so.'

'But why Gibraltar?'

'I'm not really sure...'

I'd been thinking about where might be a good destination for a while. But as I'd flown over France and Spain on the way out to Barcelona, I'd noted how the gnarly mountains and wide open spaces 30,000 feet below looked the perfect setting for an adventure. The tiny mountain villages and small country hamlets looked really inviting. My mind brought up images of ambling from place to place, quaffing beer and wine, and entertaining attentive local folk with stories of my heroic adventures. I hadn't been on a bike for a very long time, but I wondered if it was possible to cycle here from my home in the north of England? How experienced a cyclist do you need to be to get that far? Do you really need to be a Lance Armstrong or a Bradley Wiggins? I'm not particularly fit, but I'm not too bad and anyway, I figured I'd just take my time, take plenty of rest, and try to make it and adventure to be cherished at a slow amble, rather than a challenge to be completed at record pace.

'... I guess it just seems right,' I replied, 'it's kind of the end of Europe I suppose.'

'And how are you planning to cycle to Gibraltar? You haven't even got a bike!' This was one of the questions I was ready for.

'Yeah, so I think I'm going to need to buy one.' I'm nothing like what you'd call a cycling enthusiast but I'd recently been reading 'Take a Seat' by a guy called Dominic Gill. He cycled the length of the Americas from the north of Alaska to the southern tip of Argentina on a tandem bike, co-piloted by random strangers along the way. He rated cycling as the best form of transport for an adventure due to it being quick enough for you to cover good distances, and therefore experience different locations, whilst still keeping in touch with your surroundings and being able to appreciate where you are. Even though he is an accomplished cyclist, he still took over 2 years to complete the near 20,000-mile journey, which was clearly going to be a bit too unachievable for me. But a cycling trip did seem like a good choice. I just needed to get a bike first.

'Why the hell do you want to do this anyway? Is everything ok?' She asked. She'd cunningly changed tack from crazy madwoman to caring and empathetic. I was almost taken in by the approach and considered getting into the details for a moment before deciding to stick to my plan of short sharp answers. This conversation was simply about laying out the foundations, the rest could come later when she'd calmed down a bit. And besides, I knew there were far more awkward subjects yet to be discussed.

'I just feel I need to go and do something crazy again...'

It wasn't a great answer, but it was the only one I really had. I simply wasn't sure myself, not exactly anyway. I guess, in part, I was disgruntled with getting to middle-age and finding myself stuck in an unhappy rut. I used to be quite a carefree guy, trying my luck at a number of different things but never lasting long at anything until I got bored and moved on.

I started my working life at a local go-kart track before getting a job as a Butlins Redcoat in sunny Skegness. I got the job on account of my ability to unicycle and to juggle just long enough to convince the interviewer that I was a highly skilled performer.... which I wasn't. It was an interesting job with the days spent keeping the older teenage kids entertained - which actually just meant playing pool with them and letting them smoke - and the nights predominantly filled with keeping drunk parents from arguing after being de-shackled from the duty of responsible parenting. But I was a bit out of my depth in the over-dramatic, razzmatazz-filled world of the holiday-camp entertainer. Whilst I was there to predominantly get drunk and to try and pull lonely, middle-aged, single mothers, most of the other Redcoat's seemed to be there as a springboard for their careers in the entertainment business. They all wanted to be professional singers, dancers or magicians, and seemed to be enveloped by a fake plastic sheen of happiness and superficial friendliness which I could never quite accept and adopt. I found out later that the Entertainments Manager who interviewed me for the role was sacked a short time after my appointment, although it's unclear if this was related.

I also worked as a Casino Croupier and eventually went to work on cruise ships around the Caribbean. The skills to deal the games were easy enough to learn, you just needed to be able to count without using your fingers, and to hide the smug satisfaction of taking money of some sweaty drunk customer who's been screaming down your throat for the last hour. The art of charming was a little trickier for me to learn, but I eventually found that turning your 'Hugh Grant'-ness up to 11 and smiling a lot seemed to work well enough to earn some good money. I visited some truly stunning places whilst on the ships, and met some interesting people from all walks of life, from the super-rich customers dressed in more bling than an 80's rapper, to the menial workers from poorer countries, cleaning and labouring 16 hours-a-day. I managed just 2 years at this, forced to give it up on account of my girlfriend at the time having a yearning for a more sustainable lifestyle and my realisation that I could no longer survive on a diet of cigarettes and alcohol.

Since the adventurous days of my youth, I've settled down to the normality of a regular life and a 'proper career' in the world of I.T.. But I was starting to realise this placid lifestyle was not really quite what I'd hoped for in life. I'd been trying my best to be happy with the 9-to-5 type of lifestyle, trying to fit-in to normality, whatever that was, but I just couldn't shake the thought that life was passing me by. I guess I just wanted to go and find that wild youth again before it was too late.

'Well this is certainly crazy! It's a bloody long way you know. Do you know how far is it?!' She shouted.

'Not really. I know it's about 850 miles or so from Barcelona to Manchester.' I'd seen it on the map shown on the overhead TV's on the plane home. 'So I guess it must be 1500 or so. I'm not really sure.'

'Christ, this is absurd! And what about work, what are you going to do about work?' The madwoman approach had quickly returned – although she had every right to be a tad miffed, especially for what was coming next....

'Quit.'

'Quit! You're going to quit work? How long for?!

'2 months.'

'Christ! Can we even afford it?!'

'I think so.....'

I'd expected this topic to come up and had primed myself with some high-level calculations. I had worked out I could take a maximum of 2 months off. We had enough to cover the bills whilst I didn't work, and to cover a budget of about £1500 for kit, including a bike, and about £30 per day for food and accommodation. I'd considered that I'd spend as many nights as possible wild camping, such as in a farmer's field or on a beach somewhere. The rest of the time I'd be in a campsite or, when I was really flagging, I could treat myself to a cheap hotel. It was going to be tight but if I watched the costs, I figured it should be possible. As for finding a job when I finished, well we'd already discussed me training to be a teacher – in an attempt to find a more rewarding role - so I'd simply get enrolled on a training course to start when I got back. It was now April, so if I got a bike soon, I could get 3 months of training in, have 2 months for the trip, then start teacher training in September.

'Look, I know it all sounds a bit mental,' I continued, 'but I have been giving it some real deep thought. You know I've been looking for a new direction recently and I think this might be it.'

'But I mean... Gibraltar... a bike ride ... quitting work.... I mean....' She

8

then paused for a seemingly perpetual few seconds, the tension making her words linger uncomfortably. And like I'd just pulled the pin in a grenade, I waited for the reaction, waited for it to sink in, for her to work out what to say next. I'd completed my speech and I sat anticipating her next move. Was she ok with it? Did she really think I would do it? Would she object now, or delay and wait for a better opportunity? Eventually, she pressed her lips together and thankfully forced a smile. She wasn't happy, I could tell that much from the death stare. I guess she was probably more annoyed that I'd even consider the idea of being away without her. I felt bad that I was being so selfish, but I just knew that I had to do this. I had to get it out of my system and to try, at least, to search for some inner peace. I was deadly serious and, even though she probably didn't believe I'd go through with it I knew, at that moment, that no matter how far I got, I was going to at least start this trip. From here on in, I was someone who would try to cycle to Gibraltar.

Evolution of a MAMIL

Chapter 2: ...To John O'Groats

Most distance riders will happily complete up to 100 miles per day. I found this out as I busied myself mapping out different routes to Gibraltar on the Internet. It was something I was doing with excitement and vigour at every opportunity now that I had been given the green light by the wife, well sort of anyway. She was still not completely overjoyed about the trip – which was understandable I guess - but she was coming around slowly, particularly after she'd realised how much I needed to do it.

But given my distinct lack of anything remotely resembling experience, 100 miles each day seemed quite a lot when I considered what journeys of 100 miles give you. You can get from Birmingham to Liverpool, from Birmingham to London, or even coast to coast in that distance. This seemed far too unachievable, and so I started working on 50 miles a day as a more realistic target. I also found out that a slow, ambling cycling speed is considered to be about 10 miles per hour, giving me an average daily cycling time of just 5 hours – it seemed almost too easy really when I thought of it like that.

I used Google Maps to check some different routes for getting to Gibraltar and reckoned it'd be a little over 2,200 miles from door to door. There were a few viable options available, mainly with respect to the path to take once I hit Spain or, more ominously, the Pyrenees Mountains. But the route through the UK and France were pretty obvious – to go as straight as possible to Poole, then continue straight from Cherbourg to the western end of the French-Spanish border - and so I figured there wouldn't be much deviation in the overall mileage. So, at 50 miles per day, the 2,200 miles could be consumed in a relaxing 44 days riding, well within the 60 days I had available. This would then leave a full 2 weeks for a jolly up to celebrate at the other end. I knew I'd need the odd rest day here or there, but I figured I'd mainly be able to spend the spare days drunkenly staggering around little Spanish taverns, or sat sweating it out on some sun blessed beach. The more I looked at it, the more it looked like this was actually going to be a bit of a breeze. I got to wondering if I had actually made this too easy for myself? Even though I knew I was probably right, I figured I'd better keep this theory to myself for the time being, at least until I'd got a bike and a few training rides safely under my belt anyway.

With the route taking shape it was time to buy some kit and, of course, a bike. I'd owned a couple of bikes in the past but it dawned on me that I'd never actually bought one myself – they'd both been given to me as Christmas presents - and so I knew absolutely nothing about which one to buy. How do I choose a bike, particularly one that has to get me and my gear over 2,000 miles when I don't have a clue? I did some research and quickly realised that there are so many aspects to consider such as gears, brakes, wheels, sizes, frame construction, not to mention the options on clothing. And so, after a few frustrating days and a couple of trips wandering aimlessly around local bike shops, I did what anyone with any intelligence would do, I picked up the phone and asked a mate.

'So Martin, I'm thinking of going on a bike ride.' Martin is an old friend who comes under the title of Cycling Oracle on account of him once cycling from Land's End to John O'Groats.

'Nice one!' he replied, 'Where are you thinking?'

'Gibraltar.'

'Where?'

'Gibraltar, it's the little part of Britain at the bottom of Spain.'

'That sounds great, how are you getting there?'

'Errrm, I'm going to cycle there.' I replied, slightly confused by his question. 'I'm going to take some time out and try to cycle to Gibraltar.'

'Bloody hell mate, I thought you were going for a cycling holiday or something.' The shock in his voice was very reminiscent of Sue's when I'd told her of my plans. 'How far is it?'

'Well, there are a number of routes I could take, depending on how fit I'm feeling or how hot it is, but I think it'll be about 2,200 miles or so. I'm going to take 2 months off and see how far I can get. Do you think it's too far?'

'Well, it'll be tough mate, but it'll be great, I'm very jealous,' he replied, being distinctly non-committal on my chances of completing it. 'When did you get into biking anyway? I didn't know it was your thing.'

'Errrm, about a week ago! Well actually I wouldn't call myself "into biking" at all really, I just want to go on an adventure and I'm simply choosing a bike to do it on. I guess, at a bare minimum, to consider myself a cyclist I would need to own a bike!'

'Christ, you haven't got a bike?!"

'Naah, not yet anyway. Which is why I'm calling, I was wondering if you could tell me which bike I should get?'

'That's not an easy question to answer mate. There are a lot of different things to think about. How much money do you have to spend?'

'Dunno, about 1500 quid I think but I'd prefer to spend less.' As a Yorkshireman, he was in-tune with my financial frugalness.

'Go to a good bike shop and tell them what you're doing and how much money you've got and they'll sort you out. Actually, tell them you only have £1300 and spend the rest on good padded shorts - it's all about padded shorts'.

'Thanks Martin, I'll keep you posted.'

I put the phone down and pondered his response. This seemed crazy to me. If you go to a car showroom and tell them your budget and that you don't know what you're doing you'll more than likely get some banger and a Christmas card for the next 10 years from the happiest salesman in the showroom. You need to know your stuff, at least enough to be able to know what you're getting and that you're not getting ripped off. But I was running out of time and so I begrudgingly did as the Cycling Oracle said and trusted the man at the shop with my hard-earned cash. I went to a specialist bike shop called 'The Cycle Centre' in my local town of Congleton and, in contrast to my concerns, the outcome was a fantastic machine. I couldn't believe how good they were. I ended up spending £950 on a DX9 cyclo-cross bike by Orange in charcoal grey which seemed quite good, got some good reviews, but most importantly looked really bloody cool. Predominantly a road bike, it has racer style drop handlebars and a skinny frame, but has mountain bike features such as oversized tyres and disc brakes - perfect for the Spanish 'off-roading' I'd been seeing on Google Street View. They even threw in a decent pair of shoes, cleats, and pedals, although I was kind of surprised pedals don't actually come as standard when you're spending best part of a grand!

Their customer service was superb as well. On reflection, it's clear they rely on you coming back and so they deal in keeping you happy as well as the tangible products they sell. They even gave me a shop fitting by putting me on the bike and performing some adjustments to the handlebars and saddle to sit me in a good riding position. They told me I could swap out the headstock for a 'better one' but it cost £35 more and 'better' simply meant 2 grams lighter. I decided to stick with the one I had and to have an extra-long poo to compensate.

After a few days of admiring my new shiny steed, I finally bucked up the courage and went out on my first training ride. I decided to go and see my mate Carlos who works as a petrol attendant, or as an Oil Distributor as he likes to tell women he's trying to charm, at a garage about 5 miles away from my house. Wrapped in my shiny new Lycra, I made it there in about 40 minutes and was fairly happy with how it went. I was blowing a bit in places and my thighs were throbbing a little, but this was to be expected I guess, and I was encouraged by just how enjoyable it was. When I got to the garage I pulled onto the forecourt and looked through the wide shop window to see Carlos doubled over, in tears of laughter.

Now it's fair to say I am no Bruce Lee, but I'm not exactly obese either. However, there is something that happens to 90% of people that means you look a bit silly in Lycra once you hit middle age. I'm sure most cyclists know it but most don't really care, or they are the 10% that get away with it, or they're just sheer disillusioned. But most people accept they look absurd and are not really bothered - it is far more important to be comfortable, and streamlined. This matters when you're on the bike, when you're ploughing through the miles, head down fighting a headwind. But when you're stood on the forecourt of your mate's garage... you look an idiot. I walked into the shop to be greeted by an onslaught of abuse.

'HAHAHAHA! What the hell are you wearing you tool?' he said trying desperately to stifle his laughter long enough to speak.

'Shorts and a cycling top,' was my deadpan reply. I knew I wasn't going to enjoy this.

'HAHAHAHA! You look an idiot!'

'I look like a cyclist.'

'You look like a right gimp! And why do you need sunglasses anyway, it's not even sunny?!'

The beasting went on for some time and I had nothing really to reply with. I did look like a nob and I knew it. I tried to defend myself with a tactic of disinterested nonchalance, but the battle was lost.

I had deliberated for some time over what gear to wear for the trip. I'd seen some videos of people doing long cycling trips in T-shirt and shorts, but I wasn't sure whether I'd be able to do the type of miles I'd be hoping to achieve each day without getting saddle sores. I figured the trip was going to be tough enough without having an ass like a baboon. Besides, the Cycling Oracle had spoken and strongly advised on padded cycling shorts. And by the time I got to the continent, no one would know me anyway.

Finally, the battering stopped once Carlos decided to have a fag. We went outside, just far enough away from the fuel pumps to not get blown up.

'What do you need all that gear for anyway?' he asked.

'I'm going to try to cycle to Gibraltar.' I replied.

'Bloody hell mate, how far is that?'

'About 2,000 miles or so, although I am not sure yet on what route to take yet. I've been mulling it over on the maps and am not sure on the best route to take once I hit Spain. I've been looking at going straight through the centre but it looks a bit desolate. I'll be doing it in July and August so I'm also a little worried about the heat.'

'It is desolate, and it'll be bloody hot. You wanna look at going along the coast.' Finally, some useful information from the guy. 'If you stick to the coast it'll still be hot but it may be a bit more bearable. And besides, you'll have all those Spanish women sunbathing with their tits out! What does Sue say about it all anyway, is she OK with it?'

'Hmmm, I think so, though I think she still reckons I'll get over it and bin the idea.' I could see from the smirk on his face that he was having exactly the same thought.

'I guess you'll be wearing all this gear then?'

'Errrm, yeah.' I replied sarcastically.

'Well I'd probably do it in jeans and a t-shirt if I was going to do it.' He continued smugly as he drew down another lung full of smoke.

'Well you wouldn't do it would you? You wouldn't make it to the end of your road before you'd be ringing me up for a lift!'

He then coughed up a large lump of phlegm, the realisation of the prospect of such a trip straightening his face. 'Huh, spose not...' he replied. Let's just call it a draw.

Over the following weeks, I tried a number of different rides, no more than 15 miles or so at a time, ambling through the flat country lanes of Cheshire farmland. I was fine on the rides and felt good generally, not too fatigued and getting more and more confident with my physical capabilities every time. I was doing all the right things as well. I was eating correctly, stretching out after each ride, always wearing a helmet and glasses, and generally being the poster-boy for the perfect novice cyclist. These short rides came with so little effort that I rather naively considered I must be a natural and so I progressed quickly from ambling across the flat plain of Cheshire to smashing out 30+ mile, high-performance rides over the hills of the Peak District. With my new-found confidence as the latest cycling talent to come out of the British Isles, secretly mapping myself a career path all the way to the Tour de France, I made the mistake of trying to cycle too quickly and too often. The aggressive training regime inevitably took its toll and I started getting an aching pain in my right thigh, just above my knee. It started off as a small ache, but quickly ramped up till it was excruciating agony after the first few minutes of every ride.

Eventually, the pain became unbearable and as time ticked on ever closer to the start date, I became increasingly worried about failing before I'd started. With no other choice, I decided to begrudgingly part with some cash and get some professional advice. I started by trying a professional bike fitting on the advice of the Cycling Oracle. A bike fitting is where you give some guy 120 quid to put the adjustable components of the bike - such as the seat, handlebars and cleats - in the right position to put your body in the optimum position for riding. Sadly, this made little difference, other than smashing a £120 dint in my rapidly dwindling budget, so I tried a physiotherapist instead. The guy who saw me was the owner of the practice named Rick. He was a tall, straight-backed, balding guy of about 50, and was dressed in a tracksuit. Portraying an obvious sporting history from his stature and approach, I was convinced I was with the right guy as I took a seat and proceeded to tell him about my leg pains and about what was now becoming the hopeful journey to Gibraltar. I also told him about an injury that occurred during my stag do where I broke both my fibular and tibia. It was a bad break that had me on crutches for 8 months and so I had thought this might have been attributing to the pain in the same leg. He listened, gave me the familiar smirk of doubt I was now getting quite used to seeing, then proceeded in his examination.

'Fuckin' hell mate, your damaged leg is a centimetre longer than the other!' I was shocked by his choice of words, but more so by the information I was being told. 'Christ you've made a bit of a mess of that leg haven't you!'

'Errrrm yeah, I guess.' I replied, holding back a desire to break down in tears. He'd asked me to stand in front of the mirror and put a pointed finger across the lower edge of each kneecap. And I could clearly see the right leg was significantly longer than the left. I was speechless. I had never really noticed this lengthening before and I don't ever remember being told I have a limp - I'd not seen one anyway. I have suffered small aches and pains over the years, and had accepted the resetting process was never going to be perfect, but this did look a big difference when displayed in front of me in the mirror. It had been a few years since the incident and I guess my body must have just adapted to the unevenness.

'It looks like your wonky leg is putting extra strain on your Vastus Lateralis' he continued, returning to a more professional tone.

'My what now?'

'Your Vastus Lateralis, it's one of the 4 muscles that makes up your thigh. You must be overusing it and it's causing it to spasm.' That cleared that one up then. 'You're not scared of needles, are you mate?'

'Naah.' I replied, straightening up and pumped my chest out a little in a feeble attempt to meet Rick's bullish approach head-on, and also to hide the lie about the needles.

'Good. Jump on the couch and wait there, I'll be back in a sec.' I lay there in fear, reminiscent of the last time I lay on a surgery bed with my leg as the focal point, till Rick returned with acupuncture needles. 'Right, this might hurt a bit.'

My attempt at bravado quickly wilted as I lay there wincing while Rick proceeded to flick needles into the thigh of my leg. There were about 7 or so needles I think, I lost count after 2.

'Right, I'll be back in a bit.' He shouted over his shoulder on the way out of the room. I was left there for about 15 minutes in excruciating agony, water leaking out of my eyes. I mean, I was not crying or anything, and those were absolutely not tears.

When he returned, Rick removed the pins, then got one of his therapists, Gemma, to come in to perform a sports massage on my already throbbing leg. Gemma had the looks of a pretty, petite young woman of about 20 and was no taller than 5 foot, but this gentile outer shell hid the inner strength of a sumo wrestler. Thoughts about her good looks were quickly stripped from my mind as she proceeded to handle my thigh like a child playing with Play-Doh. She tried to explain what she was doing and why it would help but I couldn't really focus over the pain, I just held on to the sides of the bed to prevent myself from crying again. I left the practice about 3 hours after entering, feeling very much worse, and having now procured an unexpected limp!

When I woke the next morning I could not believe the positive results from the abuse of the previous day. It had released the muscle spasms, and with it all the pain worry about whether I was going to be able to even start the trip. I was happily surprised at how much of a success the treatment had been.

I went back to the practice a week later for a review session and I took the opportunity to thank the team, holding back the desire to kiss them both. I asked Gemma if she wanted to come on the trip to provide her massaging skills, though sadly she declined.

With the thigh pain back under control, I continued training for the next few weeks, trying a few undulating hills of the peak district but mainly sticking to the flat Cheshire lanes. The thigh pain came back a few times, only I was now prepared. Gemma had told me about something called self-myofascial release which sounds far more sexual than it actually is. Using a foam roller, which is a knobbly 6-inch diameter hard sponge tube, you simply lie on it with your full weight and roll about till you find the point in your muscles that hurts the most, then you rock back and forth so it hurts even more. It's excruciating pain but it works a treat, simulating a deep muscle massage that makes the pains magically disappear. The downside however is that it makes you look like you're trying to have sex with the roller as you rock back and forth, grunting and groaning with a pained sex face. I figured I'd better think carefully about where and when I perform the activity on the trip.

With a new-found confidence about my physical prowess, I started spending more and more time map gazing. Cycling from Mow Cop, my home town on the Cheshire-Staffordshire border, to Gibraltar looked impressive, but it didn't quite have the ring to it that I'd hoped. I also started looking at the number of days I had available. I had originally considered that 50 miles per day was going to be achievable. But with the training rides now going so well, what if I manage significantly more? Given that I would have nothing else to do each day but to cycle, I could be doing 60, or even 70 miles per day and potentially be back in a month, sat at home complaining about the British summer with everyone else.

I went back to the maps and looked at a number of different options, just to make sure I was choosing the right trip. I looked at going from the top of Norway, but that seemed a little too far and way too remote for my limited survival experience. I also thought about changing the destination to Sicily and riding through Italy, however it turns out wild camping is illegal in Italy and there were not many campsites as far as I could see. The obvious choice was to keep with the target of Gibraltar but stretch it out a bit. What if I started from Scotland instead? This would mean getting all the way up there then passing home on the way down but that was ok, I could factor in a day off at home for recuperation. It would increase the distance by about 500 miles, which was good, but it would also mean travelling through Scotland in July, the peak of the midge season. I'd been in Scotland in July before and I know for certain that I have the type of skin, or blood, highly desirable to midges. I did some research and found out that midges are actually only found in specific areas, under specific conditions, and don't like winds over 6 miles per hour. So, I figured as long as I was travelling over that speed I'd be fine, even if I did hit an active patch, which was not guaranteed. And anyway, Sue had told me she wanted to come for the first part of the journey in our campervan so I considered we'd have protection in the evenings when I'm not cycling so surely it'd be fine. So, that was it; John O'Groats to Gibraltar. It was going to be somewhere between 2,400 and 3,000 miles depending on the route I take, which I'd decide based on my fitness, capability and budget as I go. And Sue was going to come with me for the UK part of the trip in our campervan providing both a place to stay each night and the emotional support I knew would be invaluable. I mean, being the intrepid explorer I was now clearly morphing into, I didn't really need a support vehicle, however she wanted to come to proudly cheer me on and I could not refuse her that. I also decided to let her feel really useful and to let her carry my camping gear in the van. What can I say, I'm just nice like that.

I finally set about sorting out what kit I'd need. I had some lightweight camping gear from my walking days, such as a one-man tent and sleeping bag, but I needed to get my hand in my pocket and go back shopping for the many items I was missing. After a crazed spending spree that left me with cold sweats, I put all the gear in the 2 rear-wheel pannier bags I'd borrowed from the Cycling Oracle, and the handlebar bag I'd bought. I was amazed that it all fit, and also that the full kit came to a surprisingly lean 23 kilos. My bike riding clothes consisted of 3 sets of bib-type, padded cycling shorts (the Cycling Oracle was right, it really is all about the shorts), 3 long-sleeved tops, 3 pairs of socks, and some waterproofs. I reckoned I'd get about 3 days out of each set without killing unsuspecting holiday makers with body-odour asphyxiation, meaning I'd need to find a laundrette roughly every 10 days or so.

There were also some relaxing clothes consisting of a short and long-sleeved T-shirt, a pair of normal shorts, a pair of lightweight trousers, a couple of pairs of pants, and some flip-flops. I also packed my digital SLR camera, a tablet computer, and other stuff such as toiletries, a small travel towel, reading books, a small selection of bike spares, some Gaffa Tape, and a set of headphones and a wind up radio to keep me company in the evenings.

I also decided on using paper maps rather than a Sat-Nav as I didn't want to rely on electronics that needed charging, especially if I was going to do any wild camping. Anyway, aside from the £300 the Sat-Nav thingy costs that I couldn't really afford, there is something about the tactile-ness and the sense of perspective you get with a physical map that I like. When you use a Sat-Nav, all you see is where you need to go, where your next junction is and the direction you need to be heading. With a map, however, you get to see where you are with perspective of what else is around you, you see the undulation of the land and the way the roads navigate around the differing landscapes. I also think you're far more likely to make detours and to experience places you perhaps wouldn't have done when being given ordered directions by the posh speaking electro-dictator. I packed maps for the UK and for France. I'd buy the one for Spain when I got closer to the country to save on weight, and to save me a few quid for the train fare home if I didn't make it that far.

With my panniers packed, the bike in good working order, and the legs just about holding on, deadline day came around surprisingly quickly and so Sue and I threw everything into the camper, including our border-collie dog, Jazz, and we were off to Scotland for the start of what would be either an epic adventure, or an epic fail.

Evolution of a MAMIL

Evolution of a MAMIL

SCOTLAND

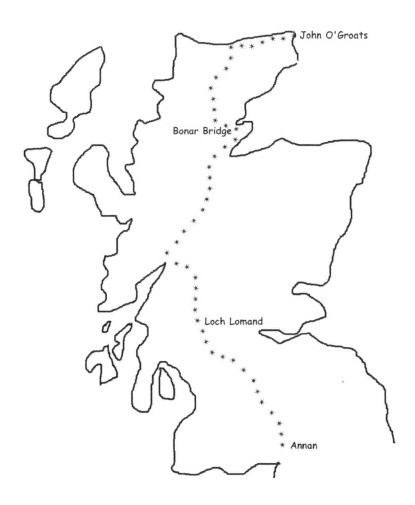

Evolution of a MAMIL

Chapter 3: ...To Bonar Bridge

'Christ, I feel nervous!'

'You'll be fine.' Sue replied. 'Besides, we'll be there in 20 minutes so there's no turning back now!'

There was a deep tense pause, in part so I could concentrate on a sharp hairpin in the coastal road we were now on, but mainly due to the million thoughts rapidly spinning through my head.

'Do you think I'm being an idiot?' I asked as the campervan chugged its way back up to its modest cruising speed - it may be slow, it'd be the fastest I'd be travelling over the coming months.

'How do you mean?'

'Well, I'm not exactly young, and all the leg problems I've had. I'm not what you'd call experienced am I. Do you think I'm making a bit of a tit of myself?'

'I think you're doing what you always do and are jumping in feet first. You've got plenty of time. Just enjoy it, no matter how far you get.' It was nice to hear her encouragement, even though there was still no mention on her thoughts of success.

'Thanks, I needed that.' I'd been getting more and more tense all the way up to John O'Groats. The road had been getting increasingly undulating and the van had struggled with some of the steeper hills, leaving me worrying about my own capabilities of negotiating them. I guess in part she was right, I do always jump feet first into things, but I normally have at least a vague idea about how I'll fair. I normally know if I'll at least be able to give it a good shot. This however was by far the biggest thing I'd ever tried to do. And with the realisation from the pains of the previous 3 months, I knew I wasn't exactly in the optimum condition. I had absolutely no idea how this was going to pan out. It was going to be either one of the most amazing things, or one of the stupidest things I'd ever tried to do.

'Anyway, you do know I'll divorce you if you don't make it don't you? I couldn't handle the embarrassment!' Hmmm, I hoped to God she was joking...

John O'Groats is actually a sleepy little hamlet consisting of no more than 20 houses and a petrol station. But the more interesting focal point for me, as well as the masses of tourists that descend on the place every year, is the small port about half a mile away. The port is used by the Orkney Islands passenger ferry, but it's the famous white signpost, indicating the distance to a number of different locations including New York, Edinburgh, and Land's End - though thankfully not Gibraltar - that most come here for. An opportunity to evidence that they've been to the very top of the British mainland. It has to be one of the most photographed sign in the world - up there with the one above Hollywood and the one for Abbey Road - and it was getting its fair share of attention this morning as I jostle for position to get my picture taken next to it. I wait patiently behind 3 Lotus cars, a couple of cyclists, a walker, presumably all at the start or end of the more popular journey between John O'Groats and Land's End, and a family of Asian tourists. After getting my turn, I stand waiting next to the post with a concocted feeling of excitement and trepidation at what the next 2 months might hold. As Sue gets the camera ready, I look around hoping somehow for some appreciation and admiration for the mighty journey on which I am about to embark on. I want to tell everyone about my achievement in getting this far. I want to convey my plans to cross 4 countries by bicycle and to describe the mental and physical challenges that I know lie ahead. But no one seems particularly interested. The only people to notice me were the Asian family as they tut impatiently for me to move away from the post, and away from the background of their photograph. It wasn't quite the fan fared start I'd imagined.

Once I'd had my picture taken I complete a few other traditional things I'd heard you do at the start of an adventure. I dip my tyres in the sea, and put a pebble in my bag, the smallest and lightest one I can find that still constitutes a pebble, to be carried to Gibraltar and thrown in the sea at the end – if I manage to get that far anyway.

I start out heading west across the top of the country. I had considered travelling straight south out of John O'Groats down to the A9. But we drove up this road to get here and so I knew just how treacherous it was. As the main route to the Orkney and Shetland Islands' ferry crossing terminal at Thurso, it's really busy with fast driving trucks on tight schedules. I had decided, instead, to head west first, where I could pick up some of the smaller lanes, bypassing the dangerous commuter traffic.

The road is thankfully flat although, given its exposed location at the top of the country, it is also horrifically windy and I have to lean heavily to my left to compensate for the wind coming directly from the south. I travel through farmland of manicured fields housing what must be the hardiest sheep known to man. The weather up here on the top-shelf of the country gets really bad with freezing conditions and driving rain. But judging by the way the sheep are shedding their coats, draping off them in matted Rastafarian-like dreadlocks, I guess you must kind of get used to it.

Due to the lack of any real cycling experience, as well as the leg issues I've had, every ache and pain seems to resonate during these first few miles. I can't quite find a rhythm, which I suppose is only natural, and I'm hyperaware of every little niggle. Every time I find a small incline, or am fighting into a heavy headwind, my legs give in to a deep lethargic ache, exacerbating the nagging thought of just how much stick I'll get off Carlos if I fail to at least make it through the first day. I always knew it would probably take a few days to get the fitness levels and endurance up, I just need to try and stay calm and focused till it happens.

I ride along, head cocked over to one side in a feeble attempt to shelter from the wind, and start getting passed by a steady stream of cyclists on the final leg of the 900-mile journey from Land's End up to John O'Groats. The diversity in ages of the people who pass is as large as the differing approaches they take. Some look like youthful sprinters, hoping to achieve the trip in record pace on bikes that cost more than most cars. Others come plodding past carrying copious amounts of gear wrapped in waterproof covers and strapped to every inch of spare bike frame. There are solo riders as well as groups, and it is really warming to see teenagers and people in the latter years of life taking on the challenge. They all seem really happy, which isn't surprising given they're only a couple of hours from the end. A solo rider, in his mid-30's, dressed head to toe in yellow waterproofs gives me the thumbs up and a shout as he comes towards me, 'Good luck fella!'

'Thanks, you're nearly there mate.' I bellow, trying to counter the buffering sound of the wind, as he passes.

'I know, thanks!' He cries back, rising out of his seat and craning his neck backwards. 'Watch out for Cornwall though, it's bloomin' hilly.'

'Thanks, will do.' I reply instinctively. Then, as I realise what he's said, I'm filled with childish injustice and I can't help but shout back, 'No, wait!! I'm going to Gibraltar!'

'Where?!'

'Gibraltar, I'm not going to Land's End, I'm going to Gibraltar!' But he's travelled agonisingly out of earshot and just shrugs his shoulders and heads off. I have a desire to turn around and catch him up just to tell him about how I was on a quest to complete nearly 3,000 miles to Gibraltar, and not the mere 900 to Land's End. But, on realising that it would have been a bit foolish to waste so much effort for something so futile, I ride on with a sulk instead.

After about 2 hours of worryingly tiring riding, I get to my first major town of Thurso. I follow the road through the town and stop at a shopping precinct in search of the first of what I anticipate will be a continuous stream of pies and other highly nutritional foods I will be consuming on the trip. I once watched a program about the training of the Marines from the 80's where the trainees were encouraged to eat pies when they'd finished exercises. The PT trainer shouted them home with a 'Go on, have a pie lad!' as they got over the finish line. I figured if it's good enough for the Marines, then it's going to be good enough for this intrepid explorer. I find a pie shop and go all native with a Macaroni and Cheese Pie as a starter, and a Scottish Pie for the main course. I'd never had a Macaroni and Cheese Pie before, and as unappetising as it sounds, and indeed looks, it's actually amazingly tasty. With my new-found ability to consume food without getting fatter, I was hoping this was not going to be my last.

I trundle through the afternoon, continuing on the relatively flat and forgiving coast road. But eventually the manicured farmland changes to scrubland as I head inland and into the true Scottish Highlands. The environment becomes more and more rugged and desolate as the neatly segmented and organised fields of the coastal farmland is replaced with expanses of emptiness. The wild and unspoilt environment of rugged mountains and open moorland is engulfing and I start to get the feeling of freedom I'd been hoping for. I get the rush of the open road and the excited feeling of being on an epic adventure. I am far away from the boss, away from normality, and am putting myself out there again, fulfilling an ambition that's been festering in me for a long time. It is very early days, but I am already feeling the giddiness of knowing that this is what I've been searching for. And no matter how far I get, I know it is going to be one hell of a trip.

The day continues through to a dull, overcast late afternoon. I check the map, set in a plastic cover on the top of my handlebar bag, and find I am closing in on the first stop off location of Betty Hill. I also notice the road taking a number of tight, spaghetti-like turns as it meanders through the mountain peaks to take the easiest path over the craggy ridge that I can see ahead. My first test of true Scottish mountain riding. The road starts rising and I start flicking down the gears at an alarming pace till I am eventually in the lowest gear with nowhere else to go. It gets steep, unnervingly quickly and my thighs respond with deep lactic acid burn. Christ it hurts! And as if to augment the agony, the dark clouds suddenly open, providing me with a really wet Scottish welcome. I spend a few frustrating minutes getting my newly purchased cycling waterproof out – which turns out to have the waterproof qualities of a woollen pullover - and get drenched in the process. I am extremely thankful when it stretches around the girth of my belly, though it makes little difference to my already saturated Lycra.

The road continues over the mountains and the steep climbs leave me with the only option of getting out of the saddle, putting my head down, and to just keep fighting the pedals around. By the time I make it to Betty Hill I am wheezing, hurting, and very, very wet. But I've made it to the finishing point of the first day and am elated to see the uplifting sight of the van parked up in the village's information centre carpark. Betty Hill is a picturesque little place, popular with holiday makers looking for the more restful type of stay. There are 2 beautiful white-sand beaches, a pub, a campsite and, well, that's about it, except for the chip-shop, which is only open on a Friday and Saturday night. But its remoteness and nothingness is its selling point and is a perfect place for my needs for the night.

After a well-earned beer, I dump my bike in the back of the van and change into more appropriate attire for the pub. We find the only pub perched at the top of a large looping hill at the other end of the village where I stuff my face with more nutritional food of burger and chips before finding a beachside carpark to overnight in.

With the first day done, albeit a half day, I still wasn't really any the wiser as to how far I'd get on the trip. I'd done about 50 miles, which was more than I'd ever done before, but it was a real effort. Every mile was hard-fought. This might have been in part due to the horrendous wind, but at least this was a side wind and I hope it eases off a bit for tomorrow as from here on in, it's all south bound travel. So, that's the first day done, only 49-ish to go… I hope.

I wake the next morning with excitement about the new day in the saddle. I jump out of bed, nearly booting the dog in the process, and check out the legs. They were a little tender, mainly in the thighs, but not too bad at all for a 40-year-old invalid. Happy with the thought of what the new day may hold, and that the wind had thankfully subsided overnight, I squeeze into my Lycra, and open the van door ready for a pleasant day's ride, 'Shit, midges! Arrgghhh!' There are thousands of the little buggers just waiting in ambush outside the van door! I contemplate closing it back up and climbing back into bed. But instead, I put on my war face and run around to the back of the van, remembering the 6-mph rule, and swiftly retrieve my bike from the boot of the van.

When I get back to the starting point, back where I met Sue last night, I notice a guy walking out of a beachside path and see it is the Australian guy called Paddy I passed in the mountains the previous day. We'd done the usual exchange of pleasantries whilst coughing and sweating our way up one of the hills - although I have to admit that was rather more me than him.

'G'Day mate!' he shouts, not wanting to break any stereotypes. He was a stocky bloke in his early 20's with red, shoulder length hair and a long ZZ-Top style beard. He had gone for the scruffy shorts and t-shirt look and made me look a bit of a pleb stood next to him head to toe in Lycra.

'Hey up! So, where are you off to?' I ask whilst checking out his bike. It's a pretty robust looking mountain bike with massive panniers front and back, and loads of electric gadgets strapped to the handlebars. He's also sporting a pair of under-crackers drying on the back rack. He's a boxers man, which I consider is quite a brave choice for a male cyclist.

'I dunno, I'm doing some of Scotland then over to Iceland for a bit I think.'

'Wow that's brill! How long you got?' I ask whilst happy-slapping midges gorging themselves on my bare legs.

'I should be out for about 4 months. And you?' He asks whilst observing my bike, looking rather puzzled at the distinct lack of anything resembling travelling gear.

'I'm off to Gibraltar.'

'Where?'

'Gibraltar, it's at the bottom of Spain. I've got 2 months so I should be ok I think.'

'Awesome! You sure travel light mate!?'

'Actually, I have a support vehicle for the first part of the trip in the form of my wife and our campervan, though I will need to think about getting used to carrying my own gear soon. I'm not really a cyclist and so I need to get fit first. I only bought my bike 3 months ago.'

'Wow, that's awesome. That's a sweet ride dude.'

'Is it? Thanks, that's awesome.' I wasn't sure why I'd said that last bit, it just seemed appropriate. The word awesome from a cool looking, 20-something hipster with a beard and an Aussie accent sounds great, but from a balding, Lycra-clad 40-year-old from Cheshire it just sounded like I was trying too hard. I fought off the urge to use the word sweet, as that would have been very un-awesome.

On leaving Betty Hill I drift into a moment of reflection on just how magical an experience this really is, and how lucky I am to be able to do it. It feels amazing to be out challenging myself again and I get a rush of anticipation and contentment I've been missing. I just hope my aging and damaged body isn't going to give up on me too soon. I fly down the steep hill out of the town at break-neck speed, completing a few furtive looks to my right at the stunning sight of

Torrisdale Bay. It is a beautiful view with a wide, sandy beach banked by craggy rocks and scrubland. I consider stopping to take a picture, but thoughts of the midges quickly dismisses the idea and instead I take full advantage of the steep descent with some inspiring, head-down coasting.

The morning is spent following the River Naver which runs from Loch Naver in the south to the sea at Betty Hill on the north coast. The river sits at the bottom of a valley and is about 20 metres wide, very shallow, and runs quite slowly with Bovril-brown water. The Scottish rivers are popular for salmon fishing and it isn't long till I pass a fly-fisherman on the hunt for Atlantic Salmon on their way back to spawn. Fully dressed in green wax-cotton, and wearing thigh-high waders, he's stood in about 2 feet of water, rhythmically casting the fly, and appearing to be in the pleasant comfort of his own thoughts. And it wasn't long before I was in my own reflective daze as I continue along the relatively flat, single-tracked, riverside road. The wind had dropped, thankfully, and it's a really nice ride with the road rolling steadily underneath my wheels as the natural structure of the wilderness passes by. I could feel I was finally finding some riding rhythm in the serene and remote environment and was starting to understand why so many have taken to cycling. When you're out on a ride, you get time to think and time to reflect. There is something that occurs whilst completing any simple activity, such as riding a bike or even casting a fly, where you lose yourself in the moment. Some call it Zen, some call it Flow, or positive engagement, but it's the act of doing something mentally undemanding, that allows the mind to drift into nothingness. It could be from cycling, or fishing, or even the simple act of washing the dishes, but having time to let your mind drift is something that's been lost in the busy lives of modern day living. The opportunity to be alone in your thoughts and to be surrounded by nature is an experience so often missed. Cycling just has the bonus side effect that you're able to eat like a king without the fear of getting too fat.

I stop for a break and I am treated to a close up encounter with a young deer near a bridge over one of the many streams that cascade down the steep sides of the valley to feed the main river. As I sit admiring my surroundings, the deer appears from along the riverbank, then nervously tries crossing over the bridge. I go for my camera, but I am no match for its acute senses and as soon as I move it stops dead, before recoiling to the sanctuary of the shadows under the bridge. It was a lovely moment, and, although I didn't get my picture, a feel a surge of excitement and anticipation at what other experiences this amazing adventure might bring.

The road takes me past Loch Naver and onto another single tracked road running by a river, this time the River Vagastie. Up in the Highlands, and indeed anywhere where it's mountainous, nearly all roads follow rivers. The path of least resistance that rivers naturally take make the best locations for building a road as the terrain is as level as possible for the area. As the rivers navigate around the large mountains and cut through the gorges and valleys, they have found the optimum paths between places, making it the most favourable location for roads in this difficult terrain. But sadly, it's not without its flaws. The rivers came first in this arrangement and so they don't always flow where the road needs to be and so from time to time there is no choice but to tackle the big stuff. And up here, they are really, really big. As I cycle ever further away from Loch Naver, the river becomes thinner but faster running as the mountainside start to climb. Rising gently at first, the road becomes increasingly inclined, turning the riding into long arduous climbs as it makes its way up to the summit. It goes on for far longer than is comfortable, and my weak body and damaged legs are not liking it to the point where I start getting a serious stabbing pain in my right knee. Every time I hit a steep bit of road, of which there are many, I need to rise out of my seat and heave myself upward causing a rush of acute pain from under the kneecap - it feels like someone's trying to prise it off with a spoon. I persevere, coughing and sweating like a 60-a-day coalminer, trying desperately to maintain composure. But it's no good and the worries about making it to Gibraltar come flooding back.

To fix my broken leg after the stag-do incident, I needed an operation so a plate could be attached to the side of my fibula, and a rod could be pushed through the inside of the tibia to keep it straight while it healed. To do this, they moved my kneecap to one side, drilled a hole in the top of the bone, then forced the rod right through the marrowbone centre, before inserting 4 screws, 2 at the top and 2 at the bottom. I once tried to watch a YouTube video of this type of operation and made it as far as seeing them smashing the rod home with a builder's lump hammer before I had to turn it off and try to un-see it, heavily traumatised by the experience. And the way it is hurting now, I'm worried I might be doing it some serious damage. I had decided during the planning of this trip that I would not do anything that could cause permanent injury. A bit of muscle fatigue I could cope with but, if my knee was hurting, this was a major concern. If this is how it is handling the moderately sized Highland mountains, then the Pyrenees would likely be a game-ender – I am starting to wonder if I might be needing a plan B.

Ever since I started the planning of this adventure, I had considered the Pyrenees as my nemesis. Being a 1000-metre, raising to 3000-metre, high mountain range spanning the 300-mile border between France and Spain, it is not only a big bugger, it's also right in my way. I had reviewed it over and over again on the map, searched about it on the Internet and posted the question on a few blogs: 'What is the best way to get over the Pyrenees?' There are a number of passes over it, and a few through it, but which would be the best one to take? Which would be the most suitable given my age, experience, fitness, and the fact I'm travelling on a humble bicycle? I'd first considered keeping to the coast and going 'around them', where I suspected they may be at their lowest. But would I see this as chickening out when I looked back in years to come? And if I did go around, would I still be able to complete the trip in the 2 months I had available. Would I run out of time, or money, given it would add at least another 500 miles or so to the journey? If I decide to go over the top, in a more direct route, apart from the satisfaction of achieving the challenge, it'd take far less time to do it meaning I could keep to a more relaxed schedule for the rest of the trip. And with the extra time it would provide, I'd be able to take a few extra rest days to recuperate.

All that planning and decision making seemed to make perfect sense back then, when I was slurping tea, sat in a reclining chair at my desk. But with my knee screaming at me to stop on any sign of an incline, none of these options really seem to matter. I am starting to wonder if plan B is actually going to be a 2-month piss-up in Glasgow. It is only day 2 and I am already having serious doubts about my ability to even make it out of the UK. I can't help thinking I might have underestimated this trip just a tad…

Everybody says that cycling is full of highs and lows and I now realised what that actually meant. If the morning was best described as like a trip to the ballet, all pleasantness and tranquillity; and the midday grind was like being in the mosh pit of a thrash-metal gig, battling through it as a sweaty heaving mess; then the afternoon was like a day at a theme-park. After the massive effort it had taken to get up and over the mountains, it was payback time as I get catapulted down the other side like I'm on the world's biggest-dipper. I spend most of the afternoon free-wheeling down to Loch Shin, again following a river, and passing the famously remote Crask Inn pub along the way. The pub is quite surreal, a single building set in the middle of nowhere, and I momentarily contemplated stopping off for a quick pint. But I decide against it as I'm not sure an afternoon beer is a good habit to get into at such an early stage. I was sure that as time went on, particularly when I got to into France and Spain, that I'd be able turn this trip into a bit of a jolly-up and to enjoy the local entertainment. For now though I need to stay professional and keep concentrating on getting some cycling experience. A MAMIL is not born, a MAMIL needs to evolve before he can flourish!

As the road continues on, with me a happy passenger being transported along by my freewheeling bike, I feel the positivity rising again. Maybe it's the scenery that picks up my spirits, or more likely the 4 miles of almost continual downhill slope, but I start to feel the buzz of the journey again. I start to get really excited about what I am doing and am taken aback at just how much of an emotional roller coaster the trip is, even at such an early stage. One minute it is euphoric highs and a feeling of inner strength and positivity, the next I feel old and knackered and way out of my depth. Given that I had no experience to fall back on, every little creak and click feels like a game changer. I guess, due to the fact I was still untested and inexperienced, I am feeling every little knock and tweak with the worry that it could be serious. In the same way that you hear every knock and creak from a newly purchased car. I need to get some miles done and to get some confidence. These first few days were always going to be about simply riding and about finding my feet. I just needed to focus on getting myself in shape and getting into the journey, and about finding my inner MAMIL. I knew it was in there somewhere as I'd had flashes of it during the morning's pleasant riding, I just need to find it and set it free. I wasn't what I'd call a fully-fledged cyclist yet, but provided I didn't run out of effort, I knew it would come eventually.

Bonar Bridge is a lovely little Scottish town on the Kyle of Sutherland and I make it there by early evening. The town sits beside a 50-foot wide river that carries the Highland rainwater in the west into the Dornoch Firth and on into the North Sea to the east. The town used to be a busy transport link as the bridge – from where the town gets its name – used to be the only place to traverse the waterway for people going up the East coast to Thurso, and beyond onto the Orkney and Shetland Islands. Sadly though, from an economic point of view, the opening of the Dornoch Firth Bridge to the east has meant that all that commuter traffic now bypasses the town and travels straight over the Firth. The Kyle was also a hotbed for commercial salmon fishing before the stocks dwindled, which is not surprising given the efficiency with which they were caught. Dating back as far as the 1600's, Bonar was known as a 'Centre for Salmon Excellence' and with almost 400 years of experience, the men that worked there had mastered the art of 'net fishing' (mauling a large net right across the 50-foot span) until it was stopped in 1986. On the bank on either side of the river are the remnants of the brick built ice houses used to store ice for preserving the tonnes of salmon that was extracted from the river every year. Up on the hills, about a mile to the east of Bonar Bridge, is Loch Migdale which, due to its exposed location, is highly susceptible to freezing. Allegedly it freezes so thick that a lad once drove from one end to the other in a Mini for a bet. It is this ice which was used to fill the ice houses of the Kyle. Commercial fishing in the Kyle has long since become unviable as the stock levels are now so low, however it still draws in fisherman, though more for the sport and the beautiful setting.

We spend the evening in the town's hotel pub. We visited the place last year on a holiday and were hopeful of bumping into some of the characters we had met back then. It's an old-world looking place, no bigger than the front room of a terraced house, with threadbare carpet and a coal fire that's never left to go out. One wall of the pub is covered in 1950's risqué cartoon pictures, which are completely out of character with the rest of the decor, but somehow seems to add to the feeling of welcoming such unpretentious places hold. Sadly, none of the locals that we'd met were in, although given how drunk we'd been last time we were here, along with the difficult riding conditions, I can't help thinking I'd had a bit of a lucky escape.

Chapter 4: ...To Loch Lomond

I woke early the next morning with the eagerness that even blurry eyes and aching legs cannot suppress as I struggle into my tightfitting riding gear ready for another day as an intrepid explorer. I'm feeling ok this morning, except for some mild leg-throbbing. I am just glad the scare of the knee pain from yesterday is behind me and it is now just a mild niggle. I'm realising that this will be a continual switching of emotions, matching almost equally to the extreme fluctuations of the terrain. At the moment, the only constant irritation I do have is the midges and they're driving me insane. Every time I stop moving, even for a moment, I'm getting ravaged, and my legs are starting to look as blotchy as an adolescent's chin. I've been bitten in places you should only get bitten when a safe-word has been agreed, and it's driving me crazy. The 6-mph plan is simply not working and unfortunately I don't have a Plan B, so it's a case of sticking with Plan A and to either grin and bear it, or to scream and shout like a psycho. I am generally going with the latter.

I travel east out of Bonar Bridge along the south side of the Firth towards the town of Tain. It's a beautiful sunny morning and it's the sort of conditions that make it a pleasure to be travelling by bicycle, particularly as it's relatively flat, and I'm being helped along by a gently caressing tail wind. The road is lined by dense pine trees on either side, casting the road into shadow. But every so often the trees to the left break and I'm presented with a picture postcard view across the Firth, with the Highland mountains in the background, and the morning sun bouncing off the rippling water. The views are truly spectacular.

Just as I turn one of the many corners that follow the contour of the water's edge, I look up to see an absolutely massive bird sat about 100 metres in front of me up in the trees. It is brown and white and looks a little over half a metre in height. I'm not sure, but it looks like an eagle and I get excited at the opportunity of getting so close, something I guess I could only achieve by the stealthy approach of a bicycle. I slowly glide towards it and stop, but as I go for my camera, buried under a mountain of uneaten fruit in my handlebar bag, I look up to see the jaw-dropping, yet frustrating sight of massive, wallowing, outstretched wings carrying it majestically over the water and away.

After the failed deer picture from yesterday and now the eagle, I guess I'm learning wildlife photography is not really my forte.

I make it to the supermarket on the outskirts of Tain and go to the in-store cafe to make use of their free Wi-Fi as well as their cheap nutritional sports food. As I devour a double sausage and black-pudding sandwich, I complete my first online blog and try to put 160 miles of travelling into a few bite-sized paragraphs and some photographs. This is not really possible to do, but I'd decided to try to keep a blog going as I'd figure it'd be a good way to keep my family and friends up to date on progress. I also post some pictures I'd taken of my mascot, 'Manion Friday' - a 2-inch plastic Minion toy I'd got off my 5-year-old nephew. I thought it would make a good travel companion and it would be funny if I posted pictures of him in different locations along the way.

Whilst I have the opportunity, I also check my Facebook page and find out that sadly the sister of a really good friend had died 2 days earlier. I'd only really met her on a couple of occasions over 20 years ago, but I'd been watching her story through Facebook posts since she had found she'd had cancer. I found her story really moving, not least as I had lost my own brother, Darren, to cancer over ten years ago when he was in his early 20's. She was an English teacher and, as such, was very articulate, and reading her battle allowed me to reflect on my brother's battle all those years ago. It somehow seemed easier to understand when it was not someone so close and it helped me appreciate the battle Cancer sufferers go through. It seems strange, and maybe a bit selfish, to say this about someone I don't really know in person but I wish I could have had a chance to thank her for being so open during this difficult time. Peace out to you Kim, you gave me knowledge and understanding.... I hope you can rest now, I know you will be sorely missed.

Back on the bike I get my head down and continue on the journey with a sadness in my heart, but a realisation that I am really lucky to be on such an adventure. I guess some people's battles are a bit more important than to get to the top of some poxy hill. I meet the support team at a supermarket carpark and we take a stroll into the town on a quest to buy some inner soles to put in my right shoe in an attempt to alleviate further pain in my knee. As I walk happily out of the shop after buying a pair, Sue looks at me mouth aghast.

'Did you see that?' She says with a smirk.

'See what?' I reply dumbly.

'Did you see those two women checking you out?' Excitedly, I turned around to see two old women of about 70 pretending to nonchalantly look around the shop in an attempt to not catch my eye. 'As you walked in they were looking at your package, and on the way out, they were staring at your bum!'

Gobsmacked, slightly flattered, and just a little bit self-conscious I walk back to the van wondering just how many other people are taking notice of the Lycra shorts. I have never really thought about being 'checked out' before as I'm not exactly your average pin-up looking guy, but it was funny to think of a couple of old ladies getting their pulse going over a balding man in Lycra. I guess there's a time in everyone's life where the standards simply go out of the window.

After an afternoon of thought-filled riding, through flat countryside full of reams of cows all on a busy schedule of getting fat, I start closing in on our meeting point of Drumnadrochit on the northern edge of Loch Ness. There's a large mountain range lurking ahead, and on looking on the map, it looks like sadly I'll be going over them. As I start getting close the road slowly starts to rise, and I can feel the anticipation intensifying of the impending gut-wrenching pain. I drop the bike down a couple of gears in preparation for the angry climb, as well as to slow me down to stretch out the feeling of not hurting. As the road steepens, the flat open fields of farmland are replaced by a pine forest covered mountain side as I frantically click through the gears searching for one that will alleviate the throbbing pain in my straining legs. But it's no good, and I quickly run out of gears and am left with no alternative but to get out of the seat, and to force the pedals around with what little energy I have left after a long day in the saddle. The road climbs at a constant, hellish angle, and after about 30 minutes of grinding it out, and losing about 2 litres of sweat in the process, I eventually get to what I think is the summit and stop for a 10-minute breather. Shaking with exhaustion, I manage to drag my 2 water-bottles from their cages - one for guzzling, the other for pouring over my steaming face like I'm in an aftershave advert.

After momentarily cooling off, I continue on, only to go around a corner and am faced with a similarly scary looking climb to the one I've just completed. I travel towards the next rise as slowly as possible, embracing the, albeit temporary, pleasure of not feeling like my lungs are exploding, but eventually I've no choice as I get back out of the saddle and into the pain again. As I climb I can feel the frustrations starting to simmer in my mind as I slow down from both the zapping effects of a long day in the saddle as well as it being really bloody hot. And as the energy goes, so does the speed, and it's not long till I drop below the 6-mph threshold and bang, the midges attack. Once again I'm filled with a raging bout of midge-madness. I'm getting battered by the heat, battered by this hill, and absolutely destroyed by the midges. At this point in time, I conclude, cycling is shit.

Eventually, my resolve gives in and the inner devil that's been sniggering at me all the way up the mountain finally breaks free, and I can see his cheeky, smug little face laughing at the stupid bald fella for thinking he could cycle to Gibraltar. I'm feeling really, really angry, the type of angry that makes you want to smash something, or to punch someone in the face. I grunt, growl, shout and swear at the midges but they seem to be preoccupied with dinner and don't take any notice. They swarm like vultures with a dinner-date before I eventually make it to the top and break over the speed safety threshold. And as quickly as they appeared, they're gone, presumably to go and pick on another unsuspecting intrepid explorer. Christ, I hate midges.... and cycling for that matter.

The pleasant-ness of riding sat upright, and on flat-ish ground, at the top of the hill lasts for only about 2 minutes before the downhill starts, but its heaven, and is just enough to calm me down and prevent me throwing my bike off the side of the steep roadside edge. Christ that was tough, but I've made it... just.

I eventually hit the downhill and free-wheel down at a nerve-jangling speed that I know would end in certain death if I crash. I've not got a speedo, but it's got to be well over 40-mph and it's scary as hell. Over the sound of the squealing disk brakes, I say a small prayer to the Cycling Oracle for strongly advising using a cycling helmet. I doubt the flimsy plastic shell would save my life at these speeds, but at least it'll keep my brains together, and easier to find, should I come off.

I eventually make it to Drumnadcochit, a little, stone-built village half way down the northern edge of Loch Ness, and find it a mecca for the droves of tourists who descend on it looking for a glimpse of Big Nessy. Looking like the Scotland Tourist Board has thrown up all over it, everywhere you go there are shops blasting out ear-piercing renditions of 'The Flower of Scotland' on bagpipes, and selling everything with either Nessy, a kilt, red hair, or all the above on it. I often wonder what it would be like to live in one of these towns, presumably appreciative of the financial security the tourist industry brings, but knowing that it's tinted in the plastic-ness of selling a shallow facade. How would it feel to have hordes of tourists descend on your town for the summer? Does it remove the soul from the place? Does it feel like you're living in a theme park, or do you just accept it and smile in the knowledge that you get to live in such a wonderful setting when everyone else has to go home? I guess, as with everything in life, it's all a matter of perception.

After a night in a campsite set on an equine farm just outside of the town, I set off early the next morning with the clouds in the sky threatening some pretty bad weather. And in true Scottish fashion, the big, black, angry looking clouds eventually give-in and I'm riding head first through a torrent of rain driving right into my face, helped by a ferocious headwind. It feels like I've almost constantly been riding into a gale since the trip started. I've heard that when people are attempting to cycle the length of the UK you are better travelling Northward from Land's End to John O'Groats as the wind generally blows in that direction... and I can categorically conclude that, yes you are, and it absolutely bloody does.

I follow the A82 from Drumnadcochit along the north side of Loch Ness and into Fort Augustus. It's a typically picturesque, Scottish town filled with stone built cottages and is focussed around a flight of 5 canal locks that facilitate access between Loch Ness to the east, and a man-made canal leading to the beautifully named Loch Oich, to the west. The locks are wide, allowing vessels of up to 35 feet wide to pass, and are an impressive feat of engineering. Interested in seeing the locks in action, I wait patiently for about 20 minutes till a large boat flying the Norwegian flag traverses the first lock. It never touches the sides as it is impressively manoeuvred through the lock with a grace unbefitting of such a large vessel. I consider waiting to see it move all the way up to the top but, whilst it is kind of interesting, I soon get bored and move on - I figure there are some things you only need to see once.

Continuing south-west along the A82, the road breaks away from the waterway for a few miles, before picking it back up at Loch Oich. The waterway is the Caledonian Canal and it spans the width of the country diagonally upwards from Fort William and the Irish Sea in the west, to Inverness and the North Sea in the east. The route is made up of 4 Lochs: Loch Lochy, Loch Oich, Loch Ness, and Loch Dochfour, and they're connected together with smaller man made sections in between. The canal was designed by the great engineer Thomas Telford and was built between 1803 and 1822. It was originally supposed to take just 7 years and approximately £470,000 to complete. However, due to a number of issues, not least due to the remoteness, the Scottish weather, and most likely the midges, it ended up overrunning by 12 years and at more than double the cost. Now that's a pretty impressive overspend, even by the British government's standards.

I follow the north side of Loch Oich by road, then spot a cycle path which the lock master tells me, in a broad Yorkshire accent, runs all the way down to Fort William and to our final rendezvous point for the day. After about 20 minutes of riding along the rough dirt-track, I realise that it's the first bit of off-roading I've done and I like it. I'd even go as far as calling it 'awesome'. I start really getting into it with a vigour I didn't know I had for off-roading. I feel the buzz of flowing over the mounds and dips and the changes in forces it brings. It's quite exhilarating, and the excitement lasts for about half an hour, right up until I hit a large stone and boom, a flatty. It's my first flat tyre of the trip and has come just at the worst possible time. It turns out that midges really love wet surrounds, like the canal I'm stood next to, and the dampness that follows rain, which has just stopped. I've no sooner got out my tools when I'm covered in the little buggers, and spend the next 10 minutes trying to change the inner tube at double speed whilst attempting to waft them away like I'm trying to perform some 1980's electro body popping.

Tube changed, and a pint of blood lighter, I'm back on my way. About 5 minutes travelling down the canal-side track, I catch up to a boat containing a party of youths on a booze cruise. As I pass they insist on toasting me with a clink of their drinks and a collective wail of appreciation. I reciprocate with a wave, then treat them to a short spell of non-handedness, which gets an overzealous roar and a round of applause. I feel awesome again.

By late afternoon I make it to Fort William, which remember from a previous visit as a busy hotspot for outdoor enthusiasts. And today is no different, as the place is filled with shoppers displaying their expensive survival clothing like sexually aroused peacocks. Everywhere you look there are people wondering about the high-street wearing very expensive, and suspiciously clean, outdoor clothing. Every other shop seems to be an outdoor pursuit's outlet, catering for the hordes of people who come to the town to tackle, or more likely simply look at, big Ben Nevis mountain only 1 mile away. I had organised to meet Sue about 2 miles outside the town along the east side of Loch Linnhe and so after stopping for some chips, I continue through the town, and get drenched in yet another torrent of Scottish rain. Still, at least I was mindful enough to bring along some reliable waterproofs.

I finally make it to the meeting point and am yet again greeted by the heart-warming sight of the van, Sue, and the dog. The rain has now stopped and it's a beautiful sight to see the support team in such a stunning loch-side location. We get organised and bed-in for a night of tranquillity. The music is on, and out of the van window we can see over the loch, which is bathed in the evening sun after the clouds have finally disappeared. The moment is beautiful and a necessary antidote from a long day's dripping wet ride. We start settling into the evening, popping the cork out of a bottle of wine, when we notice the midges circling us in anticipation of a night's feasting. The mood changes in an instant and we both become tetchy, managing about half an hour before it becomes too much and we're diving into the front seats and back down the road to the concrete haven of the Fort William pubs.

The soothing pitter-patter sound of rain droplets on the roof of the van normally brings a cosy feeling, particularly when it's heard from underneath the protection of a duvet. However, knowing I'll be riding in it in half an hour's time seems to be taking the shine off it a tad.

I've very quickly learnt over the last few days that staying dry on a bike is simply not an option, particularly given my choice of weather gear. The best approach is going to be to accept the dampness and look to stay warm instead. Warm and damp is uncomfortable, whereas cold and damp is grim, really, really grim.

As I lie in bed I look over and notice we've got a leak from the skylight. I can't bloody believe it! I lie back for a moment to first control my anger, and then to consider what the best thing to do is. As it's on Sue's side of the bed I decide the only sensible option is to hide back under the duvet and hope it goes away. It doesn't, and I'm instantly regretting my choice as I'm now faced with an even worse proposition of a pissed off wife, as well as a leaking van. Eventually, I am forced to get up and strip the van down to try and find, and therefore fix, the water entry point. I can't seem to find where it's coming from so we're left with the only option of rotating pans as they fill up with the nauseatingly unrhythmic sound of dripping water.

The morning's not started well and tensions are high. Fuelled by sleep deprivation, about 250 miles of Scottish undulating roads and the insanity of midge bites, there is friction in the air and I can feel an impending row. Even the dog has sensed it and is curled up in the corner of the seats quietly awaiting the opportunity to flee. I know how she feels.

And I'm not filled with the excitement of the roads today either. Ever since I started the planning for this journey, I have been anticipating today to be a bit of a grinder. I'm four days into the journey and my legs are fatigued, having not yet built up the strength and endurance that I am hoping will come as time goes on. There is a moment in any challenging journey where, up until that point, your energy levels and enthusiasm go slowly downward. You start off with excitement and motivation and a real sense of wellbeing and proudness. But over time, this diminishes and it becomes harder and harder to get going after each stop and you start questioning whether you can make it at all. Then you get to what feels like a crisis point and you start pulling it together again. You start getting strong, you get into a rhythm and you learn to accept the aches and pains and eventually you gain the tenacity and mind-set that keeps you going till the end. But today is a pre-day and I'm tetchy, bordering on angry, and, having driven the next stretch in the van a couple of times before, I sadly know what's in store and it's hills, lots and lots of hills.

Throughout the morning, I am passed, at quite high speeds, by loads of cyclist in the streamlined racing position of head down, eyes front. Rather than holding the handlebars, they are all using elbow rests sat on top of the handlebars and have their hands clasped together like they're praying. And they're all wearing helmets with large sloping backs that remind me of the Wolseley Pith helmet worn in the TV sitcom 'It Aint Half Hot Mum' from the 70's. I presume it is for aerodynamic reasons, but actually makes them look a bit daft. I wonder if these 'elite' level products make enough difference to warrant looking stupid and costing the earth for the average cyclist, which, judging by the rolls of fat trying to fight out of their Lycra, these clearly are. I have a lot of respect for the 'sports cyclist', but it seems there is a lot of 'for show' purchases that occur. If you're a professional racer I can see how every microsecond counts and that any competitive edge you can get is worth it. But if you're a fat middle manager from Swindon out on a Sunday race, I question your motives for spending 300 quid on a helmet that will probably make very little difference. But each to their own I guess, and I'm sure more than one person has said something similar about my Lycra on this trip.

From the town of Glencoe, the road goes inland heading east, and it goes up... a lot. I climb for about 10 miles or so, passing the 'Three Sisters' mountains, the Glencoe Ski Centre, and the Kings House Hotel. The road is a slow steady grinding uphill, but the views are breath-taking and it's one of my favourite parts of the world - when travelling by motor power anyway. The road traverses the base of the valley, which is about a kilometre wide and 500 metres high, and it's barren, save for a few splattering of trees, and, of course, a river. I can't help but take regular breaks to drink it in, to take a few pictures, but most importantly to rest the legs. The lactic acid is really building up in my thighs and I can only manage 15 minutes or so each time before I need to stop again to relieve the painful muscle-burning sensation.

As I approach the carpark used to access the Three Sisters Mountains, I can see it is overflowing with cars and holiday makers, and can hear the faint sound of the Scottish national anthem being played on bagpipes again. I pull into the carpark and am taken aback to I see a guy of about 50, in full Scottish tartan regalia, playing the pipes and being watched by a woman and a small girl standing 10 feet away hand in hand. It's a very idyllic scene with a backdrop of the craggy mountains and the attentiveness of the watching audience, and I'm really drawn in to the ambiance of the scene till he stops for a fag and performs a cough based hint for me to put some money in his tin. I stand, slightly dejected, and contemplate what 2 minutes of 'The Flower of Scotland' is worth. I eventually find a 2-pound coin and bung it into his tin, instantly regretting it. Maybe it's the cheapening of what was such a beautiful moment by its brazen commercialisation that I don't like, or, more likely, the fact that I didn't want to part with 2 quid.

I decide to get my money's worth with a picture of him and Manion

Friday side by side, but he looks quite angry and I can't bring myself to ask him to stand holding a 4-inch plastic toy, particularly as I know it is likely to come with a cough and another look towards his tin. Instead, I subtly move around the back of him and, after slowly removing my camera and my little yellow friend, I take a quick photo of me holding Manion, and the back of the Scottish piper. I get the shot, but as the camera clicks, he spins around with a confused look on his face, and I quickly scurry off, chuckling, and trying desperately to stuff the little yellow toy back into my bag. I just hope Mavo will appreciate the effort taken to get such a symbolic picture. The strangeness of the moment has me sniggering like a kid, till I realise that this might actually be the first signs that solo cycling is sending me a bit mad.

The roads today are as hilly as I remember them and its more of the same all afternoon. I continue up and over the open expanse scrubland of Rannoch Moor, and on towards the town of Tyndrum. As I get close, the road rises at a steady gradient, just on the wrong side of comfortable riding, for about 10 miles. The steady, continuous climb, along with a blustering headwind and driving rain is making my already lethargic legs feel like useless logs of blancmange. And the bleak weather, somehow made worse by being in such a remote location, is making it the most unpleasant riding of the journey so far. The weather and the environment have come together to make me feel uncomfortably isolated and the 10 miles seems to take a lifetime to complete. As the miles pass by, my face starts with a mild gurn, which turns into a wince, before finally turning into something right out of a Russell Crowe film. I eventually find myself shouting expletives in anger, however there's only the sheep within hearing distance and they seem distinctly unimpressed as they give me a nonchalant stare. But it feels good, really good. I'm not sure how or why but shouting abuse seems to help and, after carefully ensuring there is no one around, I go at it like a mad-man, screaming profanities like some mad psychotic sociopath. I feel close to the edge and I'm worried about how good it feels to behave like a mentalist, and how much I'm loving the feeling of fire rising in my belly. Maybe it's just the absurdity of it, or maybe there is actually some chemical release going on inside, but I can feel my spirits rise with every scream. I shout my way along for a good hour or so and it's just enough to stop me throwing the bike down the mountain, getting into the foetal position, and calling my mum. I'm so cold and wet and, along with the drained legs and rapidly diminishing energy, I'm starting to think this trip might have been a bit of a bad idea after all.

Evolution of a MAMIL

Chapter 5: ...To England

I journey south towards Glasgow, past the full length of Loch Lomond, and straight into the city. There is finally a calmness to the wind and I make some good miles past the serene mass of water before the need for food is upon me again. I hope for a pie shop or café, however all I can find is a McDonald's, and it's not long till I'm regretting it. Normally, I think your body lets you know when it's in dire need of a specific nutrient, such as when you crave a salty or sugary food, but when I see those 'golden arches' I have an instant desire, even though I know it's not going to end well. And I was right as it's not long till I'm riding with a brick in my stomach and a feeling that I may be seeing the greasy quarter-pounder meal again very soon. I am not sure how they've managed it but McDonald's has perfected the art of making me override my body's own self-preservation mechanism by wanting to fill it with the most inappropriate food. Damn you Ronald and your admittedly tasty produce. As I do every time I go, I vow to never indulge in their fatty, endorphin-inducing goods again.

As I get past Loch Lomond and closer to Glasgow the traffic gets noticeably busier... and angrier. Up in the Highlands, the cars and trucks were very accommodating. There was the odd vehicle that would come a little too close, but in general the traffic was able to give me a good wide berth. But as I get closer to the city things had been changing, and I didn't like it. People are obviously in more of a hurry - life just moves quicker in the city - and they are now taking chances with traffic gaps, and therefore with my life, passing way too close, and way too quickly. I decide I need to get off the road and find a different route. Luckily, as I stop to take some deep breaths to both keep down the McDonald's and to psych myself up for yet another roundabout, I spot a cycle-path signposted for Glasgow. I feel like I've been rewarded by the gods for getting this far and, after a few hallelujahs and a quick game of chicken, I'm across the road and cycling within the relative serenity of a city cycleway littered with all sorts of crap including old clothes, a used sanitary pad, and more randomly a full-sized snooker table.

The pathway leads to a canal and I follow it till I start getting worried as my compass flickers towards north, and totally in the wrong direction for my target of the city centre. I leave the canal and head down a short, wide, untarmacked path hoping that it doesn't lead me into an inner-city Glaswegian council estate. On seeing garden-gnomes with their cheeky little faces in manicured gardens of affluent-looking, semi-detached houses, I know I'm safe. But I'm also lost, and that means ask for directions.

'Excuse me', I shout in my nicest tone at an old bloke in a flat cap and black overcoat. 'Which way to the city centre?'

'The centre?' he replies looking around to get his bearings 'Aye, you go up Lewis Street, then right at the Co-op then...' I had hoped the nice English accent and the fact I'm asking for directions would have alluded him to the fact I was not local and would not have a bloody clue where any of these places were.

'Sorry, I don't know Lewis Street, or the Co-op'.

'Oh? Then you need to go up here and cross over near the train station. That's Lewis Street'. And with that he was off, clearly frustrated that I'd taken up 2 minutes of his valuable time.

I am still confused. 'Which direction is the city?' I shout to the back of his head as he walks away on the other side of the street.

'It's over there', he replies, pointing randomly to his left, clearly irritated.

'Errrm, thanks'. Note to self, don't ask for any more directions. I move on, quickly.

With my new-found knowledge and a lot of luck, I find a busy road and spot a bus with 'City Centre' written on the front. 'Follow that bus!' I mutter to myself and chuckle a little, till I notice a woman with a pushchair looking at me strangely. Embarrassed, I scurry off, head down, trying desperately to get my feet back in the damn peddle clips.

I figure my inability to take in directions was partly due to the guy being in a rush, but mostly due to me being alone on the bike for so long that my brain has gone into standby mode. Spending hour after hour in solitude has meant that when I do need to interact with other people, it feels like really hard work. It's almost like I don't belong in their world somehow. I feel like I'm a bystander, looking in, and as I get into the city centre it gets worse with the busyness and constant noise a distinct contrast to my own state of mind. I feel very uncomfortable to find myself within this hub of consumerism. After just 4 days in the Highlands, the shallowness of the money driven, superficial environment I find myself in now smacks me square in the face. Everyone seems so obsessed about having things that they're easy prey for the corporate brands who are tapping into that desire with things such as fancy shop styling, the excessively good-looking models on the 6-foot high billboards, and the 'unbelievable' deals on offer everywhere. I decide I need to get out of here as quickly as possible and so, after a few pictures of Manion Friday outside Celtic Park (the home of Celtic Football Club) I find my exit road south towards Strathaven. With a wipe of the brow, and the buzzing feeling slowly releasing from my mind, I'm out in the sanctuary of the open road again.

As I leave the city I am in a real tranquil place, back enjoying the calming countryside and its relative peacefulness. But inevitably it doesn't last for very long, as the bike starts playing up by slipping between gears, which is jolting me dangerously forward. Every time I try to put some power through the pedals, the gears slip and I'm thrown forward and downward with my man-stuff stopping agonisingly close to the crossbar. One more thing to put on the 'things to get pissed off about' list.

I continue on, grumbling to myself like an old drunk, and I realise that the landscape has changed dramatically since leaving Glasgow. The angry, craggy mountains I was surrounded by before I got there have been replaced with soft, rolling, green hills of lush farming land. Lots of the Highlands of Scotland are not really farmed, and you can see why. Beautiful as it is, the land is too rugged to be useful, however, as you head south, the land becomes more manageable and workable and, therefore, prosperous. The rolling hills may be more favourable for the farmers down here, but for me, they're still a right bloody pain in the legs.

I fight the hills, as well as the relentless wind, which has been directly into my face all day, wondering yet again why the hell I didn't choose to do this journey from south to north? I finally reach the sleepy little town of Strathaven and call the wife to try to find our meeting point.

'Hi, where are you?' I snort. I can hear the poke in my voice and realise I sound slightly more irritable than is warranted.

'Hey, I'm in Strathaven.'

I was surprised by her pleasant response given my grumpy greeting. 'I know that, but whereabouts?!'

'I'm in a carpark across from the Spar shop in the centre of town.'

'But I'm outside the Spar.'

'Can you see a hairdresser shop?'

'Yeah, I can. But where exactly are you?!' I know I'm getting unnecessarily grumpy but I can't help it. I just need a chill and a sleep. I'm done in and I feel rather tetchy.

'Hold on,' she states, 'let me come find you.' And with that she cut me off, and I see her walk from a small entrance at the other end of the square. I ride over to her, noting the significant distance from both the Spar and the hairdressers, ammunition ready for an impending row… But then she rolls out the cannon and blows me out of the water.

'So, how was it?' She asks with a noticeable shake in her voice.

'Good', I lied. And as I go around the side of the van to put the bike away, I am faced with the sight of a hole in the back corner of the van the size of a watermelon. Seeing the look of confusion and dejection on my face sends her into a frenzy.

'I have had an accident…' she states nearly in tears. So, I can see. 'I was reversing and there was a post, well not really a post, it was, well, so I was in a housing estate, and, you see, it was the Sat-Nav, I cou…….' The rest was just noise.

The look on her face was so gutted and upset that I could see the craziness of the moment. I put my piddly little row-munition back in my pocket and gave her a hug. She was so upset, and deep down, I know the van is so riddled with rust that there are places where you only need to look at wrongly and it will fall apart. It was just, well, not really what I needed right now. Just not bloody now. So, with a period of silence, followed by lots of apologies from us both, we settle into a bottle of red and forget about the worries. Just another moment on what now seems like a downward spiralling adventure.

I wake the next day to find the sun is shining both in the sky, and, rather more surprisingly, within my head. I get up and go to the café to get Sue a truce-based sausage butty and coffee. And on the way back, I suddenly realise that this might actually be the anticipated turning point of the trip. After the devastation of finding the new midge access portal system yesterday, I can somehow feel that this might be 'that point' when everything stops going crap and starts coming together. I hope I'm right because I've been increasingly struggling since I started. If I carry on like this, the chances are I'll be crawling on all fours before I even get out of the UK.

I leave Strathaven just after lunch and head ever south towards the border. Out of the town, it's immediately into the same rolling hills I'd left behind the night before, only now, there is a distinct change in my mental state. Rather than seeing each hill as a burdening challenge to tackle, I seem to be just letting them happen and am settling into my thoughts. The miles trickle by as I travel south along the B7078, running parallel to the M74 motorway. The road used to be the main access road between Scotland and England but is an eerily desolate dual carriageway now that the motorway has taken over, carrying very little other than the odd truck looking for a place to haul up for the night. It is noticeably unmaintained too, leaving it very bobbly, particularly for my bike and its lack of anything resembling suspension, though I do congratulate myself for choosing a cyclo-cross bike with its fat and rugged wheels. The quietness and isolation is pleasant, broken only by the passing of a low-flying fighter jet directly overhead, which creeps up on me quickly, sending me into some strange involuntary shouting spasm like I have a bad case of tourettes.

Passing through the non-descript, yet pleasant landscape of southern Scotland turns out to be quite enjoyable, marred only by the incessant rain. The ever more flattening hills are in contrast to the craggy sharp mountains of the Highlands. And they gently flow through rises and falls, none of which get me too exhausted, I just keep ploughing through with my new found reflective approach. This trip, I remind myself, is not something to get through at speed, it's something to enjoy, and to cherish.

I started out not really knowing why I wanted to do this trip other than the fact I knew I needed to do something, and, in all honesty, I still can't really articulate a solid reason. Although, I did know that I wanted to be inside my head again and have time to reflect a bit. I'd never really thought about this before but I wonder whether maybe this is simply the antidote for a mid-life crisis? If that's the case, I guess Sue should be thankful that it's cheaper than a sports car and far less dangerous than a motorbike.

I catch up with the support crew at our rendezvous point of Lockerbie and find them located in the town's Tesco carpark. Sue informs me that she's had a reccy of the town but sadly there is nowhere suitable to park overnight.

With the lack of an overnight spot, we hit the map and consider the options. As we stand gazing dejectedly into the map for somewhere else to stay, I see a pleasant looking old-boy collecting the shopping trollies from across the carpark and cycle over.

'Hi mate, have you got a sec?' I ask.

'Aye', he replies, stopping the juggernaut of trollies in an impressively short distance for a man of his age.

'Is there anywhere around here to stop in a camper?'

'Errrm, not really.' He states as his face turns from smiley old man to shock with a hint of a grin. 'Christ! Looks like the midges have had your legs.' I look down and am reminded just how rotten I'm looking.

'Oh, yeah, little gits. Take my word for it, my legs are not the only part that's taken a beating!' He breaks into a chuckle as I twinge slightly, remembering the more remote bite marks.

'Where've you travelled from?'

'I started in John-O-Groats and I'm trying to get to Gibraltar.' I am reminded of just how cool that sounds and I can feel my chest pump out a little.

'Jesus, how far is that?'

'About 3000 miles I think, but I'm not really sure how far I'll get.'

'Wow, that's impressive. Are you doing it for charity?' He enquires.

'No.' I'd heard this question once or twice before.

I had thought about this a lot during my planning. Losing both my brother and father-in-law to cancer had always given me a significant reason to do it for charity. But this challenge was slightly different. In the past I've done a few charity events, notably the Cheshire ring walk with Carlos and Dan, and the West Highland Way with Sue, but I've always been confident of completing them. Each has been difficult in it's own way but I had always known they were within my abilities. This one was different however as I had absolutely no idea how it was going to end. I did not know how my leg and knee would hold up and so I didn't want to put myself in a position where I pushed too hard and did some serious damage due to the feeling that I needed to get to the end. The thought of having to return sponsorship money back to people was enough to decide to not take on the extra burden. I decide to give him the short answer. 'I guess I'm just doing it to see if I can.'

'That sounds fantastic, you'll have a great time.' He was clearly as pleasant as he looked. 'If you're travelling south there's a nice little campsite at Annan. It's cheap enough and it's a lovely little town on a river. My wife and I stay there all the time.' He proceeds to give me directions and, for once, I was able to understand and remember them.

'How are the midges there?' I ask with bated anticipation.

'This is Scotland mate they're everywhere!'

Gutted. 'Do they recognise official country borders?' I reply half-jokingly.

'Aye, they're a speciality of Scotland!' He states with mock proudness.

'Ha! Thanks for the info. By the way, what's your name?'

'Charlie, my name's Charlie.'

'Thanks Charlie!' I shout back as I make my way back to the van. I couldn't really make out Charlie's age but he wasn't young. I hope that when I get to his age I am active enough to do such a physically demanding job.

I give Sue the good news and she sarcastically revels in the knowledge that she's getting treated to a campsite tonight, she's one lucky lady. We make our way down through 10 miles of sun-blessed farmland to Annan. It's still really windy, coming directly off the impending estuary and directly into my face, but with my new-found calmness, I simply tut at the injustice and continue on, although I can still feel some tension in the pit of my stomach and I know deep down that the new positivity is fragile. I wonder just how long this enlightened approach will last this time?

The short ride to Annan gives me enough time to reflect on the journey over the last 7 days as I'm now getting close to the border, and am nearly through my first completed country. Scotland truly is a rugged place, having an aggressive beauty with angular mountains and miles of nothingness in the north, followed by rolling pastoral hills of the south. It's been beautiful surroundings and very humbling as a cyclist, alone in the overpowering presence of the vastness and extremeness of the environment. There is something about such wild open terrain that fills me with excitement, and in between the continual battle of body and mind I've been able to understand, first-hand, why so many people continue to live in such remote locations. I've been to Scotland on a number of occasions in the past, but have mostly only been able to enjoy the place as a framed picture through the 2D effect of a car window. As a MAMIL, however, I've been submerged into the beauty and brutality of the place and have been able to truly appreciate how overwhelming it is. Even if it sometimes didn't feel like it at the time, it's been worth every last drop of sweat, although they do need to do something about those bloody midges!

Annan sits just above the Scottish-English border, 10 miles to the west of Gretna Green and is a sleepy town with a wide, slow running river running through it by the same name. The town is pretty with its red, sandstone buildings and its imposing clock tower set in the town centre on top of the town hall. After finding the campsite, we go into the town looking for a bit of life, however, since it's only a Tuesday night, the only other people in the pubs, other than us, seem to be the local die-hards. There is not really much in the way of entertainment in the town, and the highlight of the evening is the discovery of some free Wi-Fi where I take some time to update my blog. It's been 7 days and I'm about 400 miles into the journey, 20 miles behind my anticipated 60 miles per day. But that is fine, I'm happy with progress and am confident I'm on track.

It's been kind of a weird but half-expected turn of emotions so far. I started off with the giddiness of a kid who's found his first porno, then stooped into worry and anguish, particularly when the pains in my knee kicked in, before eventually finding nice happy, rhythmic riding. I still feel really untested though, and I am yet to know my limits. I sometimes feel like I'm out of my depth, with failure more a matter of when rather than if, but then at other times I can feel a real sense of belief. I know my body is still not strong enough to make it all the way yet, although I can only assume that will fix itself over time. But there have been brief moments where, mentally I've felt strong. I just hope this is going to be enough to get me all the way to see those Gibraltarian apes.

Evolution of a MAMIL

Evolution of a MAMIL

ENGLAND

Evolution of a MAMIL

Chapter 6: ...To Home

After yet another night of traditional Scottish rain, I wake to find the campsite is an absolute quagmire. It's smashed it down all night but I slept soundly with my new-found positivity, which even the expectation of more rain and a day being drenched cannot shift. I even surprise myself by focusing on the positive fact that at least the rain will keep the midges away.

The van, for all its flaws, of which it has many, including the new Sue-induced ventilation system, is blessed with rear wheel drive. And being twin axle, is fine in muddy conditions. The 4 wheels driving from the back mean it has no trouble getting out of boggy fields, which it definitely is this morning. As we start packing up, I can hear the high revving coming from a car on the other side of the field and look out to see a guy agonizingly trying to push his car and connected caravan out of the mud, whilst his wife screams the nuts off it, making 2 ever-deepening ruts for the front wheels to sit in. Feeling at peace with the world, and with a hope to build up some good karma, I go over and find a very wet, yet surprisingly chirpy Austrian couple of about 50. The guy, splattered head to toe in mud, is sporting a face peppered with midge bites, and his wife has absolutely none - it's like they've been on 2 different holidays. It turns out that not everyone is affected by midges and due to her dark skin tone, she was not. The guy, however, is clearly susceptible, and they'd gone for him big time, gorging themselves on his fair skin like a group of pissheads sharing a kebab. He genuinely didn't seem bothered, although this may have been due to his current predicament with the car. And he was happy with the weather too, saying the rain was a blessing as it was a constant 35+ degrees in their home town in Vienna. The grass is always greener I guess, although I wonder if the sheer volume of rain that drops on Scotland actually makes it the greenest?

After giving them a tow out of the field I'm back on the road, just in time for the heavy rain to start again and it's not long till I'm drenched, and finding sanctuary in shouting again. I opt for Trainspotting quotes in a crap Scottish accent. I make a mental note to refrain from this crazy shouting in built-up areas. Not only do I sound like a nutter, I might also be lining myself up for a kicking from the Scottish youth who may not see the funny side of my choice of phrases.

It's not long till I'm finally over the border, and my positivity steps up a notch further. Passing through Gretna Green, made famous as a place for English people to get married quickly, I am back on the road and travelling alongside the M6 motorway. The road is fairly flat, and takes me all the way to Carlisle, then onto the A6, which, as one of the longest A-roads in the UK running from Carlisle to Luton, I know will be my home for the next few days.

After passing Carlisle, the flat road disappears, and normal order is restored as the hills start again. By the time I reach Penrith, my legs are once again struggling. In my head, I feel fine, sprightly even, but when I need to put some power down for anything more than a few seconds, my thighs muscles are burning like crazy and I feel really weak. I am in need of some energy and so decide to stop for a pie, then wash it down with a nice jam and cream donut. I manage just 10 or so miles before I'm feeling sick and am doubled up, seeing both items again.

The road passes through some lovely little towns and villages but I don't really get chance to enjoy them as I'm feeling a little rough from the pie and cake combination, and the lactic acid in my legs is causing some serious pain. On a more positive note, the midges seem to have gone. Looks like Charlie was right after all. Whilst pleased that the midges are now a thing of the past, I find that midge-madness has now been replaced with an irritation from a click and a squeak on the bike that I can't for the life of me find where it's coming from. I stop every mile or so trying to locate what's causing it, each time feeling I've located its source only to be unable to recreate it once again I've stopped. It's driving me crazy and I can feel the demons of pessimism trying to make it into my head again.

I soldier on, and am awarded at the end the day with one of the most euphoric moments I've felt in a very long time. I finally pass through Shap by late afternoon and am faced with the horrifying sight of a sign stating the 1400 feet Shap Summit lay ahead. But rather than dwell on the impending suffering, I simply drop the bike to a really low gear and continue on, drifting into a Zen-like trance. As I ride up the steady inclined ascent, without any real thoughts but to keep pushing the pedals, I soon forget about the anguish of the previous days. I'm no longer angry, or particularly happy for that matter, I am just here, in the moment, focused on the task in hand and everything else somehow seems inconsequential. It is not long till I realise the thigh pains that have been with me all day have suddenly disappeared, and the squeak is sounding almost hypnotic. Just at the moment when I should be in real pain and agony, I find myself at one with the bike, at one with the world, and more importantly, at one with myself.

I'm not sure if it's taken 20 minutes or 2 hours, but I make it to the top of the summit where I stop, not because of any pain, or because I'm knackered, but because I want to stretch out the moment of peace, and to engulf myself in this feeling of elation. I can't really understand why I feel this way and frankly, I don't really care. I am just happy, the happiest I've been for a long time. I know I'm just an average bloke from Cheshire, old and slightly balding, and probably a bit boring sometimes, but just at this moment, I realise I have absolutely no cares in the world. I sit on the kerb of a roadside layby with the warmth of the sun now overhead, in silent contemplation, and I am suddenly engulfed in euphoria that makes me well up. I am so entrenched in the feeling of contentment that my eyes start to leak and I find myself crying. It's not an all-out whining fit, but a gentle trickle of tears down my previously perspiring face, and I can taste the salt from the sweat as the tears drop to my lips. I don't consider myself a particularly spiritual person but at this brief moment I feel enlightened and in love with the world, and with this trip. This, I now know, is why I wanted to become a MAMIL.

I make my way down the north of England and the roads start to get noticeably busier as I make my way through the once industrial hotspots of Preston, Chorley and Wigan. The places are a little rundown now due to all the industry having moved to countries with much cheaper workforces, but the affluent past is reflected in the grand looking town council office buildings, and the odd statue of some, once famous, industrialist. Stopping off for some food I remember back to the conversation I had with the Physiotherapist, Rick, when I asked him for some general advice for the trip. He reckoned a good diet would be by far the most important thing to take care of. At the time, I dismissed his remarks, considering that I would be completing the trip as a gentle adventure, rather than as an elite sports endurance challenge he was perhaps more used to dealing with. However, I am slowly coming around to the fact that he might have been right and that looking after my body's fuel intake is going to be critical to the success of the trip. I had thought that given the amount of energy I was using I could eat what I wanted. However, it's clear I need to stick to basic stuff like pasta and rice, and stuff that is rich in carbohydrates and protein. I'd bought some carb-gels on the advice of the Cycling Oracle, but I'd been keeping these for an emergency as he says they can make you feel sick if you have too many, and also on account of them costing 2 quid each. I've also got some electrolyte tablets to put in my water to replace the essential minerals lost through sweating. I've held off using them as of yet, again due to their expense, but I figure now is the time to start getting serious about my diet. I begrudgingly put my bag of pork scratches in the bin, drop a couple of electrolyte tablets into my water, and move on.

I get to Birchwood, just east of Warrington, and meet up with the Cycling

Oracle as he'd wanted to join me for a day's ride. I've been mates with the Cycling Oracle, Martin, for about 10 years since we both took the belated decision to go to university. Having had a bad biking accident, Martin was forced to leave his job as a fireman and lucky for me he did. I spent a lot of time with him and the other 'older guys' at university where we supported each other a great deal. We have all stayed close over the years and we meet up regularly where Martin is mocked as the sensible mate, though this is probably fuelled by jealously of his beautiful home and kids, and of his beautiful and classy wife Maris. Martin is a great friend and, being from Yorkshire, we also share the same financially careful approach to life.

We set off from Birchwood trying to natter about the journey so far but failing due to my insistence on not cycling side by side. I hate it when I'm driving and I get stuck behind cyclists riding side by side and so, as tempting as it is, I settle for sitting in behind Martin who tries to go slow enough to not leave me behind on his high-performance bike weighing less than one of my pedals. We make our way through the back lanes of Cheshire and I break my cardinal rule as we stop for an afternoon pint at a little thatched-roofed pub in the middle of Knutsford. The alcohol seems to work quickly on my dilapidated mind and it's not long before I'm jabbering away about the adventure so far and about the highs and lows I've been feeling. Martin then proceeds to bombard me with advice such as how I must eat and drink properly, and how I must wear sun-cream at all times, which, as appreciative as I am, I can't help but ignore on account of having cycled 600 miles. This clearly makes me an expert now, and I just nod at the appropriate moments and let it fly over my head. Just as Mr 'Safety-First' continues to fill me in, again, on the reasons why I must wear cycle glasses at all times, I down the rest of my pint as a hint that I want to get going. I think the world of Martin, but I realise now that I prefer to ride alone. And the isolation of being on the road, riding solo, is something I miss. The opportunity to be doing my own thing, in my own time, in my own way, is part of what is making this such a great adventure.

We make it back to my house by late afternoon via different routes so I can take the easy road up the hill to our house, and for Martin to attack the locally famous Killer Mile - a section of road a mile long at an average of 25% ascent to the top of the hill. Once we get back to the house, he proceeds to inform me about how much water I should consume, then to tell me all about the Killer Mile route he took. Aided by his GPS gizmo, he tells me his average speed, climb, heartbeat, and all other manner of statistics, which pale into insignificance as I am engulfed in the warm, yet strange feeling of being back home.

In my mind, I have achieved stage 1 of the Tour-de-Inner-Peace and I feel amazing. I am knackered, I stink, and my brain has melted, but I feel euphoric and am looking forward to the simplicities of a day in my own bed, and sitting on my own toilet. And so, after a long shower and a couple of drinks, I dive into my pit and after a quick moment of smug reflection, I'm gone to the world.

Chapter 7: ...To The Ferry

Day 12 and I'm back on the bike after a day off filled with domestic chores, including cleaning myself and my clothes of 10 days of grime and sweat. I also took the opportunity to book the cross-channel ferry from Poole to Cherbourg for the morning of the 17th of July, leaving me 5 days to get there. It should be fine, but it's the first deadline I've had since I started and it's already making me a tad uncomfortable.

The day off yesterday was a real frustration that I wasn't expecting as it felt kind of claustrophobic. I have only done 10 days riding. But in that time, I'd been through so much pleasure and pain that a day sitting about at home just seemed a bit of a waste of time. I had also expected to sleep solidly whilst at home, but I found I just couldn't stay asleep. I nodded off fine, but I kept waking with a million things spinning through my mind, not least, the ever-looming Pyrenees Mountains. I tried telling myself to stay in the moment and just go with it, but I couldn't. It was a kind of mix of excitement and trepidation at the prospect of the next stages of the journey and it kept me awake when I should have been recuperating and preparing for the next phase.

I head ever south through Stoke-on-Trent, which is on my doorstep and, similarly to the towns of Preston, Chorley, and Wigan before, has suffered greatly from the loss of manufacturing overseas. Once a thriving pottery manufacturing area, the 5 towns that make up the region are now struggling with high unemployment and other social issues that accompany it. The reams of terraced housing, once the homes of hard working and skilled potters, are rundown, with only the town council offices still showing off the grandeur of the recent past.

I'm on my way to a late breakfast meetup this morning with our friends, the Donohoes, in Stafford and I'm really looking forward to getting to them as the riding this morning feels a real effort. I can feel I'm shedding positivity with every turn of the wheel and the optimistic, upbeat attitude I had on getting home 2 days ago has been replaced with heavy legs and a feeling of fatigue. I feel like crap and unexpectedly gloomy, which is only relieved for a moment on seeing Knight Rider on the southbound carriageway of the A34. The sleek, black car cruises past relatively slowly, and is being driven by a guy in his late 30's with a blond, 80's style mullet and a moustache - I guess Stoke-on-Trent more than anywhere is in need of a crusader. The sight of the 4-wheeled hero makes me chuckle for a while, till I have the worrying realisation that seeing Knight Rider might simply have been a madness-induced mirage.

It's a real struggle this morning and I'm not helped by the fact the weather is wet, cold, windy, and miserable. I'm also feeling really weak, and, with its newly donned panniers, the bike is not only harder to project forwards, it's now infinitely more difficult to keep upright. Yet another piece of valuable information from the Cycling Oracle I chose to ignore was to use both front and back panniers, even if you don't need the space. He suggested using front wheel panniers to make the bike far better balanced, and I can now safely say he's correct. Every time I want to get off the bike it takes me 10 minutes to lean it against something so it stays upright, and as soon as I lift up the front wheel to move it, the heavy weight on the backend counter-levers the bike and flips it sideways. And if I'm straddling it as it goes down, the front chain sprocket scrapes oil up my calf, and I'm left with an oil-based tribal tattoo design on the back of my leg and the bike lying sideways between wide spread legs. Today's not starting out too well.

Throughout the day, the weather brightens up. Whilst it's making the scenery of flat farmland light-up, accentuating the yellow of the rapeseed-filled fields and the green of the livestock pastures, it's making riding a bit exhausting. I decide to take a rest and find a country pub which, by the look of the advertising boards, has followed the general trend of British pubs and found survival by replacing droves of beer drinkers with selective country dining. It's an idyllic looking place with a thatched roof and black-and-white, wattle-and-daub constructed walls. It's also furnished with loads of hanging baskets, all trying desperately to cling onto the masses of flowers overflowing in beautiful summer colours. It's the sort of place that I imagine foreign people think of when you mention that you are from England. It's a stunning, stereotypically English setting, which is marred only by the two young teenagers trying to knock the living daylights out of each other with tree-branches in the beer-garden. I can't help but watch as they go at it with the brutality only brothers could get away with. The action is only tempered by the odd half-committal shout from a severely overweight Dad to 'put that tree down!' before turning back to his pint and a fag. Now this really is a true English setting that they don't show in Hugh Grant films. It's at moments like this that I'm glad I don't have kids.

Perked up after a pint of ice-cold lemonade and having watched an epic gladiatorial battle, I head off south and in the direction of the hot afternoon sun. After a few hours, I make it to the agreed meeting point of Stourport-on-Severn where Carlos had planned to meet us and would be joining us for a few days in his van. Stourport-on-Severn is a beautifully named, yet surprisingly rough, town. It's popular as a day-out destination for the hundreds of tourists drawn to the beautiful River Severn and the town's permanently resident fairground with its hook-a-duck, shooting alley and other outdated and overpriced amusements. The streets are also crammed with outlets similarly trying to entice the coins out of the visitor's pockets, such as trinket shops and mini-arcades with their flashing facades promising large pay-outs and free coffee.

After riding back and forth through the town a few times I eventually spot the team across the park. As I ride over, I can see them both sat soaking up the sun. Carlos is sat in his collapsible chair, with a cool box half full of beer, the other half as empty cans strewn around his feet. As Jazz spots me, she comes running over and welcomes me with the ever giddiness that never fails to fill me with joy. Carlos, however, is rather less welcoming.

'Fuckin' hell mate have I had dysentery!'

'Hi mate, I'm good, thanks for asking' I reply, half annoyed, yet humoured by the familiarity of Carlos' egocentric attitude.

'Sorry mate, that's good, but I nearly shit myself. I only just made it here. Lucky the bogs were open otherwise I'd have had to go in the carpark.'

'Nice.'

Carlos is my best mate, and he's a legend, or a liability depending on the situation you find yourself in. In a dodgy pub in the middle of Moss Side he can become drinking buddies with the nuttiest guys, and can talk his way out of any potentially life-threatening situation through quick wit and a strong character. If you're on an adventure, however, and all he's brought are cans of Carling lager and Chocolate Penguins, he's a liability. On one occasion, on a weekend stomp, he felt so rough that we had to leave him in a small remote church whilst we went back to get the van, before returning to collect him - I guess he needed a bit of alone time with the big guy. But that said, everyone loves him. He's the type of bloke just as happy talking to a group of the world's greatest thinkers as he is to a bunch of homeless drunks. He always takes people at face value. He does not fear anyone, and does not look up to, or down on anyone either. He rents a room of another mate's mum and works weekends, spending the rest of his time fishing, drinking, or talking about fishing whilst drinking. He lives how he lives and seems genuinely happy with it, and you've got to respect that in anyone. He pays his way in life and only ever offends people who can take it, which, at this point in time, is his Lycra wearing mate.

'You took your time. Sue said you'd be here over an hour ago.'

'Yeah, I stopped off for a drink at a little pub.'

'Pub? What did you have?'

'Lemonade.' I can see where this was going.

'HA! Lemonade! Dressed like that? You must have looked a right idiot! You should have had a lager. Enjoy yourself kiddo, you're on holiday!'

A legend he is, but an expert on sports nutrition he most certainly isn't and so with a complete disregard of his advice, I grab the keys off Sue and dumped my bike in the van. Looking at the number of empty cans Carlos had at his feet, this was going to be a very interesting evening.

As it turned out it was an interesting evening, though sadly not for me. Having not been sleeping well, coupled by being sapped by the sun all afternoon, I had to drop out after a couple of pints and get my head down. Carlos and Sue however managed to find a lively boozer housing the local gypsies and other local reprobates. In his usual style, Carlos made friends with the 'King of the Gypsies', then managed to get himself sandwiched between a couple of gay guys during some close quarter dancing. He proclaimed they were just having a laugh, although Sue insists they were rather intent on enjoying his good nature further. The man is a true legend.

It rains all day and I am victimised again by an incessant headwind that seems to be mocking my predicament, intent on making my riding as challenging as possible. As I grind my way up yet another large hill, this one a 20% sheer gradient out of Cheltenham, I'm once again absorbed in the burning feeling in my legs and I ponder on just what has turned things tough again, particularly as I remember back to how buzzing I was feeling prior to the stop off at home. On reflection, I conclude that it's either:

- Having 12 days cycling in the legs
- Now heading away from home and not towards it

- Not sleeping well
- Now carrying my fully laden panniers
- The environment getting a bit monotonous
- This being the start of the next leg of the journey
- Not drinking enough water
- All the above....

I conclude it's the latter and hope I find that inner strength once more. I'm sure it'll come back at some point, but for the moment it's just a case of perseverance. I decide to lighten my spirits by making up a story of Manion Friday. Supported by a few pictures, I post a blog of his imaginary predicament:

Manion Friday in Suicide Attempt!

Yesterday was a bad day for the big guy. It started at about lunch time when he started going really quiet. I knew that something was wrong as he didn't eat his eggs Benedict this morning but when we stopped for lunch he went to the corner and started crying. He said it was the wind making his eyes water but I could see his shoulders shaking.

Then later I went to get us a couple of drinks and came back to him poised, seemingly ready to jump.

We had a chat and he said we went past a restaurant and he saw he was just one of many 'faceless slaves'! I told him he'll always be special to me and to Mavo. I think the trip is getting to him. I'll keep you posted on events.

I find it funny to think of this little plastic toy in emotional turmoil... right up until the moment I realise that maybe this trip is actually starting to get to me a bit too. I wonder just how much of this Manion story is actually an outlet for my own feelings, like I'm trying to make myself feel better by projecting my sadness onto a 4-inch plastic toy. I feel really worried about the possibility of this and slowly, but firmly push it to the back of my mind. I need to un-think this, and quickly.

By the time I get to the support team at the Cotswold Waterpark just south of Cirencester I feel pretty done-in. I'm wet and I'm cold but, as ever, the support team manage to pick up my mood with a laugh, mainly at my state of mind, and a few cans of lager. The Waterpark is made up of about 150 lakes, with some of them bordered by hotels and shops to support the holiday makers that come here for the array of water-sports on offer. We settle up in a shopping-outlet carpark on the edge of the area, which, on seeing a couple of trucks in the carpark, must be used as a stop-off by drivers hauling up for the night as they pass through on the main A429. It's a quiet night in the vans, consisting of food and booze, and even Jazz manages to enjoy herself, gorging on the local delicacies.

'Errm, I think that's human poo she's eating.' Carlos states as we take Jazz for a walk along a path to the lake.

'There's no 'think' about it mate, how many animals do you know that uses toilet paper?!'

After saying good-bye to Carlos, who has to get back home to his Oil Distributor job, we set-off with the target of the day being Sue's cousin Simon and his family's home in Bulford, a military town about 3 miles east of Stonehenge. I figure it's about 40 miles away and, in relation to the previous few days, is considered quite a short one. It should be a relatively easy riding day, leaving a nice ride into Poole tomorrow where we've planned a day off. However, I can't shake a feeling of frustration this morning which, I think, is mainly due to being unable to sleep again. I don't know why but I just spend hours staring at the roof of the van thinking about all sorts of stuff about the trip. I am absolutely knackered after long, hard cycling days, but I'm not able to sleep and I think it's affecting me badly. I feel so tired all the time yet I can't nod-off, and haven't really been able to since I started off from home. It feels like I've been going downhill, both mentally and physically, since I left home and I guess without proper sleep, it will keep going downhill till I'm eventually found at the side of the road, curled into a ball and sucking my thumb.

After safely negotiating the busy roads of Swindon, including its Magic

Roundabout, made up of 5 roundabouts interconnected by 1 large counter-clockwise roundabout in the middle, I continue on towards Marlborough. It's a ferociously windy day, directly in my face again and, whilst it's not helping my frustration levels, I'm more concerned with staying alive right now. The road is little wider than 2 articulated lorries, and is bordered on either side by 10-foot high hedges. Luckily, the road is fairly straight, allowing the traffic to see me, and therefore avoid turning me into a sloppy mess on the front of their cars. But the long straights also mean the road is drivable at high speed and they're taking full advantage, driving past within, what feels like, inches of my right elbow. I try to tuck in as much as possible to try to reduce the target area, however knowing I have two, potato-sack-sized panniers hanging off the back of the bike makes this pretty futile. The air turbulence caused by the fast trucks whizzing past is making the day more adventurous than I'd hoped as I try to prevent being blown into a wobble.

I eventually get to the small village of Marlborough and blow a sigh of relief at making it with all my extremities intact, even though my heart's still beating faster than a bee's wing. After a short break to try and compose myself and to contemplate changing my shorts, I continue out of the town, and am immediately faced with yet another sheer climb, this time up the brutally steep Granham Hill. As I start up the rise, I immediately know this is not going to go well as I've no energy in the legs and no determination in my head. I am really struggling to keep the pedals turning around. I plod up the hill at a snail's pace, just managing to keep enough speed to keep me upright, for about 10 minutes but it's no good. I'm done in and, rather scarily, I've finally hit the point where I want to quit.

For the first time since I left John O'Groats 14 days ago I am ready to stop and the thought of it makes me feel sick. I struggle up the rest of the hill, silenced by the thought that I genuinely might be giving in, then ride along for a while in the relentless, blustery wind, seriously contemplating my options for going home. I eventually find a farmer's field filled with metre high corn, and stop, dropping the bike unceremoniously to the ground, to take stock of what to do. I'm absolutely destroyed, both mentally and physically, and I feel like I want to cry with rage. I'm so tired, yet I can't seem to sleep. I fantasise of falling into a deep, baby-like sleep but I just can't. And my legs are throbbing in pain at any sign of a hill. The lactic acid burning with every turn of the pedal, exacerbated by this incessant, indecent bloody headwind. And to top it all off, the bike has a squeak and a clicking sound I simply cannot find, seemingly trying to push me over the edge of mental composure. I feel anger, real neanderthalic anger and I take to roaring like the Hulk at the injustice of it all, before turning to the inanimate object at my feet: 'YOU ARE A SHIT BIKE!'.

I realise I must look a right idiot stood swearing at a lump of metal at my feet. The daftness of the moment makes me stop shouting and start sniggering, before slumping to the ground as a broken man. I lie back in the dry tractor ruts in the dirt at the field's entrance, close my eyes and just stop. I stop thinking, stop shouting and stop hurting. The silence, broken only by the sound of rubber on tarmac of the odd passing car, is engulfing, and all I can hear is the therapeutic sound of my pulse beating in my ears. It feels good to just stop and I indulge in the feeling, and just lie there, unsure if I'm awake or asleep and just drift, trying to grasp for a happy mental place. This definitely feels like a new low.

After eventually getting myself under control I realise, slightly embarrassed, just how stupid I must have looked shouting at my bike, particularly calling it a 'shit bike'. I know it's not a shit bike, it's just got a shit rider, or, more specifically, a foolish one that thought he could buy a bike, do a few training rides, then cycle nearly 3000 miles from John O'Groats to Gibraltar in 60 days on a diet of cream cakes and pies. I just never knew it was going to be this hard. I knew it would be tough but I'm wondering whether this is worth it. Why am I doing this anyway? What do I have to prove? What a waste of cash and holiday time if I'm going to feel like shit all the way. Logically, I assume it's got to get better, I'm going to get stronger, but will I get so strong to make it enjoyable again? I can only assume the terrain will get worse once I hit the Pyrenees, if I even make it that far, and if I do, will I then be able to make it over?

So much negativity, and yet deep down, I know I'm not really going to quit, not yet anyway. I am at a distinctly low point, but I know this is not it, this is not that moment when I give in, I've got to at least try to make it out of the country! I wonder if it's the impending loss of support that has been bringing on this feeling? I know I'm going to miss Sue, but I also think I'm concerned about the loss of the support vehicle as well. Knowing I've always got somewhere to sleep, someone to make me feel better, and someone to row with is very comforting. The thought of losing that gives me an empty feeling but I know I need to sharpen up, I need to open the shoulders and get back in the saddle. I need to keep plodding on.

Feeling rather jaded by my first meltdown, I tentatively get back on the bike and make it to Bulford. As I get to Simon and Anita's house with their two beautiful kids, I come round the corner and am met by a cheering family that feels like a scaled down, but no less enthusiastic, ending to the Tour de France. How little they know of my vulnerable state, but and thought that they have more belief in me than I do right now brings a humbled tear to my eye.

I wake early the next day and am back in the saddle feeling a little more bullish, but still slightly embarrassed about yesterday's meltdown. A night of curry, beer, rest, and the company of carefree children has helped my morale, however I was still not able to sleep properly. I did manage to get online however and perform some self-diagnosis of the lack of energy and burning legs. It turns out I'm not drinking anywhere near enough water, which is clogging up my leg muscles with oxides and other things I don't really know much about. At least this is one thing I can try to resolve, simply by drinking water, however the wind, sadly, is not and it's doing its best again to prevent my progress, whipping across the gently undulating terrain of the Salisbury plain.

I continue south and I drift into reflecting on my current mood, focusing on the mental explosion from yesterday. I am feeling a bit disappointed in myself for not showing more steel, but I'm also feeling recovered and refocused, and I can feel the sense of achievement again. I should try not to think too far ahead as it's bringing on stress as I seem to be assuming the worst right now. Yes, plan as required, but just accept the darker moments, don't dwell on them, and try to ride the storm. I find comfort in the fact that if it wasn't a difficult challenge then it certainly wouldn't be as rewarding. As with life, this trip is full of yin-yang moments, the good and bad periods balancing themselves out. I need to try to stay positive and remember that I am on a journey not just physically, but mentally too. I am going to get stronger and fitter and I know I'll eventually get back to the tenacious character of old, even if I do spit my dummy out a few times on the way. I just need to have patience and to be at-one with the journey both within my mind and beneath my wheels. Contented, and slightly surprised with my enlightened and soulful thoughts, I am broken back to my typical character with a child-like giggle after seeing a sign for 'Sandyballs Caravan Park'. I'm back, I'm buzzing, and I'm ready to face the challenge again.

I travel quickly through Bournemouth and then onto Poole, stopping only to get my picture taken next to the 'Welcome to Bournemouth' sign by a surprised, and rather impressed policeman. As ever, it feels strange coming into the built-up areas with its busy commuters and the never-ending stream of traffic lights and roundabouts. As I ride in to the city, the surroundings change from countryside to housing estates, then into shopping areas and communal parks. The closer I get to the end of the country, the heavier the feeling I get that I will soon be losing Sue and Jazz, and the comfort of knowing Big-G will be waiting at the end of the day. I know I am very lucky to have a wife that's caring and supportive enough to let me do this, and to be able to pick me up when I've been feeling growly. I am looking forward to challenging myself to see how I cope alone, but I know I'm going to miss her loads. I start scouting the shops as I pass, thinking of what might be an appropriate present I could get her to somehow show the mixture of emotions I'm feeling towards our impending parting. I see a jewellery shop but decide it's too obvious, and besides, Sue's taste is too unique to be found in the usual branded shops, unless it's got a diamond the size of a fist, and, well, I'm tight, and I'm on a budget. I see a kind of interesting trinket shop, which has me gazing at all the weird and wonderful offerings till the gaze turns into a glaze and I lose track of what I'm looking for. I look for another shop and eventually settle on a small, independent flower shop set back from the busy street.

'Hi, can I help you?' The young, orange-tanned girl asks from behind a counter shrouded in a forest of exotic looking flowers.

'Errrm, yeah.' I reply as I tentatively walk through the shop trying not to get too close given it's been a few days since my clothes, or me, have seen a proper wash. 'Do you have anything that would survive being on the back of my bike?'

'Excuse me?'

'I'm on a bike but I want to buy a present. Do you have anything that won't get crushed?'

'Errrm, I'm not really sure, just take a look about.' Clearly minimum wage didn't warrant talking to sweating, stinking middle aged men in Lycra for anything other than standard issue flowers in a bow.

And then I spotted it, a kind of mini sunflower in a terracotta pot, which, to me, was symbolic enough to show how she has sprayed sunshine onto my soul when I've been at my worst, yet was robust looking enough to last being on my bike rack for the last 5 miles to the rendezvous point. So, with a 2-foot sunflower looking like it was sticking out from my bum, I head to Poole harbour and eventually turn a corner to see the 'Welcome to the port of Poole' sign high overhead above Big-G, and a smiling Sue armed with an ice cold can of Stella Artois. I've only gone and bloody made it!

So tonight, I decide, I'll mainly be getting drunk. But to my surprise, however, I'll actually be doing it in the luxury of a posh hotel in Poole. Sue had planned a surprise bit of luxury and it's not long till I'm sat soaking in a bath big enough to get a dozen playboy bunnies in. Sadly though, the bunnies had a day off, but I'm still super contented, sat quaffing red wine and feeling the ecstasy of succeeding at getting this far, along with the thought of a relaxing day off with Sue tomorrow. And to add further to the euphoria, Sue also informs me she has booked me in for a massage in the hotel spa the next day, which has me as happy as a pig in poo for about half an hour before I finally fall into the deepest sleep I've had for days.

Managing a full night's proper rest, topped off with a belly full of fried breakfast, I feel back on track and the thoughts of quitting just 2 days ago could not be further from my mind. We go for an amble around the bustling tourist town of Poole, then visit the fair, where we try to get more and more daring pictures of Manion Friday on various rides, with the winner being him sat on a 1950's style horse carousel. Once we're finished with the stupidity, we head back to the hotel for the massage.

We sit in the bar for a while before being notified the masseuse is ready. I'm led down some eerily steep steps to a low-lit room filled with the smell of fragrant oils and the tranquil sound of pan pipes. I risk a picture of Manion Friday relaxing beneath the crisp white towels covering the treatment bed before the door opens and the lucky lady enters. I had hoped to get some angry lesbian to really work out all the knots that have been growing in my thigh muscles, however she was the best part of 8 stone and looked disappointingly happy. Nicky turned out to be as nice as she looked and we ended up having a good chat that more than made up for the featherweight massage. She told me she had wanted to work on the cruise ships, which I obviously knew a lot about. She'd been planning it for a while and had even landed a job, however, she had to give up the dream as her boyfriend was not keen. I felt kind of sorry for her as I know just how good an experience it is, and how much being on the ships had a positive affect on my own life. The way she was talking, I could tell she was not totally contented with the idea of staying put and I just hope she would not regret the choice later in life.

That night we went for a nice meal and headed to the old part of the town. It was full of nice little eateries and had bunting hanging over the narrow high-street, which was clearly designed for a time before the oversized car was king. The shops too show the class of the area, selling various types of art, as well as different types of rustic, whitewashed furniture.

We ended up eating at the 'Hotel Du Vin' where the meal was really good, and Sue was pleasantly flattered by the advances of an old drunken gentleman in an expensive looking suit and a cravat. The evening was marred slightly by a young, annoying cockney couple on the next table, with the guy clicking his fingers at the 50-ish year old waiter, then talking to him like he'd defecated in their soup. To his credit he reacted with the professionalism and charisma clearly built up from many years in the trade, presumably dealing with similarly distasteful behaviour. I hate this attitude, underpinned by a status and money thing and I kind of hope he has indeed done the deed he'd potentially been accused of. The thought of this makes me smile as the couple return to ignoring each other, living out their 'e-lives' head down on their ostentatiously decorated phones.

So, that's it, 850 miles done and I'm at the south coast and what a journey it's been. It's been amazing, but it's been tough, really, really tough. I'd been a bit of a fool to think that I could just buy a bike and cycle nearly 3000 miles without going to hell and back, I know that now. But I've always been a 'feet first' kind of bloke and yes it's an approach that's caused me pain and anguish over the years, but it's the type of attitude that has presented me with so many experiences in the past and has done it again with the one I'm on now. And it's been surreal. I've been within 20 feet of a wild deer, I've nearly taken a photograph of an eagle, and I've seen Knight Rider up close, although the authenticity of the last one was not confirmed. I've not only seen stunning views, I've actually been in them, surrounded by the beauty of Scotland and England, smelling it and been engulfed in its splendour. I've ridden through some really tough moments, not to mention the damage to the camper, but I've also had euphoric waves of positive emotions I've not really felt for a long time, even able to move me to tears. I have had time to reflect on life and who I am. I've tested myself and, in the main, I feel like I've succeeded. I've had a few meltdowns along the way, but mostly it's been great and a real chance to declutter my mind.

I know it may not be as dramatic as, say, climbing Everest, or trekking to the North Pole, but it's all relative I reckon. I know I'm not Sir Ranulph Fiennes, I'm just a balding, middle-aged guy from Cheshire who had an idea and had a go at something different. To me this IS Everest, this is my quest to reach something I'm unsure I'm capable of, even now. But one thing is for certain is that I'm going to give it my best shot and if I don't make it then fine, but at least I can now proudly state that at least I made it out of the country - get in!

Evolution of a MAMIL

Evolution of a MAMIL

FRANCE

Evolution of a MAMIL

Chapter 8: ...To The Coast

Today is day 17 and after a long and slightly teary goodbye with Sue, the dog, and the trusty campervan, I make it onto the ferry just in time before my front tyre runs on the rim from a puncture. Gutted, but with no time to fix it before the ferry leaves, I just ignore it and make my way to the relative comfort of the lounge for a pricey, yet rather bland, coffee and a croissant. I figure this will be my staple diet for the next 2 weeks, which is the length of time I reckon it'll take to negotiate France.

I am really excited to be starting this new phase in the adventure and after getting a few photographs of Manion Friday on deck as we leave the port, I eagerly get the maps out to both plan the route south, and in a childish attempt to prompt someone to ask where I'm heading. Sadly they don't, but after a while I notice 3 middle aged guys with hipster beards, who I saw strapping their own bikes to the boat when I got on. We get chatting for a bit where they inform me they're on a reunion tour and we play adventure top-trumps for a while, jostling for the best story, before we end in a draw. They're doing the north coast of Normandy for 2 weeks on an adventure they did when they were teenagers, stopping in the same towns they did 25 years ago. This has me wondering if, in 25 years' time I'll be reliving my own journey, though sadly I conclude this is very unlikely. I know deep down that this is a one-time opportunity, regardless of if I succeed or fail.

After 5 hours travelling across the channel, the ferry finally docks in the port of Cherbourg. I pump up the now flat tyre, which lasts long enough to get off the ship, and to find a port service building to shelter from the rain and to sort the puncture. A rather surprised French port worker finds me mid task and, with a lot of hand gestures, points me in the direction of the sink to use to locate the hole by submerging the punctured inner tube in water. Using the international language of hand signals, he also offers to run over the high-pressure airline, but I decline in fear of overuse and creating a blast that would likely scramble the port's anti-terrorist team.

I have found throughout the journey so far that most people are really friendly towards traveller cyclists. I am not sure if it's the vulnerability of such a mode of transport that brings out the nurturing attitude in people, or maybe it's the fact you're simply not threatening in any way, but people always seem ready to provide help. And for this, I am really pleased I chose to become a mamil.

I leave the town of Cherbourg heading due south. The road starts off as a busy dual carriageway, full of artic trucks hurriedly on their way out of the port, and it's not long till I'm hit with, what can only be described as, 'a bugger of a hill'. I was warned about this by the bearded cyclists on the ferry, but it did not prepare me in any way for the sheer size of it. It's massive, and it simply adds to the displeasure of heavy legs, heavy rain, and an incessant headwind. But even such difficulties cannot diminish my excitement at being back on the road, and back being an adventurer.

After making it out of the Cherbourg bowl, the landscape becomes heavily cultivated farmland, and, if I'd not just spent 5 hours on a ferry I would think I was still in the more familiar green pastures of England. The roads are long and straight, and undulate over long steady hills, like riding a very long, yet undramatic, big dipper. The road is very quiet with only a few cars and trucks for company. It's very peaceful, and the cows that fill nearly every field are undisturbed from their daily chore of chomping grass.

It's not long before I fall back into the cycling trance, drifting off in to the nothingness of pleasant casual thoughts that I found almost unachievable prior to the trip. We spend so much time dealing with the day to day activities of living that I think we sometimes forget to just stop and think. We seem to fill the gaps in between our daily chores with updating and maintaining our online personas, rather than just taking some time to reflect and to daydream. Maybe it takes an adventure to be alone and unconnected enough to allow such inner thoughtfulness? I've often considered meditation and know a few people who swear by it. I love the quote that you should meditate for 1 hour a day, and if you don't have time to do it, you should meditate for 2. I think this quiet reflection time I've been having, in between the pain and the anguish, is what these people would describe as meditation.

I make it to the coast and to Saint Lô d'Ourville by late afternoon and find a nice-looking campsite in the middle of an area filled with sand dunes. The campsite manageress doesn't speak English, and my French is pretty crap. However, using her daughter as a translator, I manage to get what looks a quiet little spot in one of the hedge-lined pitches in the middle of the site. Thankful that all the tent parts are there, I get pitched and get a cook on of pasta and meat to supplement the ice-cold bottle of rosé I got from the site shop. With my belly full and my mind drowsy, I roll into the tent for an early night and, just as I'm starting to drift away, dreaming of what the next 2 weeks in France will bring, I'm woken to the horrific sound of loud angry techno like it's coming out of a speaker deep in the pit of my stomach. I try to ignore it for a few minutes but it's no good, I have to concede defeat and I'm out of my tent, half annoyed, yet appreciating the humour in the situation. I had wondered why all the youths on the site were dressed up. And I now realise why as I can see, on the other side of the next plot, that there's a teenage disco going on with a group of lads and girls hunched up in separate corners of the open fronted wooden barn. I had originally put this down as a games room, however the table-tennis tables had been folded and pushed to one side to make space for the mobile disco unit which was being manned by the

French version of Timmy Mallett. I wander up to the site's shop where I think I am told it will be finished at 12:30 by the French speaking manageress. It's just after 10 and so time to take a wander.

I phone Sue, who laughs when I tell her about the rave, and I have to admit it's quite funny, till I consider the prospect of this all the way to Spain. My proposed route through France is mainly via the coast. This, I'd hoped, would offer me loads of campsite opportunities, but with this new-found wisdom of it being France's silly-season, I wonder if it's going to make for a very noisy and sleep deprived journey?

In the morning, I start the day off with a frustrating 30-minute fight to get all my stuff packed into my seemingly shrunken panniers, followed by a further 10-minute struggle to get them clipped onto my unstable bike. With a tree as the only available solid structure, I lean the bike on it to try to put the pannier bags on the back. As I put the first one on, the bike moves slightly and the handlebars magically spin around, making the bike slide down and away from the tree, sending the toothed front chain sprocket into my shin. And with it, a sharp excruciating pain. I put this down as an agonising lesson and, after fighting the urge to both scream like a girl, and to smash the bike up, I make a mental note to never ever use a tree as a leaning post again.... ever.

I stop off at a tiny little village called Commune de Saint Germain Sur Ay. I really want some decent breakfast this morning, however all that's on offer at the only café in the town is coffee and a chance to experience France's typical early morning ritual. It's a small place with old fashioned decor, and the walls are covered in pictures of what appears to be both historical cycling heroes, as well as wartime generals and other significant French military figures. The windows are quite small, making the place look moody and characterful, and the vintage chairs and tables look perfectly in place in this setting. I stay sat at a table, alone, for about 40 minutes, and in that time, I see about 10 people pop in for a shot of coffee at the bar, and an animated chat with the sympathetic sounding waitress. On reflection, they might have been discussing their day ahead of slaying puppies and small children, but to me, the sound of this French chattering, in such a symbolic setting, is like listening to Beethoven's concerto. I am mesmerised by the French accent and admire the pictures on the walls to prevent myself from staring. If they had noticed me sat there, I reckon they might been surprised at my appeared interest in their wartime heroes. I feel like I'm in true rural France, and I absolutely love it.

I leave the café at about 9am and the weather is warming up nicely. I grab some food from the supermarket in Lessay and continue the journey south. It's turned into a beautiful riding day with the sun making the farmlands' grassy fields sparkle. I am enjoying the beautiful surroundings and can feel myself slipping back into the meditative trance I had yesterday. No sooner am I drifting off however, I am broken out of my thoughts by a car as it overtakes me and slams on its brakes, coming to a stop about 100 metres ahead. The driver gets out, the engine still running, and shouts something to me that I can't understand.

'Par-don?' I reply nervously, and in my best French accent.

'Sandales!' He shouts, pointing back down the road before continuing with French chatter. I still don't understand, however on seeing my confused look, he points at his feet and shouts again, 'Sandales!'

I look back to notice one of my only pair of footwear, other than my bike shoes, has disappeared off the back pannier. 'Ahhhh, Flip-Flop!'

'Oui, oui', he shouts back and gets back in his car. I smile and wave, then unceremoniously try to shuffle my completely unbalanced bike around in the road and travel back about half a mile to return the lost item. What a nice guy, he took just a brief moment out of his day and it saved me some sore feet and about 15 euros. Sometimes it's just the smallest of things that can make a difference to someone's day.

I stop for a roadside lunch on the outskirts of a quaint little village called Village Nicolle. After the now standard 10-minute balancing act of trying to lean the bike up against a low wall, I sit on a bench in front of an old church, chomping on baguette and pâté like a native. After about 5 minutes, an old, beaten up Mercedes mounts the wide kerb at speed, then stops right in front of me before a skinny, bearded guy of about 60, dressed in threadbare jumper and jeans, drags himself out and starts chattering in French. Recoiling from the shock of the break in tranquillity, I butt in, breaking his momentum and ask if he speaks English.

'Parlez-vous Anglais?'

'Uh?' He replies with a curl of the lip and a shrug of the shoulders only a French person can pull off with style. I try again, but slower, and with more pronunciation.

'Par - lez – vous - Anglais?'

'Ahh, Anglais?!'

'Oui!'

'Non.' This should be interesting. He proceeds to ignore this information and tries to ask me some questions… in French. I think he's asking me where I'm going and where I've been, but it's only a guess and I try to get my map out to show him. Having had this conversation numerous times in English, in my mind I make up what I think he's asking and so answer questions with 'about 3,000 miles', and '60 miles per day' and 'just to see if I can do it', at regular points, matching him equally for hand gestures. I have no idea if I'm answering the questions he's asking but in my crap level of French it's all I can muster. I think I hit the mark on a few occasions as he replies with an 'ah, oui'. And when I point to John O'Groats, then to Gibraltar on the map I am sure I hit the nail on the head as he lets out a large comical blow of air through rasping lips, and pats me on the back. Finally, he shakes my hand, gets back in his car and is off, continuing in the direction of his journey. I am stunned and am left reflecting on the surrealism of the last 5 minutes. What a nice guy, but what a bizarre moment as I'm stood, clutching half a baguette and a tub of pâté, dressed head to toe in Lycra, and wearing a smile from ear-to-ear on the brilliance of the people you meet when you get out of your comfort zone.

I continue through the early afternoon with a fast, slow progress over the undulating hills of farmland countryside. I make it to the large medieval town of Coutances and take some timeout to watch a young female artist in the street making a collage out of strange random photographs on a 4x2 metre board. It's very surreal and has collected a crowd, who, I can only assume, are all doing the same as me and are trying to work out just what the hell she's actually trying to make!

Back onto the rollercoaster roads and I notice I am starting to get a feeling of real isolation. I have only been away from Sue and the support vehicle, and of course Jazz, for about 30 hours but I can already feel that I'm missing them. I am only in France, and Sue is only a phone call away, but I am starting to feel strangely alone. I think the feeling is perhaps exacerbated by a lack of a strict plan as, up until now, the days had been planned out, with a target set to get to each day to enable us to meet up. And I think this subtle difference is having a large effect. No longer do I have someone to rely on, someone to discuss how far to go each day or where to stay. I have my map and a compass to rely on and all I have to do is to keep the needle pointing at the 'S' and to ride. I know that as long as I keep doing these 2 simple things, I'll eventually make it to Gibraltar. I'm completely alone, and even though I'm missing the team, for the first time in a long time, I feel truly, truly free.

I decide to make Avranches, located on the elbow between mainland Brittany and the Lower Normandy peninsula my stop off for the night. As I get there I am faced with a sign indicating a horrific 20% climb to the centre. I ride to the base of the hill, desperately trying to calculate a new route on the map, but there is sadly no choice and so I put the bike in its lowest gear and get out of the saddle in preparation. So far on this journey I have not yet needed to get off the bike and push, and I'm not planning on starting now. As I hit the slope I start grinding it out, grunting and swearing up the steep incline, but I instantly start feeling a worrying stabbing pain in the middle of my right knee, which turns into excruciating agony. It feels like the pains I had back in Scotland and I am thankful that it comes on slowly again, rather than as an instant intense pain like something's snapped. But it's still a worry, particularly when it does not go away after I complete the half mile climb and stop at the top. This will need to be monitored… but first thing's first, it's time for a beer. I find a small supermarket located within a mini-shopping arcade and stock up on a few cans before finding the Tourist Information Centre. France has it absolutely nailed on this front, as every major town seems to have an exceptionally well signposted Tourist Information Centre. There is also a campsite in most major towns in France and the one the nice lady at the tourist centre directs me to is an absolute beauty.

'Campsite Zoe' turns out to be an eco-friendly site, displaying a welcome sign at its entrance painted with hippy-styled daisies and a peace sign. Its owner, Zoe, is out when I get there but it gives me time to chill and to have a look about. It's a real scruffy place with wild flowers and long grass everywhere, and has 2 large greenhouses growing organic produce. I also find some writing painted on a dilapidated old caravan stating 'Education is the greatest need for all people… but first they must be fed'. It has me intrigued about what sort of person Zoe might be.

After about 20 minutes, a dishevelled, yet pretty, hippy looking lady of about 35 turns up, and I am surprised when she talks with a home-counties English accent. It turns out Zoe has been running 'Campsite Zoe' for about 5 years and runs it on a donations basis with her main income coming from the substantial amount of organic vegetables she grows around the place. There is a shower available, which is pretty rundown, and an eco-toilet, complete with sawdust, and not really a lot else, but it's absolutely perfect. I pitch my tent next to the house, on the opposite side of the plot from a massive pile of manure. I really hope it's horse-based, especially considering the drop-toilet is only 20 feet away.

Half-cut from the lager and an overwhelming sense of well-being, I wander into town to find some food. While I eat, I take advantage of the free Internet connectivity and I put a post out on Facebook about my unrelenting burning thighs. I get an almost instant reply from an old school friend who it turns out is an avid cyclist. He informs me that I must drink more water, and must consume more potassium, which can be found in bananas, and more favourably in dark chocolate. I am very happy about the last part and, after dinner, make a beeline for the shop and buy a kilo of very dark chocolate and a small banana.

Avranches is a beautiful old fortress town, which played a large role in the Second World War due to its highly defendable location set on top of a large imposing hill. The war connection is reflected throughout the town with wartime relics on show including statues and an old American tank in the centre of its main roundabout. There is a music event on in the town tonight, but I'm tired and drunk and so decide to get my head down, and I fall into a sleep even the bellowing thud of the massive speakers, about 500 metres away, cannot prevent.

During the night, I wake in a haze amid a really vivid dream. I'm not really sure what the dream was about, only that I no longer had a bike... and appeared to be extremely happy. As my brain starts to click slowly into gear, the realisation that I'm actually still on this trip comes flooding back, along with the severe, thudding pain in my right knee.

I spend the rest of the night staring at the roof of the tent, contemplating the implications of the injury. I'm just not ready to quit yet, particularly as I've had a real spurt of positivity since hitting France, but this knee pain is definitely worrying, not to mention painful. I decide that lying in contemplation and pain, listening to the pitter-patter of rain on the tent, is not helping, and I am pleased to eventually see the morning sun light up the tent. I get up, dressed, pack all my gear, eventually, and I'm gone, dragging my heavy heart behind me on what I fear is going to be an exceptionally tricky day.

Stopping off at a café in the village of Pontaubault, located at the foot of the hill out of Avranches, I order breakfast of coffee and 2 massive pain-au-chocolats. These, I conclude, will be the perfect start to the day as the sugar will give me an instant energy hit, whereas the carbohydrates of the pastry will give me slowly released energy, lasting me till lunch. I shovel the food down, hoping that they'll prise me out of this worried mental hole, but sadly they don't. Instead, I find myself staring into my coffee, slowly swilling it round, stretching out the opportunity to not be on the bike as I am really not looking forward to what I anticipate today will bring, particularly as the weather is looking particularly wet and windy.

I eventually concede, and get begrudgingly back on the bike, heading in the direction of France's west coast. The roads are similar to those I was on yesterday, undulating hills of about 300 feet climbs and equal falls through farmland of grazing sheep and cattle. But the weather is a lot different today; the rain is smashing it down, and there's a severe wind blowing directly into my face. The never-ending hills, along with the incessant headwind, have me out of my seat almost all morning and my already painful knee is really feeling the affect and is reacting with a continual heavy throb, which turns into an agonisingly sharp pain on the more difficult climbs. It feels like someone is stabbing a knife into the middle of my kneecap on every downward force of my right pedal. I persevere for a few hours, but I know I can't continue in this pain and I'm really worried I'm starting to do some serious damage. I start scanning the map for a place to stay. I need a hotel, a bath, and a day off to assess my knee and to rest my now flailing body.

I fight my way to Vitré against the continual torrent of driving rain, and with the still debilitating pain in my knee, to find a hotel. I find one easily in the tourist driven town, but the manager of the one I choose doesn't speak any English and it takes a few attempts before I manage to find the mime for a bath, which is actually a lot trickier than it first appears. I smash my day's budget with a €60 room. After dumping my gear in the room, I go for a hobble through the town to find some wine. I find 2 supermarkets, which are both closed, and I suddenly realise it's Sunday evening and therefore it's likely that all the supermarkets will be the same. Bloody French, with their admittedly great ethos on the whole work-life balance thing. I go in search of a French off-license, but again, fail. How can I not find wine in France for Christ's sake?! I guess I could go to a bar, but I just want wine and a bath, it's been the only thing keeping me going all day.

Just as I'd started to give up hope, I find a pizza shop and get giddy when I see bottles of ice-cold rosé in its glass-fronted drinks fridge.

'Bonjour. Parlez-vous Anglais?' I ask the young guy behind the till after waiting my turn. He's about 6 feet tall, very skinny, and dressed head to toe in a bright red uniform complete with matching baseball hat. The sullen look on his face shows he's clearly not seeing a pizza-shop assistant as a long term career plan.

'Oui, Yes.' YES!! 'What would you like?' He continues.

'Rosé please.' I could feel myself getting excited at the thought of being drunk. I wonder if this trip might actually be turning me into an alcoholic?

'OK, what pizza would you like?' He asks.

'No, I just want wine.'

'No, you must have food.'

'Huh?' I was getting confused and slightly frustrated.

'You must only have wine with food.' He demanded.

Now I appreciate the art of choosing wine to complement food, such as red with meat and white with fish and all that, I really do, but I just want a drink and a bath. 'No, I just want wine?!' This is all very confusing for my peppered head.

'No, to buy wine you must buy food.' He reiterated. I can see he's starting to get quite agitated, as is the line of people stood behind me in the queue.

'Look, what's the cheapest pizza you have? I just want some bloody wine.' I realise the more frustrated I'm becoming, the more I'm looking like one of the local drunks, particularly given my body stench which must now be filling his shop. He goes through a number of specials options, which are a blur, and I settle on a meat feast and a bottle of cheap rosé before hobbling back to the hotel for a bath and an evening of bottled TLC.

I wake the next day with a fuzzy head and instantly search for any pain in my knee. There's a dull throb, but nothing major and I allow myself a momentary feeling of relief. I'd posted about my knee issues on Facebook last night and was happy to see the comments of encouragement I'd been left overnight. I needed these and they really cheer me up, however I was shocked to see a post from my cousin, who is a doctor, telling me to be careful as I could do irreparable damage. I pragmatically, or more probably naively, consider that it would not be possible for her to give anything close to a proper prognosis from over 300 miles away and ignored her advice.

I go down for breakfast and book straight in for a second night, before taking a gentle stroll around the town.

Vitré is a very old town with thin, cobbled streets and is dominated by a 15th century Château. It a popular tourist spot, clearly the reason for the many hotels situated above the bars, cafés, and souvenir shops that line the pedestrianised streets. The town looks like it's thriving, feeding off the many tourists drawn to the old world feel of the place. In the centre, I find a signpost stating that Lymington in the UK is 440KM away, and Villajoyosa in Spain is 1450km. As fascinating as it is, I can't help wondering why they've chosen to reference these 2 places as relevant locations, maybe they're 'twinned' with each other? I like the town, and would normally love to just amble the streets, tanking up on French amphetamine-based coffee, but I have a different agenda and head back for a rest.... and another bath.

I phone Sue for some sympathy, then my old friend James who cheers me up no end, particularly given his request to pick him up some wine while I'm in France, though I sadly have to decline given the lack of space in my panniers. I also complete some myofascial release, grunting and sweating in the privacy of my room, then head down to the garage to complete some general bike maintenance, such as oiling the chain and trying to find the location of the squeaks and clicks that seem to be getting worse. I am so happy with the bike and its rugged wheel rims have saved me a number of times when I've, intentionally or not, gone off-roading. But the noises it's started making have made it sound like a bag of spanners, and it's become really annoying.

In the misery of yesterday's riding, I found solace in focusing on making up another story about Manion Friday by expanding on his story after his suicide attempt back in England. I decide to post his story on my blog:

Manion Friday is in a bad way...

Manion Friday is loving his new-found freedom a little too much. After all those years as a servant, I think the pressures of freedom and fame have gone to his head. I came back from breakfast to find....

He says this was the first time but I was always mindful of that friendly yet sinister grin.... and just look at those eyes! Off to The Priory when we get back I think...

When I'm at my low points on this journey, my thoughts always seem to move towards my little yellow plastic travelling companion and, more specifically, to putting him in some sort of emotional predicament. Back before I started, I had considered it would just be a funny thing to take a toy on the journey and would make my young nephew laugh as he sees pictures of it in various places throughout Europe. But the more things are panning out, the more I think I may be using it as a focus for my frustrations in the same way that Tom Hanks used the 'Wilson' volleyball in the film Castaway. I wonder if I'm using it simply as a distraction, or if there is some deep-level psychological behaviour going on. My head hurts at this thought and so I park it, and go to a bar for coffee where I watch the Tour-de-France with a room full of excited French blokes.

The French are passionate about the Tour-de-France in the same way we are about the FA Cup. Every time there is a change of leader or a breakaway, there is a raucous cheer or a communal raspberry blow, depending if their man has gone up or down in the leader board. I watch the race on one of the tiny, old-fashioned, pushbutton TV's hung around the room, high up on the walls. I watch for about half an hour, smugly noting the riders only manage to cycle for a couple of hours per day... the losers.

In the morning, after another 10-minute fight to get the panniers back on the bike, I'm on the road and am feeling positive again. The day off yesterday seems to have done the trick and the knee pain seems to have settled down to a mild numbness. When I was back talking to the Cycling Oracle he warned me about being out of the saddle when riding and insisted I should try to sit down as much as possible as it was, supposedly, a more favourable riding position. Given that my actual more favourable riding position was sat upright with the heaters on and the radio drowning out the gentle humming sound of an engine, I guess I didn't completely accept this piece of information. I make a mental note to now try to sit down where possible, and to try and get my chilled approach back on.

With the roads flattening, and perfect riding weather of no wind, mild heat, and bright sunshine, I breeze through the morning's riding, only stopping off to say a few traveller prayers at a 15 feet-high, roadside, religious cross - I figure it can only help. The last 2 days have been tough, both mentally and physically, but I reflect on the period with real optimism. The physical issues I guess I could not really have done much about, it was out of my hands and I will just have to evaluate any injuries as and when they arise. But from a mental perspective I feel I have come out of the situation a little bit stronger, and with a reminder of why I took on such an ambitious journey. I had a genuine opportunity to quit yesterday and I chose not to. I could have gone home with my head held high at getting this far, with the excuse of being denied by an old war wound. I could have got on a train, and headed to somewhere hot and sandy and seen out the rest of my budget drinking Mojitos, telling people 'if only...' stories whilst inwardly regretting an opportunity missed. But I didn't, I fought on, and for that I feel awesome.

The day passes quickly and the knee has thankfully settled right down. My only stop off, on what is a beautiful and productive day, is in the small quiet town of Saint-Mars-la-Jaille. I find a small bar called the Café des Sports, and sit at one of the tables and chairs that have spilled onto the street, though I'm left wondering just how much sport actually goes on here as a couple of drunks fall out of the door in need of a fag. They try to get me into conversation, then into the bar, oblivious to the fact I speak very little French or, at this moment anyway, drunken French slur. But I need to stay focused and, after declining the offer of a drunken hug and filling up my water bottles, I set off to the sound of drunken French cheers and laughter.

After a final short spurt for the day I make it to Ancenis, lying on the northern bank of the Loir River, and follow the signs for the municipal campsite. The French love their camping and it's not hard to see why with the favourable weather and fantastic facilities at these council run sites. For €13, about £10, I get to pitch on the edge of the massive river, and to spend a good half an hour in a pristinely clean shower, removing sweat and grime after a day's great riding. It's been stunning scenery today, bathed in a bright sun, bringing out the rich colours of the countryside. I've been through some quaint little French villages, all dressed up in bunting and proudly showing off their patriotism with high flying French and regional flags. As I sit at my tent door, gently grazing through my bodyweight in pasta, dried meat, and cheese, I consult the map and realise I've managed to cover about 120KM, about 75 miles, today and I'm well chuffed. It's been a great day and I feel proud in my achievements and celebrate, rather than the usual commiserate, with a beautiful bottle of ice cold rosé. Today I feel like an intrepid explorer again, today I'm back to feeling like I'm Sir Ranulph Fiennes.

I head off south-west towards La Rochelle on the west coast of France, which I pencilled in as the halfway point of, what I am now calling, an adventure. I had never really been able to give it a label that sticks, sometimes calling it a challenge, sometimes a trip or a journey, sometimes an enlightenment. But right now, with the physical and mental strength I'm feeling, it's a full-on adventure.

I cross the Loir River where I find the environment seems to change. The corrugated-like terrain of constant hills has almost completely gone, replaced with field upon field of grapevines - it seems Manion and I have hit wine country. It's getting noticeably warmer as well and by midday the roads are giving off the shimmering effect that make it look like I'm in the setting for some desert-based film. I'm half expecting to see Mad Max in an over-engineered killing machine coming over the horizon at any moment.

After a stop-off, just outside of Chantonney for another night camping, I make good progress towards La Rochelle. My mood is good, the knee issues have dwindled and the legs feel powerful. The bike is also good, save for a few clicks and squeaks which have been causing some mild irritation ever since Scotland, and the terrain is facilitating a nice, flat, sun blessed ride. It feels like the biking gods have finally come to treat me for all the hard work I've been doing and to thank me for persevering through their perverse games of 'destroy the MAMIL' for the last 2 weeks. Even the wind is finally onside and gently caresses me towards the halfway goal and a well-earned day off. The day is stunning, and there are just a few cotton-ball type clouds in the rich blue sky making me feel like I'm in the opening credits of 'The Simpsons' TV show.

Given the distinct lack of rainfall in this area, coupled with the slate flat terrain, the natives have built a rather complex network of irrigation channels from the nearby Sèvre Niortaise River to distribute water to the parched fields that fill the area. And it seems to be working as, after turning a sharp corner, I am blessed with a view of a field, about 1 square kilometre, of sunflowers all with their heads pointing at the sun, almost directly over my head. It's a massive carpet of yellow that butts up directly to the crystal blue sky behind and it's beautiful, the rich array of colour makes it feel like I'm stood in a computer screen-saver image.

I make it into the costal town of La Rochelle by mid-afternoon and the place is crammed with tourists and shoppers, which brings on the inevitable anxiety of heavy traffic and a need to speak to people again. After fighting through the traffic, I find the Tourist Information Centre where the assistant directs me to the town's municipal campsite. I cycle the short distance to the site across a large, open, dock area housing chandlers and boat builders and go through the now super-efficient process of pitching the tent whilst suckling on a bottle of ice-cold rosé.

As ever, the campsite is perfect, bordered by pleasantly shading trees and mapped out with loads of designated pitches, segmented using bushes and wooden fencing. I've been put next to a scruffy-looking 2-man tent, which is surprisingly occupied an hour later by an elegant looking lady in her late 40's. She's tall, with long strawberry-blonde hair and is dressed in tight jeans and a vest-top. She has the air of classy, French chic. She is the last person I'd expected would have owned such a dishevelled tent, and after we exchange a couple of pleasant and courteous 'Bonjours', she enters the tent headfirst, leaving me with the lasting image of her pear-shaped rear disappearing into the tent doors. I spring quickly into life and frantically rip down my drying underpants from the trees at the back of adjoining pitches.

By evening, it's still really warm and the campsite has been filling up with various types of holiday makers, from families to groups of young lads and girls. There are also a few solo cyclists and I go over for a chat with a guy of about 70 who introduces himself as Frederick. He's German, well over 6 feet tall, and is broad-shouldered. He's very athletic-looking for a man of his age. He tells me he's been cycling from Valencia, in Spain, and has achieved the might of the Pyrenees. He continues to tell me how tough it's been and how hilly it was, even at the coast where he chose to go around them. He also, rather surprisingly, informs me of just how windy it's been, a northerly right into his face the whole time. While this has been a bit crap for old Frederick, I can't help but give a little smile as it'll be right behind me if I take that route, coaxing me up the steep hills. He seems really fed-up, which may have been a cultural misunderstanding, or, more likely, due to the fact that it was his daughter's idea to go on the trip, to get out there and see a bit of the world. I wonder if this idea was preceded by a conversation about life insurance, and another one about a will?

Another solo cyclist also turns up and pitches in the next bay. He's a balding guy of about 40 and is clearly an experienced traveller as he has all the gear, ferried about on a mono-wheeled bike trailer. It brings up a childish jealousy as it looks a really cool setup. The jealousy rises further when, within 5 minutes of arriving, he is in a flamboyant conversation with the pretty French lady in which he is, I can only assume, talking about the puppies he's slayed today. He has her giggling like a tipsy teenager, smoking in the provocative way that European woman achieve with real finesse.

An hour passes and I am really enjoying the fun of sitting at my tent, watching the campsite politics and listening to the French chatter in the haziness of a mid-summer evening. The moment is idyllic with the trees housing tweeting birds and the site filling up with the excited hustle of people pitching tents, making food and generally getting drunk. It appears that Mr Heroic-Adventurer may have scored as he leaves the site accompanied my Mrs Seductive-Smoker. I wonder where they're off to? Maybe he's going to show her around the place? Maybe he's going to show her those puppies? Maybe she's going to show him her puppies?! Or maybe they're just off for dinner? He looks like a man that would know where to woo beautiful ladies in every major city in Europe, presumably able to know just which restaurant would be most likely to get him a tickle with Mrs Seductive-Smoker.

After diving into another mountain of pasta, I get some well-needed sleep. Gone are the days of lying in bed staring at the roof of whatever happened to be housing me that night, mind buzzing with anticipation. I have now hit a nice steady rhythm to the days, which has filled me with confidence and with it, finally, an ability to sleep. Everything is well in the world… for the moment anyway.

I had always considered La Rochelle to be the halfway point on this adventure. I am unsure exactly, given the lack of gadgetry that would be able to tell me for sure, but a quick look on the maps puts it as close as matters as the centre point of the trip, and it fills me with a pride that I've made it this far. It's time for a day off.

La Rochelle is a historic costal port and has a population of around 75,000, which, during the French holidays, swells to over double by tourists looking to take in its significant historical landmarks, as well as enjoying the Mediterranean-style climate. It's also a significant holiday location for the Paris elite who moor their yachts in the massive marinas. Walking around, there are loads of them all filled up with boats waiting for that once-yearly moment when their rich owner will come to visit and give them a reason to be. There are boats of all types, each one trying to outdo each other in the only currency that really seems to matter, size. Some are large, others are gigantic. There is clearly a lot of money that flows through the town.

The main marina is overlooked by 2 large towers at its mouth. The first, Tour Saint-Nicholas, has a square cross-section and was finished in 1376, taking 28 years to build. The second, Tour de-la Chaine, is circular and was built 20 years later taking a mere 8 years to complete - practise makes perfect I guess. There is also a beach, which is packed out with cheery holidaymakers and, in true French style, topless sunbathing women. I decided to stop off for an ice-cream.

The old town has a nice historic feel with the buildings predominantly built in sandstone blocks with arched pillar walkways underneath. It's also very international and I am finally able to talk in English without the need to talk slowly and loudly, and accompanied by a mime. I even manage to buy a map of Spain, albeit a pocket-sized one, to start planning where to cross the Pyrenees. I'd been putting it off for a while but I knew I was going to need to make a decision very soon to ensure I head in the right direction.

Back at the tent I give the bike the once over, trying desperately to find the source of the clicking sounds that are still driving me crazy, but no joy. I even manage to rope in Frederick who reluctantly agrees to run alongside me as I ride to listen for the location of the clicking but still no joy. I also do some planning, and finally decide that I am going to go for it and try to cross over the Pyrenees from Saint-Jean-pied-de-Port in France to Roncesvalles in Spain. It's by no means the highest point to pass, but it's still a 1200-metre climb and will give me the challenge I know I would be proud of once I hopefully complete it. I'm feeling in good shape at the moment, and actually consider that I'm looking slightly ripped. Even though it'll be tough, taking this route will be within the realms of possibilities, and will also allow me to get to Spain via France's very flat west coast on the EuroVelo 1. The EuroVelos are a network of cycling routes laid out across the whole of Europe and the one I would be taking, The Atlantic Coast Route, starts out at the top of Norway and ends in Portugal, travelling through the UK, Ireland, France and Spain. I'd been told about this route by a guy in a cycle shop in Wales who said it would be a nice flat interim to the journey, and I figure will also be a good build-up for the big push over the top.

I start getting a little bored by early evening, and so my thoughts turn back to my little plastic friend and his emotional journey. I decide to post a blog update:

Manion Friday is still out of control…

And you don't want to know what is happening at the back of that goat!! I'm not sure what to do, fame seems to be destroying him. He's been seen knocking around with a gang of Columbians.

Luckily, Miss Seductive-Smoker comes back before I get chance to take it any further. We get chatting for a bit and she tells me she's called Florence. She speaks perfect English and lives in Paris where she's an unemployed florist. She's been in La Rochelle for a month on a working holiday helping a friend do up his boat. She's a really interesting lady and has the type of deep brown eyes that lure you in and make you think that she's actually interested in what you're saying. I guess my adventure is quite an interesting story but as she starts doing that flirtatious smoking thing she was doing with Mr Heroic-Adventurer last night, I decide I need to call it a night. Before I go, I can't help but ask her who her friend was on the bike.

'Oh, he is a travel writer.' She replied a little sheepishly. 'He was having trouble with his bed, how do you say, with a pump, you know, and so I said he could sleep on mine but he snores. Maybe this is what you heard, no?' No, I didn't hear a thing, but it looks like Mr Heroic-Adventurer clearly chose the right restaurant.

Evolution of a MAMIL

Chapter 9: ...To The Pyrenees

I leave La Rochelle on the EuroVelo1 under a hot morning sun. It starts out as a nice, flat, concrete cycle path running along the sea wall, giving beautiful views over the rich blue water. It's an undemanding and enjoyable ride, only providing the odd challenge where the wind has blown deep sand across the track, leaving an ambush-style obstacle for the unsuspecting cyclist riding on two, inch-wide bands of rubber. These innocent-looking sand-traps are an absolute nightmare on a bike as the front wheel gets bogged down, leaving you susceptible to a Barry Sheene-style front wheel slide and a wobble - particularly bad when your shoes are clipped into the pedals. I survive a few scares before the path disappears and sadly, so do the signposts. Still, I have all the navigational devices I need in the form of the sea to my right and the compass on by handlebars. As long as I bear left if I start hitting water, I know I must be going in the right direction.

By early afternoon the clicking sound from the bike is driving me crazy, mainly due to the fact I don't know what it is, and therefore how serious it is. I am worried it is going to leave me stranded, or worse, needing to quit. I've brought along a few spares like chain links and a couple of spare cables and inner tubes, but the sound seems to be coming from the pedal crank, or at least some of the time it is, and I don't have anything like the tools available to fix this. I am not bad at fixing mechanical stuff, mainly from spending time in my youth holding stuff for my dad – who was a mechanic – whilst he fixed it, but if I can't find the source of this clicking on the bike then I've got no way of fixing it.

The road takes me into Rochefort, located on the north side of the Charente River, when the clicking becomes intolerable and I decide I need to do something about it... again. I find the town's central square and take everything I can think of off the bike, piece by piece, cycling in a circle around the flag-paved square after every removal to see if any one piece makes a difference to the sound. It doesn't, but I do manage to make myself a little dizzy, and to entertain the group of old guys who have made the square their go-to place for a sunny afternoon drink and a chat. There's no choice, I need assistance.

I find a Decathlon outdoor goods store by way of the ever present and helpful Tourist Information Centre. After asking the girl at the counter, I'm introduced to the cycle maintenance expert who looks like the BFG's bigger brother. The guy is massive, well over 7 feet and as wide as a house. He speaks so deeply it feels like he's going to hit the natural resonance of my stomach and turn it into dust. I was a little reluctant to use this service to start with as it's not really a specialist type of place and certainly not the right place for an intrepid explorer like myself, but given my predicament, along with the lack of anything resembling a proper bike shop, I have no other choice. His massive hands delicately check and adjust various components in a grace that shows he's clearly an expert in these matters, and I'm filled with a confidence that he is finally going to find the issue. After 20 minutes of aligning and checking, twisting and poking, he stops, put his lips together, then gives out a rasping blow and a shrug of the shoulders that I've now become so familiar with. Back to the drawing board I guess, although at least it's nothing major... I hope.

The road south from Rochefort crosses the 150-metre wide Charente River using a massive bell-shaped bridge. It loops up an increasingly steep gradient to well over 150 feet high and then back again, making for an unexpectedly tough half hour out of what has been a very flat days' riding. To make matters worse, the road is a dual carriageway, and is the main traffic crossing point on this part of the river, which all adds up to a slow, painful, and rather dangerous ride. I break for a moment, 500 metres from the bridge, conscious this is the first major test of the knee since the near game-ender a few days ago. Then it's head down time, finally taking advantage of being dressed head to toe in streamlined Lycra. I approach at my albeit modest, flat-out speed hoping to carry some of the momentum up the hill. But it gets too steep too quickly, and I'm left ferociously clicking down the flappy-paddle gears like I'm trying to give them an orgasm. I'm soon plodding along again, trying to find enough strength not to get sucked under the lorries screaming past my left shoulder. Remembering the Cycling Oracles words about not getting out of my seat I make slow progress, but eventually make it to the top, sweating and sucking in lungfuls of carbon-filled air. The bridge then flattens out temporarily, before it's quickly into payback time as I barrel down the other side, trying to stay on the good side of a controlled descent, then into the safety of a small side road. The bridge was a toughie, no question, but the legs worked fine, and most importantly, no knee pain. And with this, I open my shoulders, look to the sky, and wheeze out a war cry of 'Bring on the Pyrenees!!'

After a quick check over for any lost limbs and soiled garments, I choose the safety of the small lanes and proceed through a number of small, quiet villages, stopping only to guzzle water and to admire a French bread vending machine located outside a bakery - only in France would you need 24-hour emergency access to a baguette. With the roads as flat as a snooker table and my legs now seemingly as wide as He-Man's, progress is bordering on acceptable – maybe I'm finally becoming a full-on MAMIL? With the absence of pain and anguish though, things are starting to get a little monotonous. I break into talking to myself again, and to shouting out The Fast Show's Swiss Tony style quotes about riding, improving it after each rendition.

Riding a bike is like making love to a beautiful woman...

121

You have to hold her ...
You have to take control ...
You have to guide her ...
You have to make her know you care ...
And if you do that Steve, you're in for the ride of your life!

I made sure there was no one around at this time.

I make it into Royan, located at the mouth of the Gironde estuary, by late afternoon where Florence had told me about a ferry that'll get me across the large Estuary and onward to the west coast, and to the EuroVelo1. She also told me that the crossing is particularly popular with German tourists and she was not wrong as I note the proportion of German number plates I see on the back of massive shiny motorhomes, which make up most of the 3-mile long queue for the Saturday night ferry crossing. Luckily, bikes have their own lane, but that would have to wait as I need to down tools and to have some fun, particularly now that I've seen a Glastonbury-styled, dome stage built onto the beach.

The town is rammed, presumably due to the beach concert on that evening. And I have to queue to get to speak to the Tourist Information Centre attendant who points me to the local campsite. Unfortunately it's not a Municipal site, but it's good value nonetheless, particularly as the owner offers me half a pitch for half-price due to the size of my tent.

After pitching the tent, I cycle down to the beach, and to the location of the pending concert. It's dark when I get there, but I figure there's got to be about 15,000 people, and the local stall holders are having a field day selling all sorts of tat only required by overexcited holidaying children. There are flashing-light toys of everything available such as windmills, hats, and canes, which is giving the place the feeling of a nursery-rave. There are also loads of food stalls where I gorge myself on Nutella and whipped-cream filled crepes, safe in the knowledge that it will be at least 10 hours till I'm back on the bike.

Right up until it started, I'd not really known what type of music was going to happen. The crowd had not given any clues since it was made up of all ages from small kids, to teenage punks, to old people who've brought their emergency chairs and had bagsied the front seats. But judging by the 60-foot high speakers it was going to be loud, and it was... with opera. And the crowd loved it, even the punk youths were mildly appreciative with petulant applause.

After about 2 hours of surprisingly moving renditions of music I'd never heard of, I was about to leave when the compere introduced a lady singer and the crowd suddenly lost their minds, screaming like someone had just notified them there was a 2 for 1 on baguettes. With the music slowly building, some of the crowd started to sing along. Although it sounded familiar, I couldn't quite remember where I'd heard it and, being in French, the words were no clue, but it was definitely one I'd heard before. By the time it got to the chorus, the crowd were out of control, open-armed, reaching for the gods. Then, in unison, they all just broke into song, joining in with the chorus of a French rendition of 'Let It Go', the popular song out of the Disney film Frozen! That was it. I remember hearing a version a friend's daughter had covered, and that was the song I was hearing, only in French. It felt very surreal, particularly given the hours spent this afternoon sat on a bike in the middle of nowhere. And for the fact I was now stood on a beach at the end of a summer's evening, crammed with 15,000 French tourists all bellowing out 'Libérée Délivrée' with tears filling their eyes, sparkling from the lights shining out from the top of the stage roof. Another special moment on this very special adventure.

After such an emotional evening, I felt a lie in was in order and, after filling up on the customary two large Pain au Chocolats and some more hallucinogenic French coffee, I eventually make it onto the estuary-crossing ferry by lunch. The crossing was a bit of a non-event, though I suppose that's what you're looking for from a ferry, and the 1/2 hour crossing passes quickly. On the other side, I'm straight onto the EuroVelo1, and into a heavily forested area with a perfectly flat cycle track cutting right through the middle. It's great riding, although I can't help but feel a small petulance in my stomach and I don't know why. I've had a couple of great days, some interesting entertainment, amazing views, flat riding, and great weather, what could be better? But I have this feeling that I'm grumpy and I don't know what the reason is. Maybe it's just the yin-yang effect of distance cycling kicking in again, balancing out after a few great days. It's almost like I'm trying to find something to get frustrated with and it's not long till I settle on the clicking sound from the bike again and start swearing at it a bit. Time for alternative action, and so I get the radio and headphones out. The Cycling Oracle had warned me against riding with headphones in for safety reasons as, apparently, you need to hear the truck as it mows you down. But I figured I'd be safe here. And besides, the far bigger danger this morning is from me giving the bike a good kicking if I have to put up with the incessant noises for much longer.

The path is super smooth and cuts through the deep green pine trees in almost straight lines, leading me to assume it may have once been a train line. It's Sunday, and the paths are really busy with families ambling along and it's back to a fast-slow progress. I slalom exuberantly past single riders, humoured by screaming an inner monologue of 'Attack, Attack! Attack!' to myself, like we're in a race as I pass. But then I come to a crawl when I frustratingly catch up to families riding side-by-side. I try various different tactics to notify them to move the hell over but in my Englishness, they all seem a bit too rude. My handlebar compass came with a built-in bell, but this sounds too pompous. I try an 'Excuse Me' but I figure this must be gobbledegook to them. I settle on riding uncomfortably close, producing a loud cough, and saying a curt 'bonjour'.

The path continues through the forest and is never more than a couple of kilometres from the ocean. The radio is happily drowning out the unnervingly noisy bike sounds, but it's never long till it's lost reception, filling my ears with white noise.

It's a good hour or so before the Sunday riders disappear leaving just the hardy distance cyclists, all with varying types of carrying paraphernalia from the humble panniers to the overloaded kiddie trailers piled high with camping gear and donned with various designs of flags flapping high on bendy flagpoles. I stop off to down yet more baguette and cheese. I never thought I'd say it, but I am actually getting really fed-up with eating baguette and cheese. It's stereotypically the food of the French, and I usually love it. But it now tastes and feels like rolled up newspaper as I tear off leathery strips like a medieval king with a pig's leg. It's just so dry, but it's the perfect food for this journey as it's tough enough to handle being stuffed into a pannier, it's cheap, and is full of carbs - the required fuel for a distance cyclist. I wash it down with a litre of strawberry flavoured electrolyte water and continue off with what was petulance, now bordering on anger.

Now that I've overtaken all the Sunday cyclists, performed with the vigour of a Tour-de-France winner, progress should be good, but the wind takes over, whipping unimpeded through the bare pine tree trunks of the surrounding forest, and I can feel the demons rising from within again. Wind on a bike just feels so bloody unfair. You are fighting all the time, trying to find a position with least resistance, shuffling around on the seat like you have a bad case of piles. Every turn of the wheel seemingly unjust effort that will never get rewarded. At least on the hills, you can assume you'll get some sort of payback for your hard work, but on flat expanses, even the slightest wind can leave you feeling like you're dragging a bag of coal through mud, with no chance of compensation for your troubles. Why did I get taken in by the false downward projection of cycling from North to South? As my mind continues to search for things to be pissed off at, I conjure up images of cycling in the opposite direction, spending hours sat on the bike, freewheeling along, getting caressed forward by a warm and hugging wind, presumably following a group of 21-year-old dancers on a naturist holiday. I'd have guffawed at the naïve amateurs fighting the wind in the opposite direction, knowing I was going to have yet another day quaffing wine and being fed grapes by the giggling dancers. I wonder if Sir Ranulph Fiennes succumbs to a bout of petulance when he's out doing his thing?

I manage a total of about 30 miles for the day before the devil talks me into an early stop. Spotting a camping sign on my map I trundle to the coastal town of Lacanau Océan. It's a pristine little town, reminding me of The Bahamas from my Cruise Ship days, except for the missing street vendors trying to sell me crap wooden figurines, or to braid my hair. The brilliantly whitewashed buildings are topped with red ridge tiled roofs, and bordered by cultivated gardens accommodating tall palm trees - it all looks worryingly expensive.

After being arrogantly turned down by the first campsite, I find the only other site in the town and have to wait over 1/2 an hour to speak to the attendant. I am told it will be a mere €67 for the night. Being the only place in town with availability, I try a bit of haggling, justifying the need to reduce the price based on my tent being the size of a coffin, and eventually get them down to the super-special price of €64!

'Wow, 64 euros?!' I proclaim in disbelief. 'Does that include breakfast?!'

'Non.'

My passive-aggressive tone did not lead to any further negotiations however, and I was asked to leave by the white-toothed, bronzed Adonis behind the counter.

Lacanau Océan was clearly not my type of place and so, with my financial carefulness getting the better of me, I begrudgingly get back on the bike and head due east towards the next closest town of Lacanau situated on the edge of the huge lake, Étang de Lacanau. The labyrinth of cycle paths gets me there in about 30 minutes, which is just enough time to calm myself down, and I stumble upon a camping site in the woods, 'Camping L'Ermitage'. This, I now realise, is one of the massive advantages of travelling by bicycle rather than by foot. You are never really any further than an hour away from a campsite, even if it is in the wrong direction. It turns out to be a particularly nice campsite as well, located in the woods. I'm taken for a tour of the facilities by an old lady who is surprisingly fat given the speed and distance she covers to show me to the pitches on offer and the dilapidated showers and toilets. I find a nice spot, with the trees giving ample shade from the roasting sun, and at €25 it's definitely more within my budget.

I ask a young guy sat in the attendant's hut if there is a supermarket in the town, and without looking up from his paper, I get a curt and blunt 'No'.

'So where is the closest please?'

'5KM'. He mumbles, still not looking up. He was clearly a chatty guy.

'Oh?' Pasta and dried meat again it is then. 'Is there anywhere I can buy wine?'

'Hmmm, I may have wine...' He replies with a negotiator's undertone, and finally lookup. Looks like I've found something to grab his attention.

'And how much may I need to spend to get some wine?' I replied. I could see him weighing up his price with the guile of a Wall Street trader.

'€6.50'

'Done!' I'd have paid more, a lot more, and he'd have probably taken less. It was probably really crap wine, but I didn't care. In the setting of the woods, in the warm summer evening sat outside my tent with a feeling of solitude and contentedness, and the grumpiness oozing out of me with every mouthful, it was the sweetest bottle of wine I'd ever tasted.

I wake the next morning to find a note left for me by the children of the French family I briefly chatted to last night. It simply reads 'Bon Courage et Bon Voyage!' which, even with my limited French vocabulary, I gathered to mean 'to have courage and to have a good journey'. It put a beaming smile on my face from ear-to-ear. They had already left by the time I'd heaved myself out of my tent, but they had told me they were cycling enthusiasts, and were able to fill me in a bit on the Pyrenees as they'd been over that way before. They told me there was no need to worry about it and to just enjoy the experience, but they were clearly way more experienced at cycling than me, and as the days were moving on, the 1300-metre-high mountains were taking up more and more of my thoughts.

After packing up in quick time, a process I had now mastered, I spent a further 10 minutes putting my panniers on the bike. A process I most definitely had not. Although this was cleverly done against the wall of the shower block, the scars of previously experienced mishaps still visible on my shins.

After a morning spent sluggishly ambling along with a hazy hangover, I get to the tiny town of Le Porge looking for any food that is not jaw aching crusty bread. As I hit the centre of the town, housing a single roundabout flanked by an impressive 30-metre high, sandstone church and a whitewashed block built town hall, I spot an equally impressive looking unicycle with a massive bin-lid sized wheel. It has, what looks like, a few bits of camping gear attached to two bars sticking out front and back, just below the seat. Being an ex-unicyclist, and now an intrepid adventurer, I am fascinated by both aspects of the contraption and stand, straddling my bike, in awe at the noble-looking machine. The owner of the device, a short, stocky, ponytailed guy of about 25, comes back almost immediately, presumably worried that I'll dribble all over it from my open and aghast mouth. The guy tells me his name is Morgan and he is a long-distance unicyclist who is touring in the area, completing on average about 30 kilometres per day, which is pretty impressive on such a device. He's quite humble in his attitude but I know how tough riding a unicycle is on the legs, particularly given there are no gears, which is reflected in the fact he has legs like tree trunks. I later found out there is actually a surprisingly big following of this type of traveller with the god being a guy with the unfortunate name of Ed Pratt. Ed was 19-years-old when he first set out to be the first person to cycle 18,000 miles around the world on a unicycle. He made it from Yeovil, in Somerset, as far as Kazakhstan before needing to take 6 months off due to inclement weather and being very nearly killed in a car collision. At the time of writing, he has made it back out and is half the way around and in Australia. He is one person I'd graciously accept defeat to in a game of adventurer top-trumps.

I get to the town of Biscarrosse, where I suddenly start to feel really weak and dizzy. Having covered a good 80 miles today, I decide to stop at the town of Biscarrosse. But having not eaten anything more than a couple of chocolate bars - simply refusing the stale bread and warm cheese festering in my pannier bag - my energy levels are zapped and I start to feel really lightheaded. I've been drinking well but, not for the first time, I've not really eaten correctly and I can feel myself going dizzy. I desperately search for somewhere selling food, but in the outskirts of this town there is nothing but houses. I start to prepare myself for the inevitable. I'm getting worryingly dizzy, and just as I start to concede that I'll soon be fighting through my panniers looking for the child-proof bread, I find a bakery and gorge myself on their last 4 slices of cold pizza. It's not much better than the bread, but at least it's soft, and garnished with something other than warm sweaty cheese. The slices, along with a cold coke, are consumed with record setting efficiency and I feel instant relief. I'm quite gutted at myself for such a schoolboy error. I'd been doing really well of late with a disciplined approach to food and drink and I know it's really been helping. I need to eat right, and chocolate bars for lunch is simply not a staple diet, even given the alternatives. I'd laughed at Carlos in the past for trying to survive a walking trip on Carling lager and Chocolate Penguins, and the thought of stooping to that level gives me the shivers.

After searching for a while, I find a hotel for €55 a night, again bulging the daily budget of €50 all in, and it's basic, but fine for my needs. Prompted by the scare from today's dizzy spell, along with a consciousness that nearly all I've eaten for the last week is bread, pasta, cheese, and processed meat, I settle in at a small restaurant for a chicken salad and, of course, a beer. The waitress is about 20 with long, straight, jet-black hair and a deep bronze tan, showing off her dazzlingly white teeth like she's in a toothpaste advert. Once she realises I'm English she beams in delight at the opportunity to speak to me, though I sadly concede this is more likely to do with the opportunity of practising her language skills.

We chat for a while, mainly about France, and for her to tell me about the many great sightseeing opportunities I've missed along the way.

It's really nice to be able to have a chat in English, even with her limited vocabulary, particularly as she's smoking hot. Her English is really quite poor and in some empathetic attempt to help her I can hear my own accent has gone all native. I realise I've started to speak like the policeman from 'Allo 'Allo!'. I proceed to tell her how 'I ave sexualed from Britain', and that 'I ave pissed some beautiful places, travelling for thirsty days now'. I even offer to let her 'leak at my mop' to see how far I've come, and to 'show her my bake'.

I could have chatted with her all night but I needed to get some sleep. And so, regrettably, I get the bill, and get up to leave. 'I must love you now, I ave to get up early in the moaning'. And after a slightly awkward pause we part company, and I smugly walk off, proud in the knowledge that today she's learnt that little bit more.

I'm 4 weeks into the trip now and, in general, I'm really feeling on good form. I'm eating and drinking properly, except for yesterday's error, and I'm feeling strong and fit, and more than a little bit pleased that I'm able to give a bit back by educating the natives.

I spend the morning in a self-contented air of invincibility as I trundle back to the coast in hope of picking the EuroVelo1 back up. But after an hour of cycling, consisting mainly of 2 massive hills, I arrive only to be told that the EuroVelo1 actually moves inland at this point, and through the very town I'd overnighted in the night before... gutted! As it turns out, the coastal area south is a military area, set aside for training and other gun related activity, and is out of bounds. Given the large signs stating that access to unauthorised personnel could result in impending death, I choose to return back to Biscarrosse along the very road I'd just come on.

After battling the two big hills again, in the opposite direction, I make it back to the town, albeit cutting a slightly more round-shouldered and sweatier figure than I had the last time I was here. Given I'd just completely wasted the last 2 and a half hours, I figure I may as well use the opportunity of being in a town to pick up some more provisions. I try to find something to replace my staple diet of French bread. But I have to concede to the fact it is simply too perfect for my needs and I find a bakery. It's fairly busy and I have to wait a good 10 minutes to be served, just long enough to watch a little old lady choose a baguette like a professional tennis player. The girl behind the counter offers her up three possible 6-inch versions of the same crusty loaf splayed across her forearm, from which the old lady analyses each in turn. She first goes by sight and smell. Then, after completely disregarding one, she goes in for a quick squeeze, before finally settling on the winning cob. I half expect her to then bounce it on the ground a couple of times before smashing it out the door, or to stick it up the side of her knickers for later, but sadly she does neither. Her professional approach to buying bread, along with her nonchalant consideration of the impending queue behind her, is truly commendable. I figure this may be at the core of my own bread-based issues. I wonder if this carefully considered selection approach might be the best chance of some decent soft bread, and I build myself up in anticipation for the task, palms sweating slightly, and running the opening sentence over and over in my head. I wait patiently in the queue and eventually get my turn where I bottle it, point at a lonesome loaf, and scurry out the door past the queue like I've just bought condoms. These old French ladies must clearly be made of a strong disposition.

The EuroVelo1 eventually makes it back to the coast and it's back into the long, winding cycle paths. It's kind of boring, even though they make for really good progress. Every now and again however there is a break in the trees and I get a real understanding of why this area is so popular as a tourist destination. There is an almost perfectly straight white sand beach running over 100km from the estuary crossing point at Royan, to the city of Bayonne, just north of the French-Spanish border. The beach is spectacular and, given its size, is not over populated, even with the hordes of people taking advantage of the beautiful setting and surf filled seas. Being bordered on the land side by an impressive man-made forest spanning 10,000km^2, the area feels cut off from the rest of the country and gives the small holiday dwellings a feeling of isolation. We've never really holidayed this far south, mainly due to the fact our old campervan is unlikely to make it this far, but I vow that one day I will come here again and show Sue a side of France we never knew existed.

When I finally give in on the day's rather boring riding, I head to the closest town of Leon. Just before I get to the town I stumble across a lake, the incorrectly named Étang de Léon. The translation of this is the Pond of Leon, which does not do it justice as it's a massive 2 and a half kilometres across. It has the 'Camping Landes Sunêlia le Col Vert' campsite on its northern shore. It's also massive, spanning a full kilometre of the pond's bank. I arrive to see the disappointing sight of two children's activity pools full of screaming kids, flanked by equally raucous sunbathing parents. The noise brings back memories of the techno-loving teenagers back in Normandy. I find the attendant's office is manned by a pleasant Australian lady, crisply dressed in the site's uniform of yellow and royal blue.

'Hi, do you have a reservation?'

'No, sorry I don't. But do you have space for a small tent? Preferably on the other side of the site from the children's play areas.'

'Hmm, well this is a family place, so you might be out of luck.' She sadly replied, realising my requirements for peace and tranquillity.

Spurred on by the faint sound of overenthusiastic screaming kids coming from outside, I consult the map to look for other, quieter options, but quickly realise I'm stuck. On seeing my conundrum, and my pathetically solemn face, she sympathetically offers me one of their camping pods at a cut down price of €25.

'Is it close to the children's play areas?' I ask again.

'It's a bit out of the way I guess. It should be quiet later anyway.'

'Fine, I'll take it. By the way, just what is a camping pod?' I was having it regardless, but I was intrigued at where I'd be staying the night. I was taken a reassuringly long distance away from the activity areas by a young lad in a golf buggy to find a field containing 7 fabric tents set on wooden stilts. They look like the watchtowers at some concentration camp or border checkpoint and I half expect to see an AK-47 peeping out from one of the curtained doors at any moment. I put this down as a distinct plus point, at least the threat of death may keep any noisy kids away.

The pods were surprisingly comfy and were a nice alternative to my tent, which has started smelling quite badly. I am definitely embracing the local culture with my tent, my panniers, and myself smelling like they've been smearing in 4-year-old brie. Sue should be safe in the knowledge there is absolutely no chance of any other women coming within 10 feet of me or my tent any time soon. The construction of the sleeping pods was simple: 4 wooden legs holding up a mesh bed, covered by a square tent made of heavy duty PVC. The bed is about 2 metres off the ground, accessible by ladders, leaving space for an integrated dining table underneath. They were really comfy, so comfy in fact that I was woken during the night by the giggling of a courting couple as they scoured the empty pods looking for a bit of 'alone time'.

The evening was time spent quietly supping premium strength lager under the setting sun, along with posting Manion Friday's next blog. To break up the monotony and blandness of the last few days, I'd been taken to thinking up the contents of Manion's next quest. Manion has decided to cash in on his fame…

Manion Friday to host game-show!!

Due to some outstanding debts to the Columbians for 'items miscellaneous', Manion Friday is hosting his own show. Please 'like' and 'share' as he REALLY needs this to be a hit!

So, as you know, Manion Friday is travelling with me on my trip from John O Groats to Gibraltar. However, he has formed some powder based 'needs' and is looking to take advantage of his fame to make some quick cash. Please check out the below and let me know

how many you get. They are all a description of song titles...

So, a couple of easy ones...

Some slightly trickier…

Evolution of a MAMIL

And my and Manion's favourites…

Manion and I got a grand total of 0 responses, except for some comments on my shorts seemingly giving me camel-toe. Though I did find it pretty funny to create. I'd find myself riding along in fits of spontaneous laughter as I thought of the different images. As for the answers, they were:

1.   *Caravan by Inspiral Carpets*
2.   *Cars by Gary Numan*
3.   *I Heard it Through the Grapevine by Marvin Gaye*

4.   *Elephant Stone by The Stone Roses*

5.   *Beat It by Michael Jackson*

6.   *Under the Boardwalk by The Drifters*

7.   *Would (wood) I Lie to You (2 U)? by Charles and Eddie*

8.   *She's (cheese) Electric by Oasis*

I am definitely getting worried about my sanity.

One of the major bonuses of not using my tent last night, apart from the smell, was not needing to go through the full packing ritual in the morning, particularly as the rain is absolutely smashing it down. But the panniers still need putting on and I am ready in a rather impressive 5 minutes. I find rain to be a very good motivator when it comes to focusing the mind for the 'Krypton Factor'-like challenge of donning the panniers.

I head into Leon for the customary breakfast of champions then head onward towards the city of Bayonne, the target for a spot of afternoon shopping. I'd bought a very basic, non-smart phone for the trip that cost me a grand total of £13 and it's amazing. It makes calls and texts, and, well, that's about it. But the battery lasts the best part of a week, which is perfect for this trip. What is not so perfect, however, is when I eventually needed to charge it last night, I found that I'd left my plug-adapter back in Royan, and even with my level of financial efficiency, I was not prepared to travel the 6-day around trip it'd take to go back and get it. And so, I was in need of a good-sized town to find a replacement for this, and for the camera lens cover I'd also lost a few days ago. Whilst normally these things would seem like little, unimportant issues, they somehow seem to have expanded into major problems that have played on my mind. Whilst not having power in my phone won't kill me, it will certainly add extra complexity if I have a catastrophic bike failure between towns. And the thought of getting home to find all my photographs have a big scratch mark through them is a big enough driver to have me going out of my way to tackle a city and its busy humanity again.

The rain is torrential all the way to Bayonne. I stop off half way for a rest at a tourist-filled town called Seignosse, but whilst pleasant, the rain is even managing to put a dampener on a Nutella doughnut as big as a slightly deflated, size 4 Mitre football, and a jazz quartet happily playing on the town's bandstand. Still, at least I have my trusty woollen waterproofs.

For lunch, I am back on the pâté and crusty bread. Even with the rain coming down in buckets, it's still as hard as granite, the rain simply bouncing off its impenetrable outer shell. As I try my best to focus on its nutritional benefits, I can't help but dream of a coronation chicken sandwich on a bed of crisp iceberg lettuce between 2 slices of moist Warburton's mega-thick white bread. I slobber a little at the thought, which actually seems to help the consumption of the baguette somewhat.

I get to the outskirts of Bayonne just after lunch. As I hit the edge of the city the inevitable traffic starts and, disappointingly, so do the hills. It's back to the fast, then slow paced progress as I traverse the deep, wide valleys, which reminds me of those in the north of the country, only this time with the added complication of crazy city drivers.

I can tell I'm getting near the city centre as the road gets noticeably busier. After about 30 minutes, I find myself in a nose-to-nose traffic jam and take advantage of being on the bike by progressing, albeit tentatively, down the centre of the road. Progress is slow, but eventually I start getting into the heart of the city and the modern-day constructed offices and commercial outlets suddenly disappear, replaced with narrow streets fringed with 4-story-high, pastel-colour rendered buildings. The place is bustling with people, and I'm surprised when I start to see some of them walking around dressed in all white with a red neckerchief.

There are families of 3, perhaps 4, generations, all going in the direction of the city centre, and all dressed in exactly the same attire of pure white. As I get ever closer to the centre, the numbers of uniformed-revellers increase, till nearly everyone is dressed in the same gear. It feels like I'm riding through a clichéd washing powder advert. I ride over the main river running through the centre of the city using a beautiful, old multi-arched bridge, well over 200 metres long, and into the old part of the town. It's really rustic surroundings consisting of a labyrinth of pedestrianised streets all wrapped tightly around a large cathedral. And the place is packed with a sea of white down every street. As marked on the massive sign outside the city's arena, it looks like I've found a bullfighting festival.

It turns out I've hit the city right in the middle of this year's Fêtes de Bayonne, a 5-day festival inspired by the San Fermín bull-running event in Spain's Pamplona city. At first, I'm a little surprised at seeing such a traditionally Spanish event in France, however I am soon corrected by a young drunk guy I briefly talk to who states in no uncertain terms that this is not France, this is 'Basque Country'. I have heard about the region before, particularly about their struggle for independence. I remember speaking about it to a customer I visited once in Bilbao in Spain, which also lies within the area. He told me a bit about the history of the region, which spans a small part of the south west of France, and a large section of the central north of Spain. The area used to be an independent country, however it has been swallowed up to become part of the 2 neighbouring countries. There has been political friction about the region over the years and he compared it to the struggles in Northern Ireland. As with the Northern Ireland struggles, the troubles have slowly diminished in recent years and there is a lull in activity, although as history has shown, this type of thing often has the habit of coming back again.

The festival includes its own bull-running event, along with bull fighting performed in the city's purpose built Arenes de Bayonne arena. And the natives seem to be going for it big time. There is bunting everywhere, as well as alfresco catering and bars on every street. Every shop seems to be selling food, booze, or both, and the locals are making the most of what's on offer, creating a real drunken buzz to the place.

As I'm worried about leaving my bike anywhere, or more specifically the unlockable panniers, I try to walk my bike through the narrow streets, but with limited success. I try to fight my way through some of the less busy streets, straddling the crossbar of the bike, making sure the front wheel stays firmly grounded. I get a few strange looks, as well as some drunken French, or rather Basque, heckling, followed by a sea of raucous laughing. I like this place a lot. I deliberate for a while about staying the night as this looks good fun, and I feel a strong yearning to join in on being drunk and stupid.

I am not really into bull fighting, and actually think it seems quite cruel, although I concede to the fact I don't really know much about it. I am however a fan of tradition and so would love to see the natives in full swing in such an event. To be immersed in the full spectacle of pure local custom and excitement would be yet another amazing experience for the journey.

After a while I start cycling back around the outskirts of the main centre, away from the crowds, looking for accommodation. But sadly, I can't find anything. I end up going back over the same bridge about 4 times till a Good Samaritan spots me staring, rather confused, at my map and cycles over. She's a middle-aged French woman wearing glasses and a cream coloured Burberry mac, and is riding a black Dutch-styled shopper bike with a covered chain-guard and a wicker basket on the front. I ask her about the possibilities of finding somewhere to stay, but she informs me I have more chance of growing tits than getting a room - or words to that effect anyway. I also ask her about campsites, but sadly she gives me a similar response. I guess I'll have to surrender to the fact that this is not going to be my day. And so, regrettably, I bin the idea. I just hope my journey through Spain will bring other opportunities of such events. I also take the opportunity to ask her about finding a replacement camera lens cover, and after seeing my pathetic, helpless face when she started giving me directions, she decided to take 10 minutes out of her day to take me directly to the camera shop. What a thoroughly nice lady I thought, though I was slightly miffed to find the shop keeper had just started his 2-hour lunchbreak when we got there.

After loitering around the streets for a few hours, I eventually bought a replacement lens cover. The €10 I had to pay for the small disc of plastic seems a little steep, but that was nothing considering the €15 I paid for a new plug adapter! Still, I was in no position to either haggle, or to find an alternative so I begrudgingly parted with the cash and rode off mumbling my disappointment in true British fashion.

I leave Bayonne in the direction of the stereotypically French sounding town of Saint-Jean-Pied-de-Port, which will be my basecamp for the big push over the Pyrenees. The road takes me back inland, and into more of the same undulating hills I'd experienced on the way in to the city. As I get further out of the city, the surroundings slowly morph from city centre urban sprawl, into dense, natural woodland, and further into beautiful expansive countryside. The undulations in the land start becoming less uniform and more intense - it definitely feels like I'm getting into another phase of this epic adventure. The 5 days or so riding prior to today were relatively flat, and the land was quite dry and parched. The vegetation seemed to be the type at home in the dry, arid climate, such as pine trees and long grasses. But up here, as I start to climb, things are a lot more fertile and everything seems more fruitful and less harsh. The trees now seem a lot greener and bushier, and the grassy fields seem denser. The land looks less barren and more rich, which reminds me of England - a place which is also synonymous with pissing it down all day.

I make it to the town of Ustaritz by late afternoon and stock up on a bottle of red, a nice-looking tin of pre-made beef bourguignon… and some more French bread. With my budget-busting purchases today still gnawing away in my mind, I decide I need to rebalance the books with a campsite. After cycling around for a while failing to find one, I stop a guy who informs me I'm out of luck. I am, however, pointed in the direction of one in Campo-les-Bains 10 kilometres away.

As it turns out, there are two ways to get to Campo-les-Bains from Ustaritz, the easy one and the near impossible one. And my French mate, in his wisdom, decided I needed a challenge. Instead of pointing me back to the modestly inclined main road, he directs me through the country lanes where, after 20 minutes of riding, I tentatively pass over an unmanned train crossing and see what looks like a near impassable hill ahead. As I get closer, I can feel my once powerful legs suddenly getting sluggish, screaming out in desperate submission. And my bike seems to get infinitely heavier and harder to ride. I get to the foot of the hill and realise I am faced with a rise that's so steep it's difficult to imagine even a car getting up, let alone a piss wet through old guy who's already done about 100 kilometres for the day. It's unbelievably steep and, as it disappears into a wood above, I have no idea on how long it goes on for. I don't seem to recall the Cycling Oracle ever mentioning I might need crampons and pickaxes.

After staring at it for a bit, then looking for an alternative path on my map, I decide it needs to be conquered. It's getting late and to turn around would be both a waste of time, and somehow feel like I'd be cheating. So, after psyching myself up with some repetitive deep breathing, I approach with the vigour of a man half my age, or twice as fit, hoping to carry some of the speed up the hill. I get to the near vertical face at a fair old pace, then come immediately to a halt like someone's just run up and grabbed onto the back of my seat. No sooner have I started climbing that I have to ignore the Cycling Oracle's advice and get out of my seat. I force each pedal down, whilst pulling up on handlebars, each downward force of a pedal putting my muscles into shivering agony. Straining every sinew, they provide just enough momentum to carry the other pedal over the top, ready for the next down-stroke of pain. It brings a lactic acid burn like I've never felt, but with it, the success of slow, steady, upward progress. I stagnantly grind up the hill, hoping desperately that one of the bike's many creaks and clicks will choose this moment to turn into a terminal malfunction. That something out of my control will bring this pain to a stop because, I know for certain, I am not going to give in and walk. Not now. Not after a full month on the road. I have managed to stay on the bike the whole way here and, as tempting as it is, I am not getting off and pushing any time soon.

As I fight my way to the top, I can't help but conjure up images of old 'garçon' back in Ustaritz walking along laughing his French head off at the thought of the silly Englishman and his excruciating agony. I want to turn around and go back just to punch him in the face. But I can't forgo the amount of effort it took to get here. And besides, he was quite a bit bigger than me.

I eventually make it to Cambo les Bains, and to the campsite Camping Bixta Eder. I get the tent pitched in super quick time, spurred on by the torrent of rain and the thought of red wine and tinned beef bourguignon, which turns out to be surprisingly good. It appears that in France even the 'meal in a can' tastes like it's been prepared by a band of Michelin starred chef's. By late evening, the rain is still coming down in buckets and I take sanctuary in the games room with only a couple of kids playing table tennis for company.

After hanging my sodden riding gear on anything resembling a hook, along with making use of my new €15 adapter and getting some charge into my tablet computer, I decide to update my blog on what has been a great few days riding. I left the north of France in a state of mental and physical recovery after a low couple of days that saw me dangerously close to needing to quit. Since then, I have been through a very definite transitional phase where I have started to feel strong, and with it I have found an air of confidence. When I think about it, I reckon I'm actually the fittest I have ever been. I started smoking when I was 14, and was quite a scrawny kid. I also started drinking as soon as I was able to get served and, I suppose, my health has been going downhill ever since. But over the last few days I have found a strength and a stamina I never knew I had. Even though I know that the best part of the last 5 days has been spent on relatively flat terrain, I know I'm as ready as I'll ever be for the Pyrenees. I spotted a range of seemingly massive mountains ahead as I came through Ustaritz today, with their peaks hidden by the clouds. And whilst they did look intimidating, I didn't feel fear like I'd expected. I had a feeling of excitement and anticipation, a feeling of eagerness, like I am seemingly ready for the challenge. The psycho hill I went up today was really tough, and if the ride over the top is going to be like that then I think I will have some serious problems, but this I decide was a freaky hill on the back lanes. I figure as long as I stick to a more popular route, I should be fine... I hope.

I settle on this thought for a while, leaning back on the plastic chair, fingers interlocked behind the back of my smiling head, savouring my newfound confidence in my physical abilities. I remind myself again that I am a lucky man to even be here, to be able to test myself and to have some time out to think. And as I drift off into a slightly-drunk haze of self-fulfilled euphoria, I'm brought back to life by a wayward, forearm-smashed ping-pong ball hitting me square on the side of the head. The little shits!

I wake early with a now familiar muzzy head... and a horrendously full bladder. As I stare at the roof of the tent, trying desperately to revitalise myself enough to shed my toasty, down feather filled sleeping bag, I can hear the unhappy sound of raindrops clattering the tent. I search for my torch, thrown into the tent as I struggled into my pit last night. I scurry around for a good few minutes, desperately fighting the impending need to piss myself. I eventually find the torch and do the 100-yard dash to the toilets, slipping about in the mud and the puddles along the way. I pray to the cycling gods that they'll sort out this bloody weather in the next hour or so otherwise it'll be another day of being drenched. This is definitely not the image I had in mind when I was sat dreaming this trip up on the plane back from Barcelona 6 months ago.

After packing up a very damp and muddy tent into even damper and muddier bags, I get the bike loaded up with a lot of grunting, and even more swearing.

I get back into the town and fuel up with some croissants and anabolic-coffee, then begrudgingly onto a very damp Pyrenees-bound road. Prior to yesterday, I had about 10 days of glorious sunshine, yet since then it's not stopped raining. It's really not helping morale and, to make matters worse, my so-called waterproof jacket has now become so saturated with water that it's started becoming quite heavy, hanging off me like the skin of a thin man who used to be really fat.

The road follows the path of the River Nive. It's a beautiful mountainous environment with the river running in the opposite direction about 50 metres below at the bottom of the narrow valley. The scenery is really green and lush, with overgrown natural woodland all around, and is presumably a result of the incessant rainfall here, which has actually stopped, and is now going in the opposite direction, raising as steam from the trees. The sound of the river below is therapeutic, and again I find myself drifting off into thoughts about myself and about my journey. One of the countless amazing things about this trip, I now realise, is the simplicity of the activity. I just cycle from place to place, no more and no less. At times, it is horrifically challenging, and sometimes just a little boring, but it feels really pure and somehow stripped back. It's beautiful in its minimalism, and is in stark contrast to the complex world I'd created in my head prior to setting out. I had spent so much time trying to overcomplicate my life that being out here, with myself, and my bike, and with a single goal, has made me appreciate myself and my place in the world. For today at least, I've decided that I'm cool again. Today I feel like the Fonz.

Evolution of a MAMIL

It's a cloudy day, but the rain stays off all the way to the target of Saint-Jean-Pied-de-Port. I make it to the town to be faced with the daunting sight of hundreds of holiday makers, all sporting various waterproof gear, and all excitedly admiring the historic architecture. I fight my way through the hordes of people and find sanctuary in the ultra-modern-looking, glass-sided Tourist Information Centre on the main street. It takes a while, but eventually I get my turn to annoy the young lady behind the counter with a million questions about hotels, about the foreseeable weather, about the various possible routes for passing over the mountains, and unfortunately to also nauseate her with my now appalling body odour. Through an obvious grimace and a keen desire for me to leave her alone, she informs me there is little chance of a hotel in the town for less than €100, and that the rain is forecast to absolutely smash it down tomorrow. She also tells me that, given the altitude over the mountains, it is not advisable to travel over when the weather is bad as, apart from the obvious fact of getting very wet, I also won't get to see much as I'll be in the clouds the whole way. More worryingly, she also mentions that the many truck drivers that use the pass will not get to see me either, till they're peeling me off the front of their cab. I decide this is all the excuse I need and so after an exceptionally brief description of the directions to the campsite, I was once again pitching a soaking wet tent onto soggy ground. Time for a day off I think....

I wake the next morning to find I'm lying on the damp floor on a semi-deflated airbed. I'd noticed it feeling a little soft over the last few nights, but last night it had gotten so bad that I needed to give it a couple of interim blasts throughout the night. And this morning it was down again, my weight pushing all the air to the parts not supporting me, leaving me lying on a cold, wet floor, cocooned in a ballooned coffin. Not the greatest start to a relaxing day off.

I head over to the attendant's office to pay for another night, stopping off for a natter and a game of traveller top-trumps with a group of about 15 Dutch cyclists huddled between a couple of yellow vans with a tarpaulin sheet stretched overhead. They tell me they're on a week's organised holiday package, completing about 30km per day, with the support vehicles carrying their camping gear. After about 10 minutes or so of them telling me about the hardships and gruelling riding they've been doing, they ask me about my own adventure where I dutifully fill them in, sending them into silence. I figure I've smashed this round of traveller top-trumps, and trundle off with a smug smile.

I make it to the attendant's small, brick-built shed just in time before the heavens open like I've not seen since the monsoon showers in the Caribbean. The attendant is a stern, authoritative-looking guy with a perfectly manicured moustache and dressed in a deep blue 1980's Adidas tracksuit. He can't speak much English, but understands enough for me to ask about how long the rain is forecast to last, supported with the rather impressive mime of pointing to the sky, wiggling my fingers to the ground, and then pointing to my watch. He then leans his orange, plastic, waiting-room-style chair over onto the two right-hand legs, peers out of the tiny window on the side of the building, then looks at his watch and bluntly states 'Dix heures trente'. Very impressive! I work this out to be '10:30'. And given that its 10:15, I settle myself onto the only other chair in the hut in wonder at his prediction. I wait it out, dying to talk to him, mainly to break the awkward silence brought from us sitting in such close proximity in the tiny hut. But I know that any attempt at conversation would be in vain and would be an agonising waste of time.

The rain drives down in massive droplets that leave visible crowns of splashback in the ever-deepening puddles. It continues till 10:33, when it stops, dead, and the sun beams out. I want to ask him about his absolutely momentous weather forecasting capabilities, excepting of the minor error of 3 minutes. But after a quick thought, I realise my miming capabilities are not going to cut this one, and so I trudge off to the town trying to stay upright on the slippery, cobbled-stoned path.

I get some breakfast at one of the many cafés and bars that litter the streets, then go for a wander. Saint-Jean-Pied-de-Port is an old world looking place, and is popular as a stop-off point on one of the Camino de Santiago religious pilgrimage trails. The trails consist of a tree of hundreds of branching paths that start out as far afield as Paris and Vezelay in France, and Seville in the south of Spain. They all congregate at the main central cathedral in Santiago de Compostela in the west of Spain. It is said that the cathedral is the burial site of the biblical apostle St. James and the journey there is supposed to bring some sort of spiritual reflection. But judging by the people I see in the town, it's now performed more as a walking holiday, and to indulge in a stronger type of 'spiritual enlightenment'. The old town is awash with typical tourist establishments to support the mass of people who stop off on the trail. As with other historical towns I've seen on this trip, the roads are really thin and cobbled, and are fringed by old stone buildings, constructed in massive block stone. Running through the centre of the town is a 20-foot wide river carrying the recent heavy rainwater away with efficient ease. It is spanned by a historical-looking foot bridge, which is furnished with a stunning 50-foot-high clock-tower at one end. It really is an idyllic place and has kept its rustic charm, managing to refrain from turning into yet another plastic, tourist-driven money maker.

After a bit of sightseeing I get down to some more essential chores, starting with a badly needed haircut and shave. I usually have a bit of stubble and a short-cropped, shaved head. However, after seeing my reflection in a shop window, I now realise I am starting to look like ZZ-Top's unemployed cousin. I really am looking rough, and just a little bit scary, and so after finding a hairdresser shop on the outskirts of the town, I complete some rather unchallenging miming and get a full trim for a very reasonable price of €10. I also manage to find a decent bike shop, and again give in to my paranoia and get the bike's various clicking and squeaking looked at. And again, I am given the shrug of nonchalance by an irritated assistant. I guess I'm just going to have to grin and bear it - and to turn the radio up.

With the afternoon to spare I decide to get back into the maps and do some planning in the sanctuary of a café, sheltering from today's almost continual torrent of rain. I have been keeping my options open about the route to take through Spain, mainly to see how my body, budget, and available time were holding up - on all 3 counts I seem to be doing ok. By choosing Saint-Jean-Pied-de-Port as the Pyrenees crossing point it means that I can either go straight south, through the centre of Spain, or take a more coastal route along the Mediterranean coast. The many people I've spoken to about these two options have all told me that the centre of Spain can get really hot, and I remember looking on Google Maps and seeing the inordinate amounts of arid nothingness that fills the area. I also remember Carlos stating that he thought the coast would give a cooler climate and be more entertaining. The heat has always been my biggest concern about Spain however, particularly as it's now August and at the height of summer.

So, after weighing up all the options, I've decided to take the longer, but hopefully more enjoyable route around the coast. I spot a route that will take me south east to pick up the Spanish coast just north of Valencia. I plan out some distances and I think that I have about 1500 kilometres, about 1000 miles to do in at about 21 days, which is about 50 miles per day, well within my current capabilities. I also work out that if I keep a good pace up I might even make Benidorm for the 10th of August, which is my birthday and which I've decided I will spend being drunk and smoking fags - both of which are by far and away my most favourite past-times.

The next day, I wake after another night of sporadic sleep, interrupted by a head filled with a mix of emotions from excitement to anxiety to full on terror - as well as the regular need for bed re-inflation. I go through the potentially agonising process of loading up the incredibly unstable bike without losing a finger on the pannier clips, or rasping a shin on the sharp crank teeth - looks like I'm becoming a proper MAMIL!

I spent last evening getting comfortably drunk at a bar whilst the barmaid tried to unsuccessfully explain the Basque Country dynamics to me. I had originally thought her desire to talk to me might be down to my new physical prowess, along with my entertaining British wit, but I actually think it was more likely due to the fact I was her only punter. Every time she stopped talking I would ask her yet another question to keep her in conversation, and to prevent my mind from concerning itself with today's potential suffering. But I can't put it off any longer and the day has finally come to meet my nemesis. Today's the day I've been dreading, been agonising over, and been excited about for the last few months. Ever since I thought up this crazy trip, going over the Pyrenees has always been thought of as a defining moment, the moment I was going to test myself on the biggest physical challenge of the trip. By the end of today, one way or the other, I'll know if I'm going to make it to Gibraltar.

I start the relatively short 35 kilometres, about 21 miles, trip over the mountains after the usual indulgences of coffee and sweet pastries. I leave the town on an immediate slow steady climb, with the population of surrounding houses, all uniformly presented with whitewashed render and painted wooden window-shutters, slowly replaced with the lush countryside I left 2 days ago. The environment is green and fresh smelling as the road meanders through the hills on easy rising slopes, and I slowly drift gracefully from anxiety to acceptance. I cycle along, pleasantly eating up the miles with an air of confidence, though still mindful of the rocket-shaped, side-on-profile maps of the route I saw on the Internet yesterday. I know I must still be in the foothill, but after half an hour into the ride I'm still feeling ok. This is turning out to be not that bad.

I eventually get caught up by a whipper-snapper of a man who introduces himself as Andreas. He's an Italian guy of no more than 20, who very excitedly tells me his decidedly short life story of having spent the last 2 years living and working in Tenerife before coming to live in Spain.

Annoyingly, Andreas speaks really good English, and never seems to shut up. Even on the steeper climbs, he's never out of breath, which leaves him with the ability to speak constantly, taking advantage of my own breathless induced muteness.

As time passes, with Andreas continually jabbering away in my ear, the roads go through various levels of gradient, but never really get to the ball-busting, out-of-the-seat level I was expecting. As instructed by my new travel-guide companion, the roads over the mountains are constrained in their steepness to a historical requirement to be passable by horse and cart. And it's true, all the steep mountainsides have been engineered out as the road zig-zags up, with sharp cutbacks reminding me of the ending scene of the film 'The Italian Job'.

Eventually, Andreas breaks from his wittering about something to do with Italian bread and proclaims: 'Congratulations Stefan, you are now in a Spain!'

'Oh?' I stop. I look back down the road but I can't see anything around looking remotely like an official border. I was expecting a line on the road, or a barrier, or even a control hut or some other relic leftover from the pre-European Union days. But there was nothing, not even a sign. 'How do you know we're in Spain?' I asked, slightly perplexed.

'Because I have done this road 3 times in the last year, I have the border marked on my map!'

After another mile or so of Andreas telling me about the other colossal climbs he seems to do for fun, I realise I don't like him anymore. I slow down to allow him to get ahead, then stop for a breather, just long enough to see him ride off out of sight... Ahhh, finally some peace and solitude.

The road continues to cut through, and over, the mountains, on the slow steady ascent. The monotonous riding goes on for about another hour and I suddenly realise that this is it, this is the scary climb over the Pyrenees I'd been preoccupied with for the last 4 weeks... and it's actually rather boring. I was expecting a momentous challenge of man versus mountain, pushing myself to the limit up punishing hills, really testing my guile and tenacity. But it's not, it's simply a nice gentle ride up the forest covered mountains and I can't help the feeling of being cheated slightly. Back before I started the trip, when I'd been planning my route, I had hoped for it to be as painless as possible, even considering the options of missing it out completely. However, now that I'm here I want more from it. I wanted to know I'd really done it. I wanted to be sweating and wheezing, to have my legs throbbing from the enduring pain, to have a moment to be really proud of. But I'm not, I'm simply drudging up the side of a hill, albeit a really massive one.

The views are turning out to be pretty crap too. I thought I might get glimpses over massive expanses of terrain the likes of which I'd never seen before. I'd hoped to see scenery to make my toes curl. But I'm not, I'm riding through a forest, uphill, and can't see anything but trees, just lots and lots of trees. And when the surrounding trees do break, the views are made up of other surrounding hillsides, also covered in trees. It's nice, but not in the level of nice that has me giddily logging every view with a photograph. It's the kind of nice that puts a pleasant smile on my face and the kind I've felt a hundred times before travelling around the UK. What a really big disappointment today's turned out to be!

After a total of just over 2 hours riding, I get to the Roncevaux Pass and to a sign that finally tells me I'm at the top of the highest point of the route. And the most overriding emotion I'm feeling.... is that it's really bloody cold. I remember the feeling I had when I got to the top of the Shap summit, back in the Lake District in England, and how ecstatic I was. I remember the euphoric feeling of being on top of the world, both physically and metaphorically. I remember the tears of elation rolling down my face, eagerly anticipating how it'd be if I ever made it to the top of the Pyrenees. It's this searching for moments of elation that I realise makes cycling such an epic activity. But nothing. All I want to do is take a symbolic picture next to the summit sign as quickly as possible, and to get down the mountain to a warmer climate. I think all the built-up imagery of what I thought it'd be like to get here has actually worked against me, diluting the experience. It's often the case that the more spontaneous events turn out to be the best ones and I think the counter-case has happened here. I've spent so long building up to this climb that it's just not lived up to my expectations. I guess, deep down, I do feel proud of my achievements, after all, it's a pretty big hill, particularly considering how I was a month ago. Maybe it's a measure of how far I've come that I actually did it too easily! Still, one things for certain, for the first time on this trip, after travelling across 3 full countries in 32 days, I can be certain that I've now got more than a fighting chance of getting to Gibraltar.

After making it down the mountain, the road flattens out and I start to slow. I can feel the temperature rising as the wind-chill factor dissipates. It's a really dry and arid terrain and is a surprising contrast to the last few days. It's remarkable how much of an effect this massive clump of mountains must have on the conditions here as it's only about 15 miles from Saint-Jean-Pied-de-Port, but the environment is a complete contrast. On the north side, it was lush green vegetation, and was very damp and humid. On this south side however, even though it's green, the vegetation, as well at the air, seems dry and hungering for a heavy downpour. Even the roads have been feeling, it, with the blistering sun creating large cracks, filled in with rubbery tar. I guess all the wet weather must hit the north side of the mountains and drop its goods, not making it to the Spanish side. It feels, well, almost like I'm in another country.

I cycle along under the mid-afternoon sun through freshly manicured arable farming land, the crops long since cut and consumed. I am absolutely gobsmacked by the heat. It is so hot that even the fields are giving off heat-shimmers. I'm sweating really heavily, even when I stop, making me give serious thought to my water stocks. Up until now I've always carried a maximum of 2.5 litres, 1 litre in a metal water bottle strapped to the top of my pannier rack, and the rest split between 2 cycling water bottles in cages attached to the bike's frame. And I've been drinking as and when I got thirsty. Now however, I think I might need a new approach and need to actively start slugging it back. I am sweating constantly and I remember reading that dehydration kicks in well before you start feeling thirsty. I need to make sure I manage my water stocks right, particularly given the lack of services in this isolated environment.

I make it as far as the tiny industrial town of Lumbier by late afternoon and decide to call it a day. The place is desolate which is not unexpected given the heat, and I ride around for a bit in search of a hotel or, worst case, a campsite. I ride up the main street, no wider than a single car, but there is nothing except houses and a couple of bars. Then just as I get to the top end of the street, feeling slightly worried about my chances of finding anywhere to stay in such a small place, I spot a young woman sheltering from the sun at the side of the road 100-metres away. I cycle over, then as I go to ask her for directions, I open my mouth, and absolutely nothing comes out. I am stopped dead in my tracks with the sudden realisation that I know absolutely no Spanish whatsoever. I just stand there gawping, mouth wide open, quickly rummaging around in the back of my brain for anything to fill the void. But I have nothing, and she just stands there smiling, waiting, staring into my dejected eyes, willing me to continue. I don't even know how to ask her if she speaks English. I feel myself falling into a very deep and lonely hole, the thoughts of 3 weeks of awkward conversations ahead just rattling around my now empty head. Then, on seeing my inability to continue, she simply states 'Hotel?'

'Yes, wait, Oui? Oh, please.. Oh? Errm...' She starts laughing and reassuringly grabs my forearm, then points down a side street and starts giving me some directions... in Spanish. But it was enough. Enough to give me hope, particularly considering the size of this town and the lack of other options I'd passed along the way. As long as there is a hotel, I know I'll find it and, after 5 minutes of circling the few roads there were, I locate 'Hotel Irubide', or 'Hotel Bloody-Fantastic' as I have now rechristened it.

I was pleasantly surprised when the short, skinny, and very stressed-looking hotel manager asked me for a mere €37 for the room. But this is quickly overtaken with absolute shock when he then carried my baking-hot panniers up to a humungous-sized suite consisting of 2 single beds, a 3-piece suite, an open fireplace, and a balcony you could have a game of 5-a-side footie on. The furniture is slightly outdated and I'm not really sure I'll be needing the fireplace today, but it really feels like a mansion, particularly given the 2x1 metre tent and deflating bed that's been my only accommodation over the last few days. I do wonder if I've got the wrong end of the stick and will actually be having another sweaty traveller occupying the other bed later tonight?

So, after 32 days of heart-warming companionship, I've finally decided to kill off Manion Friday...

Manion Friday found in suspicious death.

Today Manion Friday was found lying face down dead in the sink, which police are treating as a suspicious death.

After the flop of a recent music show attempt, it is thought that Manion had some difficulties coping. It is also known he had illicit dealings with a drug cartel, however this is unconfirmed. It is also known that he was having some financial difficulties.

More news to follow….

I had thought long and hard about this decision over the last few days, but I now feel it's time. I think that now I have finally overcome my seemingly largest potential pitfall and have made it over the Pyrenees with such ease, I no longer need the support of my trusty companion. No longer do I need to use him to deflect my own pain and anger as a means of finding mental-soothing. The evidence of the ease at which I conquered the mountains this morning, particularly the lack of any knee pain or lasting muscle fatigue, has made me realise just how fit I am now both mentally and physically, meaning I no longer need the comforting feeling of projecting my pain onto the little plastic 4-inches of joy. His companionship has been useful, no question, but the conversation had run very dry very quickly. And, quite frankly, so has the fun of taking his picture in funny locations. Just like any other adventure I've completed, my travelling companion has outstayed his welcome and has actually ended up becoming a right, major pain in the arse.

After completing the deed and laying him to rest, I go out in search for food. I sweat it out walking the 200 yards uphill in the still baking heat, back to the main street and to the 2 bars I saw on the high-street. On entering the first one, I find it empty, and the barman busily wiping down various food preparation paraphernalia ready to close. As I get to the second one, I am depressingly faced with exactly the same scene. Gutted, I just want a beer and some nice food. As I start staring at the menu on the bar, the barman starts jabbering something in Spanish.

'English?' I ask hopefully, but I get no response. 'Anglais?' I try, hoping he'll speak French, but again I get a shrug of the shoulders and a turning downward of the corners of the mouth. Time for a mime, and with that I perform the international sign-language of pushing all my fingers and thumb together on one hand and bringing to my mouth.

'Ahhh, Comida?'

'Oui!' I guess.

'No,' he replies with an embarrassed smile. He proceeds to jabber away again, but then graciously points to the only thing he has on offer.... a 6-inch loaf of crusty baguette! I cannot believe it. I'd been dreaming all day about chomping into something interesting, something succulent, hopefully something Spanish, but I find myself back once again to ripping chunks off a dry, breezeblock of cob. Still, at least this time I was able to soften it with glugs of ice cold El San Miguel.

After today's communication issues, I now realise I need to learn some Spanish phases, and quick. Back at the hotel, I write down a list of what I think are the bare minimum, which ends up being about 20. Too much. I then revisit it and surmise that as long as I can ask, 'Do you speak English please?', then even if they don't, at least they'll know I do, and either we can settle on a common ground of miming, or they'll know they can safely swear at me and walk off. On looking it up on the Internet I find it to be 'Habla usted Inglés por favor?' So, as long as I can say that, as well as 'Gracias' for 'Thank you' for the moments when they do walk off, I'm sure I'll be fine. Well, I guess it was going to have to be, because for the next 2 weeks, it was going to more than a little bit useful!

Evolution of a MAMIL

Evolution of a MAMIL

SPAIN

(AND GIBRALTAR)

Evolution of a MAMIL

Chapter 10: ...To The Spanish Coast

I wake with the familiar eagerness brought on by knowing I'm in a new country, and from having spent the night on a non-deflating bed. Last evening, I had tried to take advantage of there being a bath in the suite to find the bed's puncture by submerging it into the bath, but no joy. I ended up trying to fight the 2-metre bed into the three-quarter length bath, with it thrashing around like I was wrestling a crocodile. I put this down as the second item on my to-do list, the other simply being to ride to Gibraltar. It feels rather nice to have such a small to-do list.

After a short, excitement-fuelled, early-morning ride, I stop for a moment and am taken away by the scene I'm leaving behind. I'm midway up a small range of hills and as I look back, peering above the wispy morning mist-line, I see a plain about 3 or 4 kilometres wide, with the mountains of the Pyrenees bordering it in the distance. The sun is still low, set in a crystal blue sky, and is casting long shadows from the sporadic clumps of trees, which extenuates the moodiness of the scene. The landscape is a mix of cropped fields and wild scrubland, and, set against the craggy silhouette of the mountains behind, gives a holistic view of the true beauty of this area. It's a very special moment and, mixed with my already excited emotions for the new phase in the journey, my eyes begin to water once more. My mind starts to flood with memories of the trip so far, flashing though poignant moments like they've been used in a dance music video. I take about 10 almost identical pictures of the scene, trying desperately to capture the moment. But on looking at the 4x3 inch screen on the back of the camera I know it hasn't done it justice and I guess it never will. I realise that I'm trying to take a 2D picture to capture a 4D world; the 3D scene in front of me, and the buzzing euphoria I feel in my head.

As I venture almost perfectly south along the beautifully smooth roads, the land becomes more dry and barren and the heat of the day really starts to kick in. Whilst merrily riding along this almost perfectly flat terrain, graciously cooled by the air as I cut through it at a good pace, I take the opportunity to practise my new Spanish phrase in various different pronunciations. I have not really needed to speak Spanish before, mainly due to speaking the now international language of English. I guess the only time I have been around Spanish-speaking people is either through work, where everyone also speaks English, or during my time on the Cruise Ships when we went to South America. But this phase in my life was spent very drunk and it was a long time ago. I try a number of different ways of saying the phase, which I've written on the border of my map strapped to the top of my handlebar bag. 'Hay-bla usted Inglés por favor?' 'Hay-blusted Inglés por favor?' 'Habl-usted Inglés por favor?!' But not having anyone to tell me otherwise, they all sound right. I figure I'll just need to keep trying it and hope that the recipient can hear past my dodgy northern accent.

I reach the outskirts of the hill-top town of Sos del Rey Católico by late morning and the road instantly starts to rise. The temperature, which has been increasing all morning, has thankfully been alleviated by the breeze of riding quickly. But as I hit the slope up to the walled town, my speed inevitably drops and I'm hit by a wall of heat like I've just opened a furnace. I climb to the top, hampered by really exhausting heat, and I am rewarded with another amazing view of the flat expansive valley I've just ridden across.

Conscious of my already falling water levels, I look for a shop in the town but there's nothing obvious so, on spotting a balding man coming out of a hotel, I figure it's time to try out my native tongue.

'Habla usted Inglés por favor?' I shout to him as he walks across the carpark.

'Hello mate!' he replies with a broad Birmingham accent.

'Ha! So I pronounced it right then?'

'Dunno,' he replied, 'I'm not sure what you were trying to say, but I heard 'Inglés' and by the look of your bright red face, I assumed you were one of ours!'

Brilliant. So, I'm still none the wiser on my ability to speak Spanish, but at least I can ask him where the shop is with confidence so I can get some water. Sadly though, he tells me I'm out of luck as there is a shop in the town, but given that it's a Sunday, it's closed. I go on to ask him about his trip, before we complete a 5-minute conversation on the only appropriate topic for two English strangers: the weather. He tells me he's driving south as he points at his massive, black, 4-wheel-drive 'Chelsea Tractor', which I assume has air-con. And that the forecast is for it to be very bloody hot. On hearing this news, coupled with the beads of sweat making their way down the side of my face, I feel like I might be in for a rough ride. I figure I must be the only English person in Spain right now who is hoping for a spot of rain.

The road out of the town continues on a steady rise, then starts to zigzag up the side of a mountain sparsely populated with pine trees. It's tough, uncomfortable riding under the ever more scorching sun, and I can feel the sweat dripping off the end of my nose and the damp heat from my face is making my sunglasses steam up. I'm hurting and am reminded of the need to drink more by a drying in my throat and the lack of energy in my burning legs. But I am running low on water and I curse myself for not trying harder to find some when I had the chance. It's really remote around here and the opportunities for procuring water are few and far between.

After only about a day's travelling, it's clear to see that up here, in the very North of Spain, the terrain is made up of long west-to-east ranges of mountains, segmented by vast open plains of part-cultivated land. The mountains all seem to be utilised for growing pine trees, whereas the flat land is used for either nothing at all, or for growing arable crops. I guess the heat is just too much for the farming of animals. The land is made up of cultivated farmland, scattered with pockets of scrubland, presumably where the conditions were just not quite right for effective use. It's easy to see that with the heat, and with the distinct lack of water that must fall in these parts, that there is a fine line between usable and non-usable land.

The journey over the other side of the mountain is a gentle glide down and provides some well needed respite, and I'm back into the comfortable meditation of long-distance cycling. I really cherish these moments that have now become a main-stay when I've been riding. At first, back in Scotland I was very conscious of everything, reacting to every ache and pain, and to each and every town or place I saw. But now, I tend to find more and more opportunities to simply turn over the wheels, look about a bit, and to reflect on anything from my family and friends, to more obscure things like how a gearbox works. It's a mind-set where I don't often get to in my normal life, mainly due to living such a busy lifestyle, but it's definitely something I promise myself I'm going to make time for when I get back home. And I've decided the first step to finding such reflection-time is going to be to deactivate my Facebook account. Out here, having that connection to my life back home makes sense, but in my normal life I think I have been filling any gaps in my day with looking at my account, hoping to find something funny or interesting to read. I could be sat on a bus or train, or even just sat at home, and I'd be on it, hoping to see a funny clip or meme. But I figure these moments would be better served in thought, just stopping and giving contemplation to, well, anything really. I know it's the right thing for me to do, but boy am I going to miss seeing those videos of funny cats.

The rest of the morning is filled with blistering heat and nice gentle riding, including travelling through a mini-desert, whatever that is, called the Monegros Desert. Since leaving the Pyrenees, I've been on the bike for about 15 hours and I've only seen a couple of towns, a few cars, and no petrol stations or shops. If I don't stay hydrated, and get better at keeping the amount of water I have available high, then I fear a few small errors of judgement could make my little jaunt get really serious, really bloody quickly.

I make it to the next town of Sadába before my dwindling energy becomes too bad. And after being unnervingly jabbered at by a local drunk, then saved by the intervention of a more-friendlier native, I find an eatery at the other end of the town. The oversized pavement outside it furnished with a large plastic, 3-sided gazebo protecting 6, tightly-packed, white garden tables and accompanying chairs from the blitzing sun. After frustratingly trying to lean my bike against the wall outside, I enter the bar through its small door and its only source of natural light. As I step down the couple of steep concrete steps I am faced with a small room filled with local Sunday revellers, all eating and getting nicely drunk. I stand at the entrance for a moment, unsure if I'm to just get a table, or to go to the bar to order. I can see I'm getting some inquisitive looks, I guess they don't get many sweaty, red-faced, Lycra-clad Englishmen in here. The harassed-looking waitress eventually spots me, and jabbers her Spanish opening line to me from across the room. Nope, I've not got a clue, time to try my Spanish. And so, with the awkwardness of an adolescent asking out his first date, I mumble out, 'Habla usted Inglés por favor?' Nothing. I try again using a different pronunciation and a little louder, but still nothing. The tables around me slowly go quiet as they eagerly enjoy the afternoon's entertainment of watching me self-consciously wilting at the door of their boozer. After a few more failed attempts, a fat, jovial-looking man on the table next to me shouts some Spanish to her over the din of the bar, which brings a rupture of laughter from the surrounding tables that leaves me crying inside as I try to style it out with an embarrassed chuckle and a smile.

I can only assume he'd twigged onto my predicament and wanted to help, albeit with a hint of piss-taking, as the waitress suddenly states, 'Oh, Inglés?' with an inquisitive, yet comforting smile.

'Yes, err, I mean Si, Oui, no Si...'

'No Inglés.' She replies with a wag of her finger.

'Oh.' At least I noticed the lack of any tones of swearing coming from her. I proceed to defiantly walk across the room, shuffling myself between the hordes of eaters, to the glass-fronted display cabinet showing off a vast array of really juicy looking tapas. I feel like a kid in a sweetshop as I stand there, all doe-eyed, pointing to the tasty, snippet-sized chunks of food I want. I end up with some cured meats, some cheese, some strange fishy thing, and some Spanish omelette - or do they just call it omelette here?

With the crowd now back to their own conversations, and me with an overflowing plate of goodness, along with 2 cans of ice-cold coke, I proceed back outside, where I am reassuringly patted on the back by the fat Spanish comedian along the way. I like the Spanish.

As I tuck into the tasty and succulent foods, contented at finally not eating crusty bread, I am joined in the gazebo by 2 separate guys who set about reading the Sunday papers. Both are supping rosé wine with condensation gathering on the outside of the cold glass. After a morning's sweaty riding, I'm grateful to be out of the sun, and I get out my book for an afternoon of downtime. I also take the opportunity to phone Sue who is currently away with some of our friends at a music festival. She tells me she's making a spoon-based puppet of me, comprising of a life-sized picture of my face, set on top of a tiny cut-out shirt and pair of trousers. The thought of it makes me smile and well up a little, and I can't wait to see the pictures of me getting drunkenly danced around a festival. As we chat, I notice a rather swanky looking black Volkswagen T5 campervan with English number plates has pulled up on the other side of the road. As the conversation with Sue continues with us swapping our respective stories, the line goes a little crackly and I ask if she can hear me ok? I hear her say she can hear fine, but I also hear someone shout something in English behind me.

'Excuse me?' I ask to the couple that have sat down on the table behind me.

'I said she can hear you, you know!!' He shouts again, angrily, and in a posh home-counties accent. 'We can all hear you!!'

I am so surprised by the obtuseness of this idiot that I just smile as my brain slowly processes the situation. He's about 60, balding, and is sat with his wife, leaning back in his chair with fingers interlocked behind his head. He doesn't even have the grace to look me in the eye.

I know I speak loudly sometimes when I'm on the phone, but no one else seems to be put-out by my conversation, only this tool. The rudeness of this guy's approach really throws me off and it angers me that I've managed 33 days on this trip, across 3 different countries, and the first bit of aggravation comes from a pompous English twat. I can feel the anger inside me welling up as he starts huffing and tutting as I continue my conversation. Eventually, I can't help myself but put Sue on hold for a moment, spin around to look him square in the face and instruct him to simply 'fuck off' through gritted teeth. And I'm absolutely astounded when he does just that! He gets up and wanders across the road to sit back in his campervan. I'm more used to getting a bloody nose when I swear at people than I am of them actually doing as I ask.

It's a very surreal moment that, after finishing my chat with Sue, has me reflecting on what just happened. I replay it in my mind and, whilst I'm not proud of my actions, especially considering being so isolated and the possibility of it escalating, he was a twat and he did need to do one. I was clearly on a call with my wife, and I was obviously excited to speak to her. This guy was simply being a prize prick who, judging by the way his missus didn't even flinch from her book, was already in a mood before he'd even arrived. I figure the heat must be getting to him a little and I'm tempted to childishly go over with a Solero ice-cream to help him cool off, though I decide against it as I'm not sure it'd be appreciated too much.

After a few hours break to cool off from the mid-day sun, and from the annoyance of the English idiot, I eventually head off again with my water-bottles now reassuringly full. The road rises up a short, steep hill out of the town, then on an arrow-straight, steady downhill for the next 15-mile stretch to the next town of Ejea de los Caballeros. I pass a campsite on the way but considering the heat, as well as the relatively cheap cost of last night's accommodation, I am interested in more exuberant surroundings for this evening.

I make it to the town by early evening and again, I find a ghost town as the native's shelter from the sun. I again fail to find a hotel, but I do find an old-boy sat on a bench outside the closed tourist office. When I mime sleeping to him he just points back in the direction I've just come, presumably letting me know about the campsite I passed on the road in. I consider my options and, given the near full water bottles, I decide to keep going in hope that the next town will come up trumps.

Just as I get to the edge of town, ready to begrudgingly continue on the day's riding, I pass a restaurant, which looks like it might also be a hotel, with a couple of waitresses, all dressed in black, stood outside smoking.

'Por favor, habla ust… oh, sod that… Hotel?'

'Uh?' She replied, squinting from the sun now low in the sky.

'Hotel?' I repeat, coupled with the mime of praying hands tucked under my tilted head.

'Ahhh, Hotel!' She states, with the surprised realisation of understanding my request. And just as I get my hopes up from the response, she points to the restaurant and declares 'No'. The two women then proceed to get into a rather excited conversation, presumably arguing about who was going to be the lucky lady to take home this sweating, stinking Adonis tonight.

The conversation continues for a few minutes before one of them instructs me with a curl of her finger and a 'Come' as she walks to her car parked on the other side of the road. Looks like she's the winner, however she then continues with a shout over her shoulder of 'Hostel'. I follow her in her car as she takes me through a maze of streets to a small place advertising itself as a 'Pension'. After thanking her I go inside and am amazed to find I get a room, with a bed and an en-suite bathroom, and breakfast, for a mere €25. I fight the strong urge to hug the hotelier for being so cheap and for preventing what would have been a very unpleasant evening, and quite possibly night, riding.

I settle into the hostel's small bar for a few beers and find a table of rowdy guys aggressively playing cards in the corner. The arguments get really heated at one point, with grabbing of arms and shouting into each other's faces. I'd have been really worried had the minimum age not been about 70. Seeing the animated hand gesturing and hostile finger pointing of men of such maturing age was admittedly quite funny, but also quite impressive. I just hoped it didn't go off properly as I'm not sure I could have coped with seeing that.

Today has been absolutely amazing and I figure it has to have been one of the best yet. It's been blazingly hot, but I've seen some amazing views and have met some really interesting people. I've been laughed at for speaking English, and I've been shouted at, also for speaking English. I've also been helped by the natives to find a hostel, which was a small thing, but meant the world to me and prevented what might have turned into a bit of a blag of riding at night. I think I'm going to like Spain. Surviving Spain, is going to be about being a nutty Englishman. Luckily, nutty Englishman is one of my specialities.

Another night, and another great sleep in a real bed. I'm really liking stopping in hotels at the moment, even if my budget is containing them to the bargain-basement ones. I like that I can sleep on a non-deflating bed, of course, but I also appreciate the fact that I can wake up without the knowledge I'll need to pack all my sleeping gear away before I leave. I also like the fact I can stand up while I get dressed, and that I have a toilet within feet of my bed - an important fact considering my ever-aging bladder. Given that I was paying about €20 for campsites in France, then as long as I can find similar accommodation to the one I'm in now, I know I'll be ok for budget and I'm definitely going to stick to hotels for the near future. The thought of trying to sleep under canvas in this debilitating heat is not appealing in the slightest. Last night, after the excitement of the near kick-off in the bar, I went to find food and spotted a thermometer/clock display outside a pharmacy that told me it was both 22°, and 22:03. I hate to think what the temperature was like in the midday sun?

I head through more dry, arable land and am amazed at just how many solar farms I am seeing this morning. I saw a few yesterday, but this morning I seem to be in a hotbed as I pass field upon field of these massive, shiny black plates, all strategically pointing at the sun for maximum effect. They are massive and, I assume, expensive, but here in this location, I am sure they must really be earning their keep. I have visions of an electric meter in a farmer's under-stair's cupboard spinning in reverse at 2000rpm. Although I suspect it's probably a far more professional outfit than that. I pass more and more fields filled with them, even passing one symbolically situated right across from a long-since abandoned petrol station. I figure that if this is the future, if we are going to dump our use of fossil fuels in favour of solar energy, then judging by the last couple of days of blistering sun, Spain has got to have a future as one of main providers of the world's energy.

I get to the town of Truste and to the Ebro Valley, and head south-east towards the major city of Zaragoza. The road lies on the very edge of the north side of this massive and very fertile flat-land. To my left, never further than 100 metres away, is a wall of rock and dry mud over 50 metres high. To the right is an almost perfectly flat, open expanse of well over 4 kilometres of what looks like lush, green vegetation. I'm taken aback at just how green and prosperous it is, and it's in stark contrast to the rest of Spain I've seen so far. An already fertile land due to the abundance of minerals in the ground, it has been made even more effective by the use of a labyrinth of irrigation channels, fuelled from the free-flowing Ebro River in the centre of the valley. I can safely say it seems to be working well.

As I ride along admiring the weird geological phenomena of the surrounding area, I am feeling really blitzed by the sun and am starting to re-evaluate the positivity of the last few days. It had been going so well, too well in fact. I guess it was inevitable that it wouldn't be long till I was feeling some tetchiness again. And so, in search of something to get annoyed at, I focus, yet again, on the dodgy clicking and squeaking noises from my bike. The noises are becoming disconcertingly loud and are really annoying. It's not long till I've conceded to listening to the radio again, even though it's a busy road. Sorry Cycling Oracle, I need the distraction this morning.

I slog it out and eventually make it to the town of Alagon where my naivety on Spanish roads brings a new and unwanted adventure. On looking at my admittedly crap overview-level map I hadn't realised that the only road from Alagon to Zaragoza was actually an excessively busy, 2-laned road. As I cycle up to it, I can see the traffic is mainly made up of vans and articulated trucks. And they're flying down both lanes at alarming speeds. And to add to the worries, it looks very much like it might even be a motorway.

I cycle back to the petrol station I passed about half a mile back in the hope of picking up a new map and to find an alternative route. But I am out of luck. On asking the 'Oil Distributor' behind the counter for directions, he informs me in very broken English that yes, this is the road I need to take. I ride back to the carriageway again, looking anxiously for any other options along the way, but it looks like this is it. I make it as far as the slip-road, before I lose my nerve again and spin the bike around in the road trying desperately to keep it upright. And again, I am back badgering the attendant, making sure there was no misunderstanding on the road. It really did look like a motorway, but again he insisted that this was the way. And with an air of confidence brought about from sitting in the comfort and safety of being behind the till, he adds, 'Is OK, drivers are used to seeing bicicleta on road'. Well that's reassuring then.

And so, once again, I'm cycling back to the juggernaut-filled highway. I really don't want to do this, but I need to get to the coast as soon as possible in the hope of finding cooler weather as I fear for my chances of making it all the way in this blistering heat. And the quickest way to the coast, I concede, is down this road. So, with no other real option but to go for it, I put my war face on - which actually turns out to be quite easy given my current mood this morning - and I take the left-hand sweeping curve over the carriageway. Not daring to look over the side of the bridge, I cycle down the sloping slip-road onto the narrow emergency lane of what feels like the busiest road in Spain. Head down, I pedal ferociously, spurred on by the fast-running traffic, which is actually quite accommodating and moves over to the fast lane where possible. But it still leaves me trembling, both from the air being pushed aside by the big trucks, and from pure fear. I feel very small, and very, very vulnerable. Still, at least the cooling effect of blustering air as it gushes past my face is a welcoming by-product.

I make it to Zaragoza by lunch and it's a welcome relief to be off the busy road, even though I'm now in a city. The last hour was head down grinding it out, whilst trying to navigate around various roadside debris including numerous empty water bottles, a water bottle half filled with what looked very much like urine, and a shoe. Just how the hell does a shoe make it onto the side of a dual-carriageway?

Once in the city, I get the inevitable whirlwind head from the speed of everyday city life. Everyone seems to be travelling around like someone's pressed the fast-forward button. Luckily, the city has been made cycling-friendly, and they've put a nice smooth cycle path down the middle of the oversized pavement, well away from the crazy, city drivers. They've even put up signs, which warn cyclists of going too fast, presumably to further protect the pedestrians. I'm not sure I really need to worry myself on that one.

I notice another thermometer/clock display in the centre of a roundabout and am gobsmacked to read it at 38° and 14:21. Wow! I mean, I knew it was hot, but... Wow! I can't remember ever being in temperatures this hot. I'm sure I probably have, during my Cruise Ship days in the Caribbean, but unlike those days, I'm cycling in it... day after day... right across Spain. The heat is really draining, and with the sun zapping what little energy I have, along with the need to stop every 10 minutes to check for directions in the labyrinth of city roads, my pace has gone down to an embarrassing crawl. They do say that only mad dogs and Englishmen go out in the midday sun, though I'm not quite sure which of these I'm feeling most like right now.

As I get further away from the centre, the heavy traffic subsides again and I'm left with a rather more tranquil ride though the industrial outskirts of the city, then back into the lush open expanse of the Ebro Valley. They really do take advantage of the land's fertility here, with almost every inch used for growing various types of crops. I pass a number of fields containing teams of pickers walking in unison behind tractors, making the most of the now cooling late afternoon conditions to frantically rip up the ripened produce.

As the light really starts to fade, and my body finally gives in, I decide to call it a day and head off the main road to the town of Fuentes de Ebro. It looks a small town on the map, but the first building I see on the way in is decorated with hand-painted silhouettes of naked women with massive boobs, all positioned in provocative poses such as on all 4's or kneeling down smoking cigars. When I get close, I find that the building is the home of a venue called 'Venus II'. Maybe this isn't the quiet little town I thought it was after all.

I ride through the town, hopefully scanning for something resembling a hotel, and just as I get to the other end, the anxiety rising again that I might be back on the now dark main road very soon, I thankfully find the Hostal Elena. After being told bed and breakfast is a mere €20, and finding beers are €1 each, I know I'm in the right place. During the trudge up to the room, carrying all my gear, I had been a bit worried about the low price and the fact it was a named Hostal, a place more commonly known to house massive room of bunkbeds, and hordes of sweaty Australian backpackers. However, I am pleasantly surprised as I open the door and am faced with an admittedly small room, furnished with what looked like a brand-spanking new bed and wardrobe. I was so happy I could have run downstairs and given Elena a full-on, open-mouthed kiss. But after considering that this was likely to get me thrown out with immediate effect, particularly as I'd not showered yet, I restrain and glug a beer instead. The feeling of elation I get at these moments when I've been slogging it out all day not knowing when I'll find a place to sleep, only to be given the sanctuary of a room, a bed and a shower, is simply immense. The only thing I can liken it to is the feeling after going out all day getting drenched, then immediately sitting next to a warm fire in dry clothes with your bare feet thawing out. It's like that, only better, a lot, lot, better.

I head out into the town for some food. There was a restaurant attached to the side of Hostal Elena but I like to get out in to the towns when stopping in hotels, just to see what it's like. I head towards the main street, which is again a thin, single-vehicle road banked with multi-floored, adjoined houses. As I get there, I am faced with the sight of small groups of athletically built Hispanic guys in white vests hanging out on the street. They look very menacing, particularly as they seem to be clocking me as I head their way. It feels like I'm in a Los Angeles gangster film, and have inadvertently drifted onto the turf of another crew. Feeling very isolated and a tad uncomfortable, I decide that the food at Hostal Elena looked quite good after all and, after feigning forgetting my wallet with a pat on my pockets, I turn around and hurriedly walk back, trying desperately to look cool whilst staying attached to my wayward flip-flops.

I wake again the next morning with the dejecting sight of the already hot sun blasting through the paper-thin curtains. Looks like it's going to be another stinker. I am joined for breakfast this morning by Elena, a very pleasant lady of about 50, and about four and a half feet tall. She may have been small, but her diminutive stature was in stark contrast to her business guile as she enthusiastically tells me about her plans and desires to turn the place into a massive empire. She's only owned the hotel for about 6-months and currently relies on the custom of the seasonal crop pickers - I assume these are the same customers who also require the services of the 'Venus II' club. But she has dreams and a vision as the town lies on another of the branches of the Camino de Santiago heading for the Santiago de Compostela in the west of Spain. She thinks she can open up this as an extra revenue stream. I didn't have the heart to tell her there is absolutely no way anyone in their right mind would go walking for the 6-months it would take to get there in this horrendous heat. Everyone needs a dream I guess.

So, after filling up my water-bottles, emptying them again down my throat, then filling them back up, I'm back out in the excessive heat - it's only 10:30 and already I'm already sweating like a fat baker. I continue along the Ebro valley, taking advantage of its flat terrain. It's a nice melodic ride, save for the bike's clicks and squeaks, and I'm back to the meditative state of easy riding, nice scenery, and being lost in my own thoughts. I am missing home a bit today and I wonder what it will be like when I get back. It feels so long ago now that I was leading a normal existence, slogging through the daily mundanity, that I wonder if I'll have trouble fitting back in. This trip has been such a revelation that I wonder if I can go back to greasing the cogs in the regular world. I feel so far away from that life that I'm sure it's going to take some major adjustment.

The road leaves the comfort of the flat Ebro Valley and starts to climb as I start heading due south again. The terrain instantly changes, with the greenery gone and the landscape back to arid nothingness. The surrounding land is made up of brown mounds of dirt and rock, dotted with clumps of hardy vegetation desperately clinging on to the loose, dusty ground. As the road climbs, my speed conversely drops off and again I'm left slugging it out under the ever-more scorching sun. The combination of climbing hills, even up the gentlest of slopes, and the heat, is brutal. When I'm climbing, I'm obviously using more energy, and therefore my temperature increases, but worst still, is the loss of a breeze. There's been no real wind to talk of since I hit Spain, but the wafts of air generated from riding at speed is just enough to keep my head from exploding and to help waft away some of the sweat. But on the hills, the speed drops to a slow crawl and I can feel my temperature rise, leaving sweat dripping from my nose and from the lobes of my ears. And no matter how much water I glug down, I can never quite quench the thirst. My mouth always feeling like I've got a bad hangover. The electrolyte tablets I've brought seem to help cut through the thirst a bit, but it's not enough and I start dreaming of salty, and sugary foods like a large Burger King bacon double-cheeseburger, chips, and a large coke. My body craving to replenish the lost minerals which are now showing up on my shirt as white salty tidemarks. It is just brutal riding, totally and utterly brutal.

I stop off for lunch in the small town of Hijar at a place called Bar Quemao, preferring it to the less appealingly named Bar Arse just around the corner. I spend the early afternoon sheltering from the sun outside at a parasol-covered table with a book, slurping icy cokes in an attempt to replenish the lost sugars. I am there for a good couple of hours and, just as I am about to leave, people start coming around the corner in their droves, and start settling into the place for an afternoon tournament of backgammon. The mood goes from quiet serenity into raucous activity in minutes. I go into the bar to pay, where the English-speaking barman simply slides the bill over due to the din of over 30 people all excitedly rattling dice and clicking counters, then leave. As I go outside and start saddling up, re-caging my newly refilled water bottles, a small, flatbed mini-van pulls up carrying a load of loose fruit on the back. The driver stops, gets out, gets what looks like a massive peach from off the back of his van, and puts it in my hand. When I look at it puzzlingly, taken aback by the offering, he simply states 'Strong!', whilst giving me the international mime of lifting his arms to 90 degrees, bending his elbow, and tensing his biceps. And with that, he gets back in his van and drives off before I can recount any sort of Spanish phase that could even come close to projecting my appreciation. What an amazing moment. Such a small offering but what a welcome one. Unsure of if I need to peel it or just eat, I mime the action of eating it as is to a table of guys sat outside. One of them gives a long, positive 'Siiii!' and points to a drinking water tap in the street for me to wash it first. And what a juicy fruit it was! I'm not really that keen on fruit, and so I'm not sure what it is, but this thing is so succulent, and is perfect for this hot climate. What a surreal yet magical moment. Another great experience on this amazing, albeit now bloody hot, adventure.

Back on the road and it's back to the inevitable heat, hills, and more open arid land. Even though, given the choice, I'd rather the heat and hills weren't here at the moment, they are actually giving the opportunity to see some stunning scenery, and in full, and very bright sunlight. It's beautiful in its ruggedness and is actually quite humbling when you are a mere speck in the vastness of the open land of nothingness. As I ride along there is, more often than not, no other manmade structures in view other than the road and the odd line of electric pylons, which must be carrying all that energy from the fields of solar farms I passed. I swear that now and again I can see them glowing red from the sheer amount of current that must be blasting through them right now.

I get to the large, hilltop town of Alcaniz by late afternoon and am very unsurprised to find another old-town consisting of thin streets with 3-story, adjoined houses either side. I guess all the towns here are built in the same way to maximise the more desirable land, and to provide the streets with protection from the sun. And it works, even though it's about 35°, it actually feels quite cool in the shadowed streets, and it's needed as I have to cycle up a horrifically steep, out-of-the-seat hill to get to the Tourist Information Centre at the top in my quest for accommodation. The town is set on an almost perfectly circular hill, about 200 metres high, cupped safely within the meander of a 20-foot wide river almost three quarters the way around. There's a 12th century castle at the top, and the Tourist Information Centre is situated right next to it. I reckon this place must've been a right bugger to attack in the past.

After finding the tourist centre closed, I find the closest bar and wait it out, getting surprisingly drunk of a single bottle of beer. At least being horrendously dehydrated has its upside. I wait it out for a good hour and two more beers, entertained by a Border Collie dog doing various tricks outside, instructed by a bronzed Spanish lady of about 25 in a short, electric blue dress. By the time the tourist centre opens, I am struggling to focus on either the dog or its owner and I stagger over and slur some questions in the hope of finding a cheap place to stay.

I eventually get sorted with a place back at the bottom of the hill for €40. Given that I feel quite drunk, along with being blitzed from the heat, I part with the cash easily and am shown to a single room in a first-floor apartment, which is managed and owned by the bar right below.

After sleeping off the beer, I finish off what has been a really tough day, with a walk into the town for some food. I find a nice little pizza place near the town's massive cathedral, and I get chatting to the barman who translates the TV weather report for me on seeing I'm glued to it like I'm watching my team 1-0 up in the 90th minute of the FA cup final.

'They are saying that we are breaking more records for the heat,' nice to know I thought, 'but I think this is not true, no?'

'Well I've been heavily sweating just walking here and it's like 10 o'clock at night!'

'Ahhh, this is nothing,' he replied, 'today it was only 41 degrees, it can be over 45 here.' Now don't I feel like a lucky bugger.

I pack up early to try to get some good mileage completed before the sun gets too hot. I'm a bit concerned by El Barman's words of wisdom last night and I'm worried that if it gets any hotter, I'll have to reconsider my options. I'm really feeling it and I'm getting close to my body's threshold of acceptable torture. I'm feeling like a badly aging MAMIL.

On a happier note though, I find breakfast this morning is being served by Lemmy! As I came out of the shared entry for the apartment block I stayed in, I found a gleaming chopper motorbike parked up outside the bar, and its owner, who is now behind the bar, is the spitting image of the rock legend Lemmy from Motörhead. I order, or rather ask very nicely for, a coffee and a couple of those tasty half baguettes topped with grated tomato and olive-oil I've been loving, before slating it all down in quick time. I need to get going. I need to get as far as I can before I inevitably fall over from heat exhaustion.

Back on the road and I'm back riding in more brutal heat. It's only 9:30 in the morning, and I'm sweating constantly. I'm currently consuming between 7 and 10 litres of water per day but it still doesn't ever seem enough. Given that the recommended daily intake in the UK is between 1 and 2 litres, I'd have thought 10 would be enough. But I am not really pissing, and when I do it is coming out very yellow, and almost glowing. The logistics of it are tricky too. I'm trying not to glug it down in large amounts. Instead, I'm trying to sip it regularly to minimise bloating. But I feel like I've constantly got a bottle in my mouth like I'm a newborn baby. I don't feel ill at all, and I still need to get up in the night for a wee. I have heard that the body is very adept at fluid management, so I don't think this is an issue just yet, but I hope that my body adapts to this environment very soon. I am hurting and I am constantly exhausted, but I still feel surprisingly chipper. I'm just ready for the brutality to stop now, I just really want to be at the coast.

The road continues southwards on a steady incline and the landscape changes to rich green vegetation again as I get into the national park of Benifassá. It starts out as a strange mix of dry arid land with ever increasing pockets of shrubs and small, natural trees, before turning into large expanses of pine forest. As the road rises, I get ever more opportunities to gaze across vast areas of the park, where I'm faced with a thick, dense blanket of dark-green trees. How they're surviving in this continual heat is beyond me.

As I ride along, I continually stop to rest my aching legs, to take on water, and to wipe the stinging sweat out of my eyes. I can feel the positive and serene attitude to riding I had painstakingly developed over the duration of this trip slowly evaporating, and being replaced by the angry daemon again. If I don't get out of this sun soon, then I can feel I'm going to have another meltdown. I can feel a slow build-up of aggression that takes me flooding back to when I spat my dummy out and nearly quit back in England. I need a rest, and quick, but up here, the opportunities of finding anything resembling sanctuary are few and far between and it takes another few hours to get to the next village of Monroyo.

Through gritted teeth and with an internal mental conflict of my inner-daemon trying to convince me how nice it'd feel to snap my bike in two, I make it to the hillside village. I am brought back to a nice mental place again by the sight of chairs and tables set outside a café on the main street ahead. But as I get to the start of the buildings, I am pleasantly greeted by the even more uplifting sight of a sign stating, 'Piscina' – doesn't that mean swimming pool?! I contemplate whether to check it out or not for less than 2 seconds, before blasting down the steep hill in search of the soothing, and more importantly cooling, effect of water.

I get to the main entrance and after a few failed attempts at leaning my bike against the 2-foot wall outside, I grab my swimming shorts out from the bottom of my pannier bag, and unceremoniously dump the bike on the grass verge like an overexcited toddler. I go into the white-washed reception building, change, then back out the other side. It's an open-air, 20-metre pool filled with inflatable rings, beach balls, and about 40 screaming children all running around and jumping in. Not the calming scene I was hoping for, but I'm past caring and I wander down to the deep end to what little space I could find. As I walk, I notice I'm getting some funny looks from the parents sat about the side of the pool. Confused, I simply put it down to protective parenting, but then I spot myself in the reflection of a window and notice I'm looking rather strange. I'm now sporting a nice, deep bronze tan on my arms, to where my shirt sits halfway up my bicep, and on my legs, to where my shorts end just above the knee. And presumably, on my face too. The rest of me is my natural pasty-white. I look like I'm wearing brown stockings and ladies up-the-arm evening gloves. Not the look you really need when you're getting into a pool full of young kids.

As I lower myself in to the cool, albeit choppy, water I can feel my inner daemon getting pistol-whipped into submission as I submerged myself into the coolness of the liquid. Ahhhh, nice. I lie there, floating face up for a good 10 minutes, oblivious to the surrounding chaos. I feel good again and drink in this momentary lapse in today's gruelling ride. This section of the journey is really hard and is starting to become quite unneeded. I guess I've slipped back to the mind-set of thinking too much of the what-if's rather than staying in the moment, but I can't help it. These are proper hard-fought miles at the moment and I am longing to be at, what I've now pictured as the heavenly sanctuary of, the Spanish coast. With all the information I've been told about the coast, I expect it to be filled with a cooling breeze, to be more entertaining, and of course I'll be able to have a cool down in the sea as and when I need it. I really want to be at the coast now, I'm done in with this gruelling and unforgiving environment. I'm currently triumphant in the challenge of the north of Spain, but it feels like if it continues for much longer, I'll end up as a shrivelled-up loser.

I mooch about for a while till I start feeling really self-conscious about being a weird stranger in a pool full of kids. I try to reassure the circling parents that I'm not a weirdo by facing the other way, looking outward from the pool. But as soon as I do, 3 young girls of about 16-years-old, dressed in skimpy bikinis, come to sun themselves on the grass verge right in front of me. I figure it's time to leave before the pitch-forks come out and I'm unceremoniously run out of town.

After a nice roadside lunch and a glass of ice-cold, freshly-squeezed orange juice that tasted like it'd been squeezed out of the nipples of the Delmonte Man himself, I'm back to the day job again. I did get a chance to have a nice chat with Sue during lunch and it was a real pickup to hear her voice, and her ever-uplifting attitude. It's nice to know at least one of us still believes in me.

I fly happily down the slope from the hilltop position of the town, over the brow of the next relatively small bank of hills, only to be faced with the demoralising sight of the road climbing up a steep, ball-busting hill on a steady incline, stretching as far as I can see. The upbeat feeling brought on by the mid-day cool down, and from speaking to Sue, is short-lived and I can feel the inner-daemon doing some preparatory lunges, limbering up, ready to batter my soul once again.

I stop for a moment, wallowing in my own self-pity, angrily anticipating the impending pain. I try to soften the blow with some soothing music through my headphones, safety long-since gone out of the window, but it does little to deflect what I know is going to be a very uncomfortable few hours.

I eventually conjure up what little courage I can, and I'm off. I'm straight into the lowest gear the bike has, and straight into a numbingly slow pace. It's horrible, and it goes on for miles. Every time I drag myself to the top of a slope, the road turns around a bend, or over a brow, and I am faced with another almost straight line of tarmac climbing at an unsympathetic incline as far as I can see, each stretch a good kilometre or so in length. It's agonising, and I can hear my heartbeat throbbing heavily in my head, leaving me wondering if each beat will be the final one that pops my head right off my scrawny shoulders. Balls to 'staying in the moment' and 'staying calm' and all that crap. This is raw, excruciating pain. Gone are the thoughts of just 'enjoying it' or 'high-order thinking', or any other rubbish I've been spouting over this trip. I simply feel anger. A real deep-cored, animalistic anger.

I continue to climb and continue to curse as the energy is forced from my legs, to be replaced with excruciating pain. The sun is blitzing me all the way, blinding me every time it creeps over the top my steamed-up sunglasses. I keep turning the pedals, willing myself up this never-ending hill, trying desperately to keep any momentum going. But I'm going so slowly that I'm losing my balance and meandering across the road, darting into the few, sporadic glimpses of shade for some feeble respite from the sun.

I take to shouting again, focusing on 'El Toro!', 'The Bull', remembering the benefit shouting had in Scotland. I'm sweating from every pore, even from my palms, which is making the grips on the handlebars slippy as I try pulling up on them, back arched, trying to heave every pedal stroke down. With all this excessive strain trying to force this lump of metal up the hill, the bike's clicking and squeaking has gotten worse and I hope desperately for a malfunction that'll make the pain stop, but sadly, it doesn't come. I curse the bike for being so damn good, certainly better than its owner is right now.

I eventually make it to the summit at the top of the 1204-metre high Torre Miró. I'm so incensed, so engulfed in anger that I don't care about the beautiful scenery, or about the stunning views across miles and miles of mountainous terrain. All I can think about is how unjust it is that I've had to ride up this monumental hill in such conditions. The Pyrenees I knew about, but they can't just put a mountain up without preparing me, can they? It's ridiculous that they expect me to ride up such a steep mountain in this heat! I know, deep down, that all this is the thinking of a mad-man, but I've lost it and I take to stomping around, screaming, bare teethed, seriously considering jumping onto the wheels of my bike, bringing this day-after-day agony to an abrupt end. Where the hell is Manion Friday when you need him!?

Eventually I calm down enough to continue and get to the walled hilltop town of Morella. It's a medieval town perched on the top of a steep hill in the foothills of the mountain range I've just climbed over. I enter the town through a large archway entrance in the town's stone-built perimeter wall where I find a sign stating the Tourist Information Centre is situated next to the castle... right at the top of the increasingly steep hill. I eventually get to the top, coughing and blowing, and I can feel I'm getting alarmingly close to another mental explosion, only prevented by the fact there's loads of people about and I'm worried someone might call the funny-farm if I do. I spend less than 2 minutes receiving instructions from the helpful attendant that the towns 'pension' hotel is located right back at the entrance to the old town I passed about 3-levels of madness ago. Arrrgghhh, why does everything get exponentially crapper when you're at your worst?! As I get back to my bike, I am annoyingly stopped by an overly happy couple in their 50's. They're smartly dressed and wander over waving, leaning sideways, trying to get into my eye line.

'Hello there! We saw your Union Jack,' the lady said speaking in a posh accent and pointing to the flag limply hanging off my back pannier, 'we felt we simply must introduce ourselves to you as we are also from the UK'.

'Oh.' I reply abruptly. I'm not really feeling like a chat right now. I try to deflect them with ignorance, but they proceed to completely ignore my deadpan face.

'So where are you travelling from? Have you come far?'

I just really can't be arsed, but my polite Englishness won't allow me to tell them to 'piss off', even though it does cross my mind. I proceed to give them the bare minimum story.

'Oh that sounds quite wonderful, you simply must visit....' Bang, gone, the rest is just a noise. I know the only place I 'must' visit is a bed, a shower, and oblivion from the horrendous amount of beers I'm drinking tonight. They do actually seem like nice people, but I am in no mood for talking and so with the always successful action of cutting the conversation short by walking off mid-sentence, I make it to the pension to get showered, and to get really, really drunk.

I wake the next morning with the strangely disorientated feeling of being in a room with no windows. On looking at my watch I wonder, is it 9:00 in the morning or 9:00 night? The lack of a window did add a bit of mystery though as to whether it would be sunny or cloudy outside, although I kind of knew the answer to that one already. It was the cheapest room they had but at €40 it still stung a bit. It seems that the more popular a town is, the more expensive the accommodation is becoming. I fear I'll be back in my cesspit of a tent all too soon once I get to the holiday resorts on the coast.

Before my drinking binge kicked into full swing last night, I had a motivational conversation with Carlos who, with a typicality that never ceases to make me laugh, told me that I need to change my drinking habits. On mentioning about the gallons of water I'm getting through, his reply was, 'Water? Water? You wanna get on that Mahou shit they drink over there. It's five and a half percent!' But, by the way I'm feeling this morning, beer is the last thing I need right now, and certainly not as my staple fluid intake. He also nearly wet himself when I told him about the swimming pool scene before wishing me luck as the call ended. What an idiot, but what a legend.

I really needed the release of getting royally drunk last night, even if it was spent alone at a bar staring at TV programs I couldn't understand. Looking back, I think the pressure of the relentless heat and barren environment had been building for a while and had come to a head with the explosion at the top of the hill yesterday. I'm further perked up by the knowledge that, at some point today, after days and days of heat-sapping cross-country riding, I'll finally be hitting the east coast of Spain.

Back out on the road, I get a few miles done before the road flattens out and I see a sign stating 'Atención: 30-50 – EN 4KM', complemented by a red warning triangle encasing a squiggly line. Given that I'm at the top of a hill, the warning for drivers that the road is meandering ahead for 4 kilometres can only mean one thing.... I think I'm going to enjoy this.

The road topples over the brow of a hill and my assumptions are confirmed as I see a wide, deep valley continuing for about 10 kilometres into the distance. It is almost completely covered by a dense pine forest, with a road gently making its way down the left side, taking in the contours of the hillside as it does. I stop in a small layby for a few pictures, even though I know they're not going to do it justice, and am suddenly joined by the posh couple from outside the Tourist Information Centre last evening. They pulled into the layby, beeping and flashing their lights, in a shiny black mid-sized car. I apologise for my shortness the previous evening, which is waved off without further mention. They go on to tell me they are here on a 'down memory lane' trip to revisit the areas where they used to live. We chat for a while, mainly about the weather, of course, and they are suitably impressed when I give them the details of my journey. I never get bored of telling the story and I can feel my chest pump out as I relive some of the highs and lows. I know I'm blessed to do this trip, even though know I might take to a child-like tantrum from time-to-time.

After we say good-bye, I am back in the saddle and I start the descent down the snaking road. With the advantage of a high position, I can see good distances of the road ahead and can tell when I have the road to myself, allowing full-on, head-down, fast-paced coasting. I travel for mile after mile without needing to turn a pedal and its brilliant, payback for all the hours of painstaking torture I've been through over the previous days. I just coast all the way, only pedalling to get back up to speed after completing one of the numerous tight bends as the road navigates a craggy outcrop of the hillside, or when it's corrugated together to zigzag downward.

Eventually, the road starts to flatten out but maintains its course, just about on the good side of horizontal. When I do need to pedal, to maintain my desired speed, it's always with feather-like pressure. It feels good, really bloody good, and with the crippling heat now factored out by the wind as I ride at a good pace, the morning's riding turns out to be a happy, serene experience once again.

The road picks up a river after about 2 hours of coasting, or where a river should be if it ever rained. The river bed is completely dry and, judging by mounds of vegetation that has started sprouting up in its wake, I'd guess it's been like this for a good while. The grey, stony channel cuts through the land as I follow it through olive tree-filled fields… all the way down to the coast.

I get to the coast and to the resort of Vinarós, about a quarter the way down the east coast of Spain, and halfway between the cities of Barcelona and Valencia. I pass through the labyrinth of small roads, passing rows of shops furnished in the usual beach tat such as blown-up dinghies and lilos, and eventually hit the beach… And what a sight it is! It's about 30 metres deep, and filled with hundreds of half-naked people all chilling under an assortment of different coloured parasols, saving themselves from overcooking in the blistering sun. They're all nicely relaxing and getting steadily drunk, enjoying the crystal blue sea glittering in the distance as the water-ripples catch the glare of the sun. It's an idyllic scene and I can't help but grin like a Cheshire cat. I'm here and I'm staying, I vow, from this day on, till I get to Gibraltar, that I'll stay as close to the coast as the roads will possibly allow.

It's amazing. But is it cooler? Well a bit. But is it better? Hell yes! I rest for a bit, enjoying the buzz of being surrounded by people having fun, savouring this reward for 5 hellish days of mountainous riding under a brutally hot sun. It looks like I've only been doing about 40 miles per day, which is well under the 60, 70 sometimes 80 miles I'd been hitting in France, but under these conditions I didn't think that was too bad. It's been a real struggle but it's been good. The sanctuary of it has been brilliant, the time alone to reflect and to be lost in my own thoughts was one of the things knew I wanted out of the trip. The scenery has been truly spectacular as well, and it's been interesting to visit some of the sparsely situated medieval towns with their historic castles and cathedrals. And it's also been good to test my guile again. To test how I fair in such harsh conditions. To be able to answer the question 'can I still survive out of my comfort zone?' with a decisive 'yes' fills me with a warm proudness that'll be with me forever. There were moments when I was worried, and more when I was angry, but I did it, I made it, and I survived… just.

But now it feels like the game has changed. I'm on day 37 and so I've got the option of another 3 weeks, if I need them, to get about 1000 kilometres. I know I've got plenty of time to spare, and if I don't smash the funds too much, I should be fine. I've decided I'm going to have plenty of days off from now on… I'm here, and I'm going to enjoy it. I'm going to try to squeeze the very last bit out of this brilliant, brilliant journey.

After an hour or so, I peel myself away from the beach and find a campsite halfway between Vinarós and the next resort south, Benicarló. As I enter, I'm instantly hit by a sea of Englishness. Through the main gate, there's a large entertainment area with a wood-built, open-sided building at the centre containing a bar. It has a large, decked veranda at the sides and front, which is full of horrendously suntanned mums and dads wearing boob-tubes and vests, merrily slurping down pints of lager out of 'Carling' engraved glasses. I can even hear a pair of couples comparing notes about the cost of food at various supermarkets, one with a heavy Liverpudlian accent, the other sounding from Yorkshire. In the background, hooked to the outside wall of the bar, there's a 50-inch TV showing Sky Sports and the English cricket team smashing the Aussies in the Ashes back home. Next to the bar, on the other side from the entrance, is a small pool crammed full of pasty-white kids. And to top it off, the bar's promoting tonight as 'pint night', although I'm not sure what that means because it looks like it's actually pint morning, noon, and night here.

I go to the attendant's office, which doubles as a shop, located in a small building at the back of the bar. I'm greeted by a grumpy English lady who, after taking €60 for 2 nights stay, leads me past the bar and the guzzling Brits, then around the back of the amenities block to my grit-covered pitch. As we walk, I ask about her English accent, where she informs me that she owns the place with her extended family. I continue to ask about how she came to be here, hoping to get her into conversation, where she proceeds to drudge through a monologue she's clearly said a million times before about moving here when she was young, then sullenly wandering off. As I stand there, surveying this new world, I can't stop grinning at its contrast to the one I've left behind in the mountains. This is brilliant... welcome to paradise you aging MAMIL!

Evolution of a MAMIL

Chapter 11: ...To Benidorm

So, pint night last night turned out to be that you got a free one, as long as you'd bought another, and they were both Carling. I spent the evening grazing on pasta and making my way through rather too many beers whilst watching the cricket, and enjoying the scene of watching English families abroad. The place is filled with 'Barrys and Jeans' of the world, here on their annual holiday of two weeks in the same place to do the same thing of get drunk and get a tan. I didn't really get speaking to too many people but of those I did, it was filled with conversations about how cheap Spain was, and of course, the weather. We Brits really do love nothing more than talking about the weather - I guess that comes from living in a place with such a fluctuating climate. The campsite is the kind of place I would normally hate, conjuring up images of a million different Peter Kay comedy sketches. But as I sit admiring it from my isolated perch of being on a far different quest, it really is quite funny to see, I guess 2000 miles of near solitary riding will do that. Sadly, I missed out on the darts tournament last night, governed by the more popular regulars, in favour of my book by the tent - I just wasn't quite in that place yet.

The morning is filled with domestic chores as I use the laundrette to treat my clothes to a much-needed wash. I also give my bike an overhaul, including fixing slow punctures in both tyres. I am really happy with how the bike is doing as it's been getting a right battering. I know it's new, and was a relatively costly purchase, but I'm not normally known for looking after things and so with minimum maintenance, it's literally crunched and clicked its way through the miles. I guess it was always going to grunt and groan a little as it transports my fat-ass halfway across Europe.

The afternoon was a more chilled affair, with a hot, sweaty walk into Benicarló, followed by a dip in the warm sea at the campsite. The site had advertised itself as benefiting from a beachside location, but this is like a house with no roof benefiting from 360° views. It took a good 5 minutes of walking through wasteland, complete with a few piles of dumped rubbish, to get to the pebbly beach. Still, I didn't really care, I floated about in the warm Mediterranean Sea smiling at how good it feels to be lounging about at the coast after the often-torrid affair of the last few weeks. Looks like my yin-yang has finally flipped the right way up.

By evening, I'm a tad drunk having spent the afternoon watching England taking a massive lead in the Ashes, ready to win the highly-coveted trophy tomorrow with a match to spare. I decide to get my head down early. With the temperature still well in to the high teens, I fall asleep by about 9:30 with the tent open and a gentle breeze wafting over me. I'm down to my boxers to maximise the cooling effect of the wind but it's still stiflingly hot, and now really humid. I am thankful that I'm drunk enough to drift off quickly and I'm soon dreaming of broken bikes and plane journeys home.... only to be woken again an hour later by the karaoke and an enthused teenager screeching out 'I Will Survive' at 100 decibels. It's loud, and crap, and not what is needed for my now sobering mind. I feel groggy from being sleep deprived, and from being half way between drunk and hungover. I have to restrain myself from going around to the bar and smashing the place up like a 1960's rock star. Why does it need to be so loud!? I make it through a rendition of 'Shake it Off' and another one I've no idea about before I can't stand it any longer. I need get out of here.

I find out the karaoke is set to finish at about one o'clock from the rather apologetic-looking bargirl, and so begrudgingly take myself off back to Benicarló. I stop off at a beachside bar, just out of the town, for a beer. The place is open fronted, and crammed with revellers, all drinking cocktails and chatting in the warm, and slightly sticky, night air. It's a really cool bar with low lighting and soft, ambient dance-music just audible over the din of excited conversation. I find myself a seat at the bar and it takes a while to get served, but eventually I get the attention of the over busy barman and order a beer. I sit and watch as the English expat barman makes his way through about 2 litres of sweat in about half an hour, trying to keep up with the demands of the waitresses, all under 20, and all stunningly good looking. He's a good 6-foot plus, and looks like he's been hitting the protein shakes, and with all that bulk, he's really struggling with the heat and humidity as his grey T-shirt is saturated.

'It's not always this hot, is it?' I ask optimistically.

'Yeah,' he replied in the nasal slur of a strong Mancunian accent, 'this time of year it is.'

'I guess you get used to the humidity though, right?'

'Well I've been here 15 years' mate,' he replied, peeling his T-shirt off his chest with a pinch from his thumb and forefinger, 'and no, no you don't.' Balls.

I make it into town by about midnight and wander into a housing area consisting of apartment blocks set on all sides of a communal square about 50 metres across. I set myself outside one of the many bars and eateries that make up the ground floor of the buildings and, after much deliberation, buy myself a packet of cigarettes. I gave up fulltime smoking about 2 years ago but I've always had a tendency to go back to them when I'm having a really good time, like at a music festival, or when I'm having a bad time, like now. I know it is likely to have a detrimental effect on my physical capabilities but I had promised myself a pack for my birthday and, well, that's only a couple of days away.

I actually feel the butterflies of anticipation as the bartender presses the activation pad for the vending machine and I put in the €3.90 for a pack of 20. At that price, it would be against my financial carefulness NOT to buy a pack. Smoking is a weird addiction that I have spent the last 26 years trying to understand. I know how bad they are for you, you'd need to have lived on the moon your whole life not to. But I really like it. It's not that smoking even gives you a big chemical hit either, but there is something about it that I find so relaxing. I think sometimes I like it as a breakout activity, as a thing to do as a pause from whatever I'm doing. Whatever it is, I love it.

I open the wrapper of my newly bought pack by the red pull-off strip around the middle, then slide the crisp, perfect-fitting cellophane wrapper down and off. I open the box and pull on the inner tab. It comes away with a firm and reassuring tug. I put the open box up to my nose and smell them. Ahhh, that sweet smell of a fresh box of 20. I then pull out a cigarette with a smooth glide. There's just enough friction to require a little encouragement, not too much, just enough to know they've been packaged with care and precision. I then put the newly-released, perfectly-cylindrical cigarette in my lips, and with 2 flicks of a new, clear-plastic lighter, I light it and listen to the crisp crackling of the bone-dry tobacco as I draw the smoke down into my lungs. I hold it for a moment, before blowing it out in a single, slow, savouring action. Like I say, I really, really like smoking.

It's about 12:30 by the time I leave, but the square is still filled with children playing football, and climbing on the playground equipment set in the corner, taking advantage of the relative coolness of the night. By the time I get back to the campsite, I'm thankful to see the English children are keeping a more British timetable as the karaoke has long-since stopped and the only people still out are the bartenders cleaning up.

I get straight back into my tent and wrap the doors open with the Velcro straps to let the air flow and, after re-inflating my bed, I drift off to sleep in the cooling breeze.

'Arrrgghhh!!' I wake an hour or so later with a throbbing pain in my left leg. What the hell was that? I reach for my calf and realise I've been bitten, twice, right next to each other and it hurts like crazy. I can feel it throbbing and, with a panic that the little buggers are still in the tent, I'm once again getting some clothes on and going outside. I go around to the bar area, naively thinking that being on the decked area will somehow prevent further attacks, and I sit there, head in hands as a dejected man. This is not a good evening, and certainly not what I'd expected from the mecca I had pictured as my time on the Spanish coast. I decide to have another fag.

After a night spent trying, and failing, to sleep in a baking tent with the doors closed, I wake early and with an eagerness to get out of here as quickly as possible. After packing up my gear, nervously slapping at my legs whenever I feel even a slight touch, I head to the main gate with a new-found enthusiasm to be back on the road and away from any more biting. I spot the grumpy Englishwoman busily preparing the bar for its next onslaught and ask her about the bites.

'Oh yeah,' she states nonchalantly, 'they're mosquitos. They're a bugger aren't they?'

Yes, yes they are.

'We're having a real problem at the moment, the council have given us some tablets to put in the puddles to try and kill them off. But I don't think they're working too well.'

No, no they're not.

I stop off for a family-sized bottle of insect repellent, and bite relief spray after Miss Happy went on to tell me I'm likely to get the mozzies all the way down the coast. Great. I also buy a watch to replace the one I broke in the pool at Monroyo after annoyingly mistaking water-resistant to mean waterproof. I'm feeling quite tired and sluggish this morning, the uplifting feeling of getting to the coast has long since gone. I drag myself along the, thankfully flat, road south. When I was completing the preparation for this trip, I did a lot of online trawling of Google Maps. I'd drop the little man from the bottom right corner of the screen onto various roads and use Street View to excitedly review my potential path. During these review sessions, I got an image of Spain covered in badly maintained roads full of potholes and cracks. But now I realise that I have been grossly mistaken. The roads so far have mostly been silky smooth and have been a pleasure to ride on. And the one now is no exception. It is a nicely smooth, single-carriageway.

There's not really a lot to look at as I pass through mile after mile of Spanish countryside, other than to admire the accuracy of the perfectly straight planting of the olive trees as I pass. I realise I'm quite bored, but this is good traveling terrain, and I'm motivated by the fact that every mile done now is all the more time I'll have to spend on the beaches later on. I pass the Serra d'Irta national park and cycle all morning along busy main roads, before the boredom gets too much for me and I head costal again in search of some food and the pleasant feeling of being at the at the beach.

I find the beach at Benicássim and it's pretty busy, which is surprising given it's a really cloudy day! For the first time since I hit Spain 6 days ago, I see cloud, a thin grey layer stretching right across the sky leaving the temperature perfect for cycling! After a healthy lunch of hotdog and chips, I am back taking full advantage of the relatively inclement weather. Continuing south, I hug the coastline, and travel through the port town of Grao de Castellón, thankfully missing out the large city of Castellón de la Plana situated inland just to the west. The road goes through a maze of interconnecting roads, which has me slightly lost, but always with the backup comfort of keeping the compass pointing south. From here on in, as long as I keep heading south, and turning inward whenever I start riding into the sea then I know I'll make it to Gibraltar.

With the sky beautifully covered in a thick blanket of heavy cloud, and the roads as flat and as straight as a train track, I make really good progress in spite of the lack of sleep from the debacle of last night. I do hope Miss Grumpy was wrong about the mosquitos though, I clearly have tasty skin and I don't want this to be a torturous ending to this trip.

I continue plodding through the miles, entertaining myself with my now steadfast headphones connecting me to my windup radio - sorry Cycling Oracle, but I've given up caring about safety. The roads are pretty quiet and it's easy riding, which is evidenced by the 70 odd miles I've done by late-afternoon. It's been a little boring, but I can cope with boring right now, boring doesn't hurt.

With a distinctly non-eventful day coming to a close, I peruse the map looking for options for a place to stay. I settle on a town called Sagunto about 10 miles away, which looks big enough to warrant some hotels. After last night's lack of sleep, I'm looking for the sanctuary of concrete accommodation for this evening. I ride along, merrily contemplating the pending comfort when, suddenly the heavens open and it starts to rain... really, really heavily. I'd noticed the clouds slowly getting darker throughout the day and, finally they've hit their threshold and release their large payload. I'm drenched in seconds as the grape-sized droplets fall, splashing onto the instantly saturated road, the drains unable to cope. I immediately start on the lookout for some shelter, but there's nothing, I'm in the middle of nowhere. And so with no other option, I persevere through the monsoon. I'm feeling the chilling effect of the rain, and it's actually quite fun, till suddenly there is a stunning flash of lightning to my right, followed by a loud crack of thunder almost immediately afterwards. I use the timing method to check for distance - every 5 seconds between the flash and the bang representing a mile between me and it. Wham, another flash in the sky, I start to count 'one, tw..' bang, the thunderous sound lingering slightly as it bounces about on the expansive terrain. I'm sure it's fine but it does cause some concern to be so close, especially as my metal bike seems to be the only conductive material for miles around.

I make it to the edge of town after about 15 minutes and find protection on a roofed petrol-station forecourt, which is now under about 4 inches of water. I am joined by a family, and a couple of policemen, and we all stand there on the curbed distribution pumps in the middle, watching the street slowly filling with water. Eventually, the rain slows to a heavy shower and, with the pull of some food and a warm bed only 10 minutes away, I bid my new friends farewell. I have been hoping for rain for the last few days, though I'd not expected it to come with the fear of potential death.

I find the Hotel Azahar near the train station and, given its single star rating on the board outside, I know it's the one for me. I enter and am faced with a heated exchange between the short, stocky hotelier of about 50, and a young Middle Eastern looking guy and his family. There is lots of pointing going on, both at the bill, which I assume is the focal point of the debate, and at each other. I feel quite awkward as I stand at the entrance waiting, keeping an eye on my bike outside. After about 2 minutes of angry discussions, a short, fat lady with tight, curly blond hair comes through from a room opposite the counter and sternly states something in Spanish as she passes through the mirror-walled foyer, sending both arguing parties into silence. They then sheepishly nod at each other before the Middle Eastern guy walks away - I'd love to know what she said.

I proceed to try, and fail, yet again, with my well-practised Spanish of asking if he speaks English. When he stares at me blankly I try again, this time in English, which gets a heavy shrug of the shoulders. I'm kind of getting used to this awkward initial interaction and so I persevere with some miming for somewhere to sleep, and by saying my new Spanish word 'Bicicleta' for bike. I guess he'd already worked out I was a cyclist as I stand there, head to toe in Lycra, holding my helmet, in fingerless-gloved hands with a puddle of water growing rapidly at my feet as the rain drips from my sodden waterproofs.

'Siii', he states, in a dramatically deep voice before writing €40 on a piece of paper on the counter. On agreeing, he then puts my bike in a side room before I pay him and go to my room and wring all my gear out, including my saturated socks, then hang them all out of the window on wire hangers to dry in the now warming sun. I need to get some sleep, but first I need beer and a kebab.

I wake energetically the next morning after about 10 hours of almost undisturbed sleep. I was woken temporarily by what sounded like a hen night trying to get into the adjoining room, but compared to the mosquitos last night, even the raucous giggling was a rather gentler awakening. After packing up my gear I head downstairs and, on finding there's no one around, I go to grab my bike from the side room. 'Hola?' I ask shyly as I open the door. No one answers. I start to unlock my bike from a stack of plastic chairs in the corner when the owner comes in and tries to get me in conversation. I have absolutely no idea what he's going on about and, on realising this from my deadpan expression, he then goes to a large box in the corner. He starts rummaging around a little before bringing out trophy after trophy, each with the same name 'Pepe Martinez' engraved on the base plaques. When I'm passed one with a 4-inch, plastic cyclist standing on the top, arms overhead in triumph, I realize Pepe was once a title-winning cyclist. I try to show how impressed I am with raised eyes and an exaggerated 'Wow!' which I can only assume worked as I am then taken to another room to see a white, tatty, dated-looking racer bike with cream-walled tyres, and red, white and blue handlebar tape. It reminded me of the ones I've seen on old films and photographs, usually being ridden by guys donning a cloth cap with the short peak pointed skyward. I am absolutely gutted I can't speak Spanish as I'd love to have had a good natter with him. It's people like this that I find the most fascinating. I bet he had a great story to tell, though sadly it wasn't going to be to me.

One thing that he was able to tell me about though was the water. Using rather unpleasant miming of throwing up and sitting on a non-existent toilet, he was able to explain that I shouldn't drink the Spanish water as it will give me a bad stomach. He tried selling me a couple of bottles of large mineral water. But, on refusing, given my budget limits and the fact I've felt fine so far, even after 7 days on the stuff, he proceeds to give them too me anyway. What a nice guy. I think he felt a certain level of pride to be able to help a fellow MAMIL.

I get my stuff together and travel back through the town, passing the bar I turned down the offer of some Cannabis in last night. I travel for about 10 minutes before the road rises slightly, and goes over a slip road, seemingly in preparation for joining the fast-flowing dual carriageway running parallel to me on my left. On seeing a sign at the side of the road for 'Autopista', which I've worked out to mean motorway, I stop, and look over the spaghetti of roads down to my right. I just can't work out which road goes where. Worried about the thought of getting nicked, and of course dying, and with my high-level map of little use, I do the semi-circular shuffle astride my bike and turn it around before riding back to a café I passed on the edge of town.

Time to try my Spanish again on the poor waitress behind the counter. 'Habla usted Inglés por favor?' I ask. Nothing but a blank stare. I try again in a number of different accents, even slipping into a strange version of Scouse at one point, but nothing. Let's simplify it a bit 'Inglés?'

'Uh? Ahhh! Inglés, no.' She replies before getting an idea, signalled by putting a finger in the air. 'Momento,' she states before wandering off into the back room, then coming back followed by her male colleague who has dark skin and jet black hair.

'English?' he asked.

'Si'.

'I … am … English', he states proudly with a beaming smile… and in a thick Spanish accent.

I think you mean 'I can speak English', but no worries, let's give it a try. 'Here please?' I ask pointing at Valencia, the next major place, on my map, before stating 'bicicleta', and pointing out the door in the direction of the maze of roads.

'Ahhh... Err....' He realises my predicament instantly, and pauses for a moment, thinking over his options before speaking, 'Momento'. He then proceeds to collect a pen and a piece of paper before coming around the counter and tracing out the road junction, and my required path, on the paper. The explanation is supported by lots of sweeping hand gestures and the odd grunt of attempted English. Nice thinking I thought, however my reassurance was short-lived, as when I get back to the junction, the mess of roads in front of me looked absolutely nothing like that described on the diagram in my hand. With no other choice but guesswork, I proceed to tentatively make my way down one of the roads chosen at random. The road takes me down a rough, tarmacked lane running parallel to the motorway, which then turns into a dirt track and comes to a dead-end and a massive puddle-come-lake. Crap. I turn around, using the circular shuffle I've now mastered, and cycle back wondering how the hell I'm going to get south. It's my birthday tomorrow and I'll be dammed if I'm going to spend it camped by the side of a motorway in the middle of nowhere. Just as I start heading back to the junction, a group of 8 cyclists on mountain bikes come towards me down the track. 'Valencia?' I ask as we meet, palms facing upward in a gesture of questioning.

'Si,' one of them replies. It goes against my male ego, but asking for directions does actually help sometimes.

We all ride off, me dragging along behind, through a maze of tracks and lanes I'd never have found alone with only my pocket-sized map for guidance. I resist the temptation to burst through the centre of them shouting 'Attack, attack, attack!' like I'm in the peloton on the last stage of a race, realising that I'll then be at the front, and lost again. We ride through the lanes for a good 20 minutes before they point down the road, say goodbye and then peel-off into a side street. Back on my own again.

I continue on through built-up areas, each one getting more and more busy. I must be getting near Valencia. I have absolutely no idea where I am and am thankful when I spot a group of 3 aging cyclists on exceptionally expensive-looking bikes, and with one of them wearing a shirt with 'bikesport Valencia' written on the back. I want to shout, 'Follow that bike!', but I don't. I do however try my trusty Spanish lingo when we stop at a set of traffic lights, 'Habla usted Inglés por favor?'

And it worked, first time, with a simple reply of 'No'. Ah well, getting there though.

'Valencia?' I ask hopefully.

Which is replied with a cheery chorus of 'Si!'

We ride for about an hour and the surroundings get more and more built-up as we travel through housing estates, and industrial and commercial parks. I start to get some concerns as to how I'll get across the city and so, as we stop at yet another set of traffic lights, I get the attention of the biggest guy and point to my map and my hopeful exit road on the other side of the city. 'Siiii', he replied deeply, before getting into a conflab with his crew, complemented with lots of exaggerated hand-gestures - either they're working out the directions to get me there, or we were going to a rave. There is another chorus of 'Si', before we cycle on and through this crazily busy city.

I leave my new team after about another 40 minutes of riding through the busy city they stop, instructing me to continue. I am really thankful of their help as I'm sure I would never have found this road alone. So, after thanking them all, I continue on. It was nice to have company for a while, but I'm definitely happier on my own. I pass by the town of Cullera, which is overlooked by a large craggy hill sporting the name of the town on the side in massive, 50-foot white lettering. After stopping off for yet more water from a petrol station on the outskirts, and having a natter to the 'Oil Distributor' behind the till, I head off along lanes running slightly inland from the coast, relying on keeping my compass heading south for directions. I head through flat farmland consisting mainly of olive tree, and orange tree-filled fields. At the side of the road, there's a concrete drainage ditch about 2-feet deep running all the way along, and it's filled with rubbish, mainly consisting of discarded water bottles. Given the heat, along with the undrinkable mains water, it's not surprising they get through so much bottled water, but it's disappointing to see so many discarded at the side of the road. I pass a boat cemetery, filled to the brim with abandoned and disintegrating boats, along with a number of dilapidated houses displaying scrap-art above 10-foot-high, breezeblock-built, boundary walls. There is all manner of creations on show including windmills, a smiley face, and I even see a small replica motorbike, although this could actually have just been a small motorbike. It feels very impoverished here, and in stark contrast to the holiday resorts that litter the coast less than a kilometre away. I remember back to the conversations I had whilst visiting my Bilbao customer where he told me Spain went through some difficult financial times back in the Franco era, particularly in the south. And it's easy to see how life could have been tough here without the supply of Tourist cash.

Continuing along the lanes, void of any traffic, I see high-rise apartment blocks on the distant skyline that look strangely out of place, framed above the flat open farmland. Time for a change of scenery I think. I take a left and hit the beachside resort of Grau I Platja where I'm faced with a concrete haven filled with whitewashed apartment blocks all set in perfect rows and in almost perfect order - the tall ones up front, and the smaller ones filed in behind. I travel along the outskirts on the town's bypass road and it's really quiet. Presumably the holiday makers are doing the only natural thing right now and enjoying an afternoon on the beach. I pass by a number of closed bars and nightclubs with names like the La Hacienda, Bestias, and CocoLoco. This place looks like it goes off at night, big time.

I power down the urban dual-carriageway, fuelled from the giddiness of just how great a time I'm having right now. I'm smiling from ear-to-ear at just how much fun it is to see such contrasting, yet equally amazing environments. I know it's far from over, but even up to now, I've experienced so many different places, and met so many different people that I feel truly blessed to have taken on what is, for me, such a monumental task. I am not an experienced explorer or an extreme sportsman, and I'm certainly not super-fit or super-cool. I'm just a chubby balding bloke from Cheshire who wanted to have an adventure. I got off my arse, and got myself out here, under my own steam, through a countless stream of positive and negative experiences. I've been bitten more times than I can remember. But it's been amazing, it's been an eye-opening experience that I know I'll never forget. I'm sure the revellers on the beach less than a 100-metres away are enjoying themselves, but no-one, at all, in the whole of the world, can possibly be having as good a time as me right now. I wonder if Sue would let me turn around and ride back again once I make it to Gibraltar? Because right now, I can't imagine doing anything else other than being on this trip.

I leave the resort as quickly as I arrived and, after passing a place called the 'Wanderwall Music Resort', presumably renamed for legal reasons, I am back into the greenery of the countryside again.

The road cuts inland and around the edge of the city of Gandia. I manage about another hour before I decide to call it a day. On hitting the built-up area of Oliva, I immediately spot a sign for the 'Playa', and given it's my birthday tomorrow, a day on the beach seems perfect! I follow the palm tree-lined road through the town and follow the signs for the beach in search of a place to stay.

The road seems to go on for ages, but eventually I get to the coast and follow a maze of intersecting lanes to find the Eurocamping campsite. After waiting 20 minutes to get my turn at the attendant's office situated at the site entrance, the strangely overdressed lady, wearing heavy makeup and what looks like a black ball-gown, behind the counter instructs me that the only place they have available is in a field at the bottom. I don't really know what she means, but I take it anyway as I am absolutely knackered and even a pitch on Heathrow's carpark would've been acceptable.

I ride through the site, consisting of row upon row of pitches, each one segmented with netting hanging overhead and on 3 sides, there to protect the occupants from the sun's rays. They all look taken, each one filled with varying types of family-sized tents. There are kids everywhere, playing various games or just cycling about, or crying. It seems OK here and as I get to the end of the site, I find a small, steep, upward slope with a concrete building on top (presumably the bar), and the beach. Looking good. I then turn left and follow the path around a corner and I'm faced with a rather derelict plot of land, with leaves littering the bare dirt ground, and with two beautiful, bronzed, bikini-clad ladies in their early 20's giggling, and playing a game of badminton. I feel like I've just cycled into a Carry On film. It's brilliant! It's right next to the beach, and is relatively quiet due to the kids being in the main part of the site away from this plot. And there are only 3 tents, huddled into a circle around various chairs and tables, and, rather strangely, a stand-up fridge-freezer. I start the familiar process of unloading my gear and pitching my tent. I just start to get unpacked when I'm joined by a short, shirtless man of about 25, with short-cropped hair, a goatee beard, and some missing front-teeth. He can't speak any English but we converse for a good 10 minutes through mimes, and by writing numbers into the dirt as I try to explain how far I've come. On finally comprehending my colossal ride, he lets out a raucous, raspy laugh, and I realise from his drooping eyes and grinning toothless smile, that he's holding a half-smoked Jamaican rollup, and is as stoned as a Rastafarian. It looks like I've been put in the naughty corner!

I get my tent pitched and my stuff sorted between glugs of crisp, cold beer. My tent still stinks like a welder's crotch, but I realise I actually quite like the little thing. It's been far more practical to stay in hotels, with more comfort and an easier morning pack up, not to mention the lack of killer mosquitos, but I like the cosiness of the tent, even if I do have to contend with my ever-deflating blow-up bed.

After a day off to celebrate by birthday, I'm back on the road and back to the day job. I didn't have a cake to hand yesterday, so I compromised with heavy drinking and smoking instead. It was a day filled with lying at the beach and having a laugh with the reprobates in the other tents close by. The beach consisted of soft, silky-smooth sand, with dunes behind, and a crystal blue Mediterranean Sea, filled with kite-surfers in front. In between, it was filled with cool youths sunbathing, soaking up the rays of the sun whilst getting royally sloshed to the sound of soft ambient tunes pumping out from the open sided beach-bars. It was a great place for a day off, even though being old and sporting a 2-toned tan, complete with Ronseal dipped limbs, I fitted in like Hugh Hefner at a feminist rally.

I had a nice time yesterday but it was not really what I'd had in mind for my birthday. I had hoped to be smashing it up in Benidorm, but due to slow progress back in the stinking hot hills, I'd not made it. Still, you've just got to go with what the road dictates I guess. Benidorm will have to wait till tonight.

As I pass down the long and rather straight road out of Oliva, I start seeing single plastic chairs at the side of the road every 500-metres or so. They look very odd and out of place in this agricultural landscape. I pass quite a few before I find one occupied by a woman dressed in hot-pants and a tiny bikini top made of red sequined triangles of material and string. As I pass, noticing her heavily made-up face, she stands up and shouts something with a wave. 'Uh?' I reply after removing one of the headphones from my ear.

'Hey baby!' she shouts provocatively, before giving me a smile and a wave. Ahhh, hookers, so that's what the chairs are for. They're so the prozzies can have a rest during a slow shift. I give her a smile and cycle on. I've been away from Sue for nearly 5 weeks now but given the rolls of fat hanging over her hot-pants, along with her clown-like makeup, I think I'll hang-on for a bit!

I pass quite a few more 'working-girls' along the road as the day starts waking up, and I can't help but smile at the bizarreness of it given it's mid-morning and I'm out in the middle of nowhere. I'd seen a few empty seats over the last few days since hitting the coast and had wondered who they were for, and now I know. I guess Carlos was right, this really is the party-region of Europe.

The road continues to climb and gets ever steeper as it meanders up the mountainside, trying to find the path of least resistance through the craggy, white rock. I am surrounded by beautiful scenery and stunning landscapes, and even though they're lots of effort, the hills are providing some quite magical views across 15 or 20 miles of perfectly-flat, open land and out over the sea. I eventually make it over the top, and come hurtling down the other side, desperately clinging onto the handlebars, and grabbing the brakes whenever I lose my nerve. I pass down the hill at a fair old rate and as I flick momentary glances around at the scenery, I can see hundreds of plateaus of long, thin steps cut into mountainside on the other side of a gorge. They are perfectly flat and satisfyingly uniform as they follow the contours of the mountain to permit cultivation of row upon row of olive trees and other vegetation in this difficult terrain. I can't help thinking how much hard work must have gone in to creating the terraces - necessity really is the mother of invention.

I get out of the mountains and am provided with the heart-warming sight over resort after resort of hotels and apartment blocks littering the coast for nearly all of the 10 miles of it I can see. The road takes me through each of the resorts, one by one, but, even though they look great, and are buzzing with holiday makers, I have only one thing on my mind, Benidorm baby!

Ever since I started planning this trip I have always had Benidorm on my list of places I definitely wanted to go to. I never really went on jolly-up holidays in my youth and sometimes I think I missed out. When my mates were smashing it up in the likes of Magaluf and Ibiza, I was away working on the cruise ships, and since I spent my childhood holidays in a caravan in Wales, I've sadly never really been on a resort-type holiday at all. I wanted to know what it was like. I wanted to know if it was as tacky as I envisioned it to be. Was it really 'Blackpool with the weather' as Peter Kay has made a living off all these years? Only one way to find out I figured, and that was to go for a night out in Benidorm!

After missing my first turning into the resort through excitement, I find the second one and coast down a steep, straight road towards the Brits-on-the-piss mecca. As I get further into the heart of the town I am surrounded by Union Jack bunting, cafés advertising English food, and bars promoting '2 for 1', or '€1 a go' drinks deals - looks like I'm in the right place then. On asking a very disinterested guy through the window of a porta cabin Tourist Information Kiosk, I'm directed to campsite 'Camping La Torreta' located just behind the 'Benidorm Palace' cabaret venue. I ride the 15 minutes or so it takes to get there in awe at how cheesy this place is. But when I get to the ostentatiously decorated Benidorm Palace, and instantly recognise it as the mirror-panel fronted cabaret venue bought by Mel Harvey in the TV show 'Benidorm', I go weak at the knees. It feels like I've arrived in a horribly brilliant dream.

I take a ride down to the beach, past rows of pubs draped in Union Jack flags, where I find a soft, white, sandy beach absolutely rammed with holiday makers. Everywhere I look, there are people propped up on sun loungers, strategically exposing body-parts out from underneath parasols for short blasts of the strong rays of the sun, daring themselves to stay out for as long as possible before overcooking and recoiling back to the safety of the shade. It's a nice enough beach, but I'm more interested in the town itself and I ride around for a bit. It's amazing to see just how much easier it is to get British food than it is to get anything Spanish to eat. Everywhere you look there are English or Union Jack flags and every place is advertising itself as the best place to eat or drink, or with the best entertainment. And it's all written in English! After the deserted riding today to get here, this place feels really surreal. And after overhearing a group of lads from Manchester, I'm left wondering just who the hell is Sticky Vicky?

After stopping off for a beer where I get to watch a drunken old-boy humorously arguing with himself, I ride back quickly to get spruced up ready for the evening which consists of putting on my least soiled T-shirt and trousers - I'd forgotten to pack my suit. I'm back out by 8 o'clock and the party's already getting going. I start down one of the main roads that lead into the resort centre, and straight into the exotically named 'Tropical Sports Bar'. I take a seat at one of the neatly lined up tables outside and enjoy a beer in the low evening sun surrounded by British families. A lady starts singing, what is quite a ropey rendition of, ABBA's 'Dancing Queen'. I assume it's Karaoke night, till she kicks in again with Wild Cherry's 'Play That Funky Music'. Turns out she gets paid for doing it, although by the sounds of her, I really hope she's got a plan B. I make it through a couple of other numbers, including a rather screechy version of Wilson Picket's 'Mustang Sally' before I decide to move on to prevent my ears from bleeding.

I spend the evening on a bit of a pub crawl round bars with very English names like The Yorkshire Pride, The Tavern, and the Rovers Return. There are live acts on everywhere I'm entertained by a whole host of rather crap tribute acts including Meatloaf, Showaddywaddy and Michael Jackson - though sadly Michael must have had a cold or something as he was only miming and dancing. I also got to see a hypnotherapist show, as well as some sort of Pirates of the Caribbean re-enactment, but it looked like the real Jonny Depp-alike was having a day off. Whilst watching these was very entertaining in their own right, they paled into insignificance later on in the evening as I was treated to the pleasure of finally finding out who Sticky Vicky was, or rather who Sticky Vicky's replacement was on account of the real one now being well over 70.

I was walking past The Red Lion pub just after eleven o'clock when I saw a sign on the door advertising 'A Sexy Female Magician' starting at eleven thirty. Could be interesting I thought, and so I waited around for what I genuinely thought would be a sexy female magician, which I guess it was... of sorts. At eleven thirty the lights went down and the compere dramatically introduced the show to an audience of only about 20 people, all sat at the side of a large room with a dancefloor in the middle. With the small crowd appreciatively clapping, a lady, well into her 50's, came onto the dancefloor where she immediately slipped off her leotard using a couple of quick-release catches on the side, and stood there, in the buff, legs crossed, and with her arms in the air. She was tall, with long blond hair, and was absolutely ripped. She had a protruding pair of fake boobs which were so pert it looked like someone had popped a couple of half-coconuts under her skin. She looked rather strange having these bulbous breasts given the rest of her was old, and muscular. So, here she was. Female? Clearly. Sexy? Errrm, kind of. So now for the magic. And as the music started, with not a murmur from the clearly shocked audience, she proceeded to pull an assortment of items out of her fanny. There were bouquets of flowers, ice-cream cones, pool balls, there was even a snooker cue. I assumed they were all fake, but I wasn't going to get close enough to check. She was clearly uncomfortable with the performance, not only by the contents of her fanny, but by the whole experience as she kept this nervous, over-the-top grin on her heavily sweating face the whole way through. And she was also having trouble with the magic too as she was either cross-legged, or was rummaging about 2 handed, one to get the next item out, the other to keep the remaining items in. I guess 50 years' experience will do that to a lady. So, there was the magic... well kind of, anyway.

Chapter 12: ...To Gibraltar

I wake to the crippling feeling of being horrifically hungover whilst lying in a baking hot tent, filled with the stench of a rotting, half-eaten McDonald's meal. Christ, I feel like shit this morning. My mouth feels like I've been chewing on one of Sticky Vicky's ice-creams. I do a quick check around the tent for foam toys just to be sure.

As I return to what I now consider to be the sanctuary of the open road, away from the madness of Spanish holiday resorts, I pass another of those thermometer/clock displays which tells me is 33° and 11:32. I'm pleased to see it's not the hottest I've seen it, that was 38° in Zaragoza, but cycling in it with a horrific hangover is not nice. I promise myself I'm going to start looking after myself again, although I feel I've been saying that quite a lot recently. I've been drinking too much and smoking too much and its making me feel really lethargic, like I just can't be arsed to get to the finish. Since hitting the coast, I think, deep down, I have assumed that's it, I've pretty much done it. But I haven't, and I've still got about 500 miles to do. Looks like the yin-yang has spun around once more, I need to flip it back the right way around, and quickly. I need to sharpen up.

I try stopping off for some orange juice and a croissant at a shopping mall along the way. It tastes great, but does little to improve my resolve. And its back to slugging it out in the heat again. I also have a stop off in Villajoyosa to take a break, and to get more water. Since speaking to Pepe, the hotelier back in Sagunto, I have decided to keep to bottled water, and I'm really starting to get the hang of managing the water stocks. I carry anywhere between 1 and 4 litres, actively searching out replenishments when I get to the 1 litre threshold. It's costing about

€10 per day to buy bottled water, but I don't want to take any chances. A day with a bad stomach is not really what you need on a bike, particularly with bib shorts.

Villajoyosa turns out to be quite a nice place. It's a coastal town with a large port, and full of modern high-rise buildings. And looks absolutely nothing like Vitré in France.

I continue trudging on through the miles along busy, single carriageway roads. I'm set in the thin emergency lane, trying desperately to keep from wobbling into the traffic, brought on by really slow paced progress and hangover-induced double-vision. Christ my head hurts. Hangover dehydration, coupled with dehydration from this heat, is really taking its toll today and I stop off at a petrol station for more water and a Solero. I sit on the kerb of the forecourt, feeling really dejected, cursing myself for going too mental last night. I wonder if Sir Ranulph Fiennes has ever been hampered due to a raging hangover. The answer to this one I think is probably yes, or at least I hope it is anyway.

I carry on the arduous journey, unable to enjoy anything other than the thought that it might be over soon. I'm also unable to think straight and at one point nearly make it onto the motorway, only to be saved by the aggressive beeping of cars as they pass me by. The first and second cars got a simple shout to 'fuck off'. But with a few in succession I realise there actually might be an issue and starkly look up to see a 20-lane toll station up ahead and the road I'm on veering right in front of it. Shit! I stop, and proceed to do the semi-circular shuffle, cursing like a Docker, before riding back down the road I've just come on, travelling against the traffic back to the junction 200 metres away. What an idiot.

I make it through Alicante on a dual carriageway, which winds its way through the busy city along the waterfront, and around the massive San Anton mound. The traffic is travelling really fast and it's just not what is needed. I decide to take it in stints, cycling for 100 metres at a time before stopping to get a little respite, and to prevent my throbbing head from falling off. Eventually though, I'm through the town and my mood lifts slightly as I catch views across a large bay to the Cape of Santa Pola about 5 miles ahead. It's a beautiful view and, at any other time, I'd have stuck around for a bit to take some photos and to drink it in. For now though, I just need to get to wherever I'm going.

I travel past Alicante airport and decide I can't cope any longer. I've only done 30 kilometres. But given the battering I've given my body over the past few days it feels like the hardest day's riding I've done so far, well almost anyway.

I get to the pleasantly named San Palo by mid-afternoon and get some directions to the local campsite off a passing teenager. He starts out being very friendly, but then becomes frustrated at the admittedly endless requests for clarification on directions, drawn out by my muzzy head. On completing the conversation, he gives me a strange sneer and a curt 'Welcome' before walking off. Very bizarre. Maybe this is not such a pleasant place after all, although the way I'm feeling right now, I'd settle for a night nestled into Hitler's armpit.

I wake the next morning to the sound of someone coughing up large clumps of phlegm like they're a 60-a-day coal-miner. It sounds like they're stood right outside my tent and it's a horrific sound, which, at any other time, would have me reaching for my own packet of cigarettes before crunching them into a tight ball. He goes at it for a good 10 minutes before he's all clear and ready to go. Last night was spent nurturing my body again by devouring pasta and dried meat, along with lots of water, and a beer obviously. I got to bed about 9:00 and even though the air-bed needed a few refills, I did actually get a good 10 hours sleep, which was well needed.

On leaving the town, I immediately start to see large, manmade lakes about a foot deep and about a kilometre wide. They go on for miles in all directions, and it takes me a while to work out they're actually salt lakes. I can see a network of irrigation channels have been dug to allow the seawater to navigate its way in, then presumably the sun evaporates off the water, to leave the salt, which is clinging to the side in massive clumps. It's a beautifully simple design and I can only assume they've been here a while. And given the heat of the sun now blasting my neck, I think they've put them in exactly the right location.

Travelling is good this morning and I make good progress, only stopping to admire the comical sight of a lady walking her 3 large Alsatian dogs by driving around a field in a cream-coloured estate car, with them trotting alongside in the shade. I pass over the Segura River, which is now at a mere dribble given the distinct lack of rain that's been falling. I've been in Spain for 13 days now and, apart from one momentous downpour, there has been absolutely no rain at all. I don't know if this is normal or I've just hit a dry patch but, if it is, it's a real testament to the local farmers and their ability to grow such lush vegetation which I've been passing almost all of the way down the coast.

I pass by the 'Puerto d'Amore' swingers club, rather unsubtly situated at the side of the busy main road with a massive advertising sign located overhead, before heading off in search of the beach. I head into the resort of Guardamar del Segura where I find the now familiar layout of rows and rows of perfectly straight roads and white-washed apartments. The symmetry in the construction of the town is an indication of its age. Whilst old places are a mishmash of roads created as the town naturally evolves, towns with parallel roads and matching buildings have been designed as a whole and are generally pretty young. I wonder what was here before the cheap airlines started shipping in the droves of tourists?

I stop off on yet another stunning beach for a spot of sunbathing for an hour and to enjoy the relaxing sound of people having fun at the beach. As I get stripped to my shorts, I notice again how I'm going some really funny colours. I've been using P20 sun cream since I started on the advice of the Cycling Oracle and it's brilliant as it's waterproof, not greasy, and lasts all day even given the heavy sweating I've been doing. I've also noticed it's alcohol-based so if things get really bad you can always glug it back, although I've not quite got to that stage yet. However, given that most of my time is spent sat in the same position, riding in the same direction almost straight towards the sun, places that are catching the sun's rays are really catching it, and those that are not, almost never do. From the front, my limbs are really brown, but from the back, I am still my usual pasty white.

I pass Torrevieja, and out of the weird urban sprawl of a full on beachside city. I've been getting a little bored of the main roads recently, which are the only roads recorded on my high-level map. I'd been trying to find a new, more detailed, map since being in Spain and am thankful when I finally manage to buy a proper 1cm-to-4km road atlas - with the modern-day reliance on Sat-Nav's, it is actually quite hard to find. I realise I need to get off the beaten track otherwise I'll be in Gibraltar way too early, as well as having missed the opportunity to really appreciate the beautiful coast of southern Spain. And so, after failing to find a replacement blow-up bed at a Decathlon outdoor superstore in San Javier, I immediately put the map to good use and break off the main road and head past the strange phenomena of La Manga Lake. It's a large, semi-circular sea lake about 20-kilometres in length, and about 10-kilometres across at its widest point. There is a thin strip of land almost completely cutting it off from the sea. As I ride around the mainland side of the lake, I look across and see the strange sight of a strip of high-rise hotels almost the full length of the strip of land, breaking the border between sea and sky. It looks like the hotels are floating in the middle of the sea.

Given that I was unable to find a replacement airbed, I start scouring the towns looking for a hotel for the night. I try a couple of hotels, but they weren't willing to let me stay for less than €120. And so I cycle on into the evening. I leave the more touristy area and instantly start getting an anxious feeling again that I might soon be riding in the dark, until I stumble upon the Hotel Sol Mar at Los Urrutias. Judging from the outside, it looks a right dog of a place. Perfect.

I try my trusty Spanish on the short, plump, smiley girl behind the bar.

'Habla usted Inglés por favor?' I ask sheepishly, which brings on the inevitable blank stare. Back to the drawing-board then. 'Inglés por favor?'

'Ahhh, Inglés. Pocito, err I mean a little.' she replies, performing the mime of first-finger and thumb almost pressed together. We proceed to attempt to communicate in broken English where she introduces herself as Maria. She's a really bubbly character who continues to laugh all the way through our conversation, even at the parts that weren't supposed to be funny. Her enthusiasm is really uplifting and reminds me of Sue. I can't help but laugh with her as she dashes around the place, looking for pricelists, then the boss, and then keys.

Eventually, she gets sorted and shows me up to a rather drab room, but it has a bed, the only mandatory requirement, and it has the bonus of a bath. I've been seeing the price of hotels getting increasingly more expensive as I've been heading south, and the pensions getting noticeably few and far between. I need to start looking after my budget more otherwise I'll run out of money way before I run out of road. Time to fix the airbed while I have the chance. I block off the bath's drain with a plastic cup on account of the plug being the wrong size, then fill it up before carefully placing the inflated bed in, one section at a time. I find the hole easily as a small stream of bubbles rises from right in the corner of the bed, YES! It was only a small hole, but with my weight, and over time, it must have been streaming and enough to reduce the bed to, well, useless. I patch it up, excited at the thought of knowing I'll be back to a full night's sleep in the tent very soon. Happy days!

So, as it turns out, I'm crap at fixing punctures. Given the practise I've had over the past 6 weeks on my tyres, you'd think I'd be good at it. But sadly no. I wake after a relaxing evening and a good sleep, and look over to the other side of the room to see the demoralising sight of my blow-up bed hanging flaccidly over a small table. Last night, before I went to sleep, I blew up the bed to check my repair work, however this morning, it's looking much deflated and very sorry for itself. I know the feeling.

Since I've got to the coast, it feels like the challenge has gone a little and with it, so has some of the fun. I'm still enjoying the trip generally, enjoying the pleasure at being in some beautiful and entertaining resorts, but I've started feeling like I'm ready to finish. I've been trying to fight the feeling, but I've lost some of the excitement for the trip. I guess I've lost the sense of accomplishment I had from trudging up the mountains of Scotland; from the hours and hours of pain-filled riding I had across England and France; and from cycling through the debilitating heat of the north of Spain. I have been through so much, and yet it feels like the trip is dripping away to a soggy end. I feel like a nutter for thinking it, but I really miss putting myself through those agonising challenges. So, I've decided that today I am going to find some mountains. And knowing now just how craggy Spain is, finding them is going to be the easy bit.

I stock up on fruit and water at a local veg shop and, after a breakfast at the beach with the tranquil view of the massive La Manga lake as still as a millpond, I'm off on a quest to get off-piste and to find the natural highs of mountain riding. I head inland towards the major city of Cartagena. On this short ride to the city, I realise that I've finally acclimatised and am no longer struggling with the conditions. Yes, I am still sweating like a priest in a brothel, but the sun is not killing me anywhere near like it was. I wonder if maybe it's getting cooler and that's what is doing it, but after passing another pharmacy thermometer/clock and seeing it is 34° and 10:32, I quickly dispel that idea. I guess my body has finally readjusted and sorted itself out. Maybe 40 years of abuse has not destroyed it completely after all - I resist the temptation to celebrate with a cigarette.

Whenever there are squiggly roads on the map, you can assume that either the planners were drunk, which is not unlikely on the south-coast of Spain, or that there are mountains around for the road to meander up. The one I'm on turns out to be the latter. After leaving Cartagena the road climbs almost immediately and with it, so does the heat. I'm back to the psychotic pleasure of fighting the hills, sweating heavily, and slogging through the miles. No sooner as I start getting to higher ground do I get the comforting, isolated feeling I remember from 2 weeks ago. The humbling feeling of being out in the middle of nowhere, and with nothing around except open expanses filled with wild shrubs and dry crumbly ground. I love it… for the moment anyway.

I travel on through mile upon mile of mountainside road, bordered by craggy mountains either side, jaggedly cutting into the crisp blue sky. I pass nothing manmade, other than a few farm buildings and, rather more randomly, a restaurant complete with a sea of red, plastic garden chairs and tables outside. Maybe it's not actually a restaurant, but a hotbed for roadside hookers?

The angle of undulation in the road starts to steady before starting its descent. As I start to accelerate, the cooling effect of the air as it rushes past my face is refreshing, but it's nowhere near as uplifting as the view I'm blessed with as I come to a sharp right-hand bend that makes me stop dead. I'm about 300 metres up, just below the brow of the hill, and am near the top of a valley with rugged mountainside sloping inwards either side. In front, at the bottom of the valley, there is a few miles of flat, green land, followed by the deep-blue water of the sea, and the light-blue cloudless sky. The sun directly overhead is making the scenery glisten, and, framed by the rugged mountains, it's a truly spectacular view. To top it off, I can see the road snaking its way down the side of the valley all the way to the coast. Mountain riding in the heat is really gruelling work, but when you get to experience hard earned rewards like this, it's worth every last drop of sweat. I realise that if I'd driven here, then yes, it would be a nice view, but when you've spent 2 hours sweating and grunting to get here, you truly understand how big it is, and you've earned the right to admire its enormity. You now see it as really sweet view.

I get to the seaside town of Isla la Plana by early evening and get the tent setup at the rather expensive campsite on the edge of town. After parting with €36, I take a quick shower and get back on my bike and head into town. Isla la Plana turns out to be a sleepy, somehow untouched, little coastal village, complete with a quite beautiful church set on a small rocky outcrop of land and a shaded village square containing about twenty old blokes quietly playing dominoes. Everywhere I go it makes me fall in love with the place more and more. Every part of this old, unspoilt town looks like it is right out of an airplane's inflight magazine with its stone-built houses and idyllic, and blissful attitude. I guess being protected by a large mountain range, along with the fact the small beach is pebbled, has kept away the more typical tourists. Yet another off-the-beaten-track place I feel blessed to have found on this trip.

I just about make it out of the town before the clicking on the bike is triggering another meltdown. 'Arrgghh! Bloody thing!' I don't know why it's causing me so much aggravation as it's clearly not a major malfunction, but as soon as I start to notice it, it's the only thing I can hear and it fills my ears with an annoyingly, arrhythmic sound. It was clicking badly yesterday during the hill climbs, but this morning it sounds like lose change bouncing around a washing machine. I stop off at the entrance to a campsite and continue to remove every last item connected to the bike one-by-one, cycling in a circle after each removal, trying desperately to find the offending part. It's still bloody clicking! I try everything, I loosen all the movable components slightly, then try tightening them, I even try removing some of them but no, nothing. 'Shut up for Christ's sake!' Why didn't I bring a personal MP3 player to drown out the nauseating noise? Because the radio is causing as much irritation as the bike noises now as it continually loses signal. Sod you, Cycling Oracle and your admittedly appropriate, safety conscious advice.

It's a nice tranquil morning, save for the obvious clicking noises, and there is not a breath of wind, which is making the sea flat and mirror-like, and is beautiful to see as I dip in and out of the small coastal bays. I head inland through Urbanización Playasol, then through a large tunnel and into the bottom of a massive, wide, open valley, flanked by craggy mountain ranges either side. The land is back to barren openness of rock, course earth, and the odd pockets of vegetation that have managed to survive in what is probably horrific growing conditions of blistering sun and gritty soil. There are small areas of agricultural farming, but it is being done with very careful management. There are literally hundreds of massive, plastic tents, spanning up to a square kilometre at a time, there to protect the produce from the harshest rays of the sun, as well as the insects. And there have been massive concrete water collectors cut into the ground to collect the rain water during the wetter times, whenever they might be. It's really impressive to see such adaptation to what is a really harsh environment.

I get to the resort of Aguilas by lunch. On riding down the beachfront, I see a fat guy stood aside a sturdy looking yellow mountain bike with panniers front and back, and furnished with more electronic gadgets than Mr Bond's car. Attached to the bike is a low-slung, single-wheeled trailer which is overflowing with gear. On saying hello, I realise he speaks English and after making a comment about the weather, we move quickly into the game of traveller top-trumps. I try my best, but he beats me hands-down as he informs me he's been travelling for 70 days so far and hopes to complete 10,000 kilometres in total, covering the whole coast of Spain and Portugal. He introduces himself as Gerald and he rode from his home in Germany across to the coastal border between Spain and France before sticking to the coast all the way around. Impressive, especially give he looked well into his 60's, not to mention the amount of extra weight around his waist he's been dragging up the hills. He's got to be well over 20 stone. It's truly admirable that he's gone out and done it at his age, and with his rotund physique. He clearly wasn't an experienced adventurer or an extreme athlete, he was just someone who, like me, decided to get off his arse and do something different. It goes to show that age, as well as weight, are not limits. The only limits are the ones you make up in your own head.

I look over his bike, admiring the kit he had on board and it's pretty impressive. It's not really my type of travelling but the gadgets look good and he proceeds to tell me what they all do. I also note the amount of water he's carrying. There's got to be over 10 litres strapped onto every available space - I guess it's true, fat people do sweat more. I did wonder whether he has had some advice off the Cycling Oracle with all that water, till I note a lack of anything resembling a cycling helmet.

After swapping information about tricky hills to look out for and good campsites to find, I ride off on a mission to take care of my own water supplies. I try to find a supermarket but, not for the first time, I'm stumped. As I stand straddling my bike at a junction, clearly looking confused, a scooter pulls up alongside with a plump, menacing-looking guy on it, his jowly face all scrunched-up beneath the peak of his open-faced bike helmet. 'What do you need?' He asks sternly.

Slightly taken aback by his harsh tone and his funny, rubbery face, I proceed to tell him that I'm looking for somewhere to buy water.

'Follow me.' He instructs in an equally pointy fashion, before riding off as the lights turn green. I follow him for a few minutes, half wondering if I'm being led to impending death, or worse to be used as an afternoon sex-toy by him and his cronies. Just as I'm feeling like I need to scarper, we pull up to a large white building and he simply states 'Here', then rides off before I've even had chance to speak. What a nice guy... I think.

The road out of town hugs the coast on nice flat terrain for a while, passing through more textbook-looking tourist resorts, before cutting inland and back to a craggier landscape. It's pretty tiring, especially given the long day of climbing I've had in the zapping heat. But I'm helped massively by the beeps and waves of encouragement from Spanish-plated cars as they pass. Eventually, the tough, angular terrain stops. I get to the small resort of Villaricos and spot a sign for 'Camping' pointing up ahead. As I ride up I see the site, furnished at the entrance with different international flags high up on flag poles, and notice the sign stating 'Textil Y Nudista'. Hmmm, does that mean what I think it means? I cycle to the attendant's office where he informs me, in very broken English, that to the left is normal camping, but ahead, behind the 5-metre-high, chain-link fence draped in green plastic sheeting, is the naturist section. To clarify, I ask, 'naturist?' complete with a mime of pulling down my shorts along with a double-barrelled cheeky whistle.

'Siiii'. He replies with a smirk that verifies my initial assumptions were correct. I stand there, contemplating what to do for a moment before asking where the supermarket was. I need provisions anyway, but I also need time to consider if I want to experience being tackle-out in a Spanish campsite.

I find the supermarket quite easily and fill my basket with some food and beers, all the while deciding if I want to do a bit of naked camping. I can't help but be giddy about trying something new, I've always been keen to experience new things, but am I OK with being starkers in public, particularly given my strange tan lines? I've done a bit of skinny dipping with Sue before, but it's usually been performed after dark, and typically with a belly full of alcohol. And what's behind that massive curtain anyway? It could be some massive orgy, or just a load of fat old men waiting eagerly for a 'new bit of flesh'. I get finished shopping, pay, and stuff my newly bought goods into my paniers.

I cycle back, ride past the attendant's office, giving him a curt, confident nod along the way then through the staggered fenced entrance. Sod it, no one knows me. As I enter, I'm faced with about 30 camping pitches, segmented with bushes, and with sun-blocking mesh stretched overhead. It's about half full, and it looks exactly like a normal campsite, only with naked people in it. There were no orgies and no rampant old men, just people minding themselves, quietly getting on with being naked. Not wanting to dwell too much so as to make it look like I don't know what I'm doing, I quickly pick my pitch and ride over, not really looking at anyone and am feeling ok about being here. It's a short ride to the pitches and it's going well.... right up to the point when my front wheel digs into a large patch of soft sand, stopping the bike dead, and nearly sending me flying off. I immediately try to put my feet down, but they're stuck firmly into the pedal clips. I start a slow and awkward fall to my right, just managing to grab hold of a tree before I hit the deck. Shit! I'm stuck! My feet won't release from the pedals and I'm wedged at a 45-degree angle, hanging onto the branches of a small tree, frantically trying to wiggle my feet to get free. This really wasn't the low-key entrance I was hoping for.

I eventually get myself free, and, with my dignity long-gone I get to my pitch and dump my bike. Deciding the sticking plaster approach is best, I proceed to confidently strip down without further thought, till I'm stood there stark naked. Feels good! I then proceed to pitch the tent and get all my gear sorted, still naked, although I do the courteous thing and wrap my flag around my waist when I realise how much bending down I need to do to put the pegs in. Some things are best kept to yourself I reckon.

I settle onto my blow-up bed outside my tent, get my book out, and finally feel comfortable enough to have a cheeky look about. I'm not sure on the etiquette on sunglasses, but seeing no one else is wearing them, I take mine off. There is a surprising array of different aged people here. Most are old, but there are young couples also, as well as families. It's quite heart-warming to see a young mother holding a young baby at the tent opposite. There is nothing really sexual about it, it's just naked people enjoying being naked. There are moments when I worry about getting 'too excited', but it's not really in a sexual way, it's more like the way you need to prevent yourself getting the giggles at a funeral. It feels very liberating, although it is a little strange to look down from your book to see your manservant flopped onto your leg. It's refreshing too, particularly after having the boys all squashed up on the bike seat all day. It feels really free and natural, and I just hope I get the chance to do it again this trip. I don't know when I'll get a chance to do it again back home, I'm not sure the British climate is appropriate for going 'tackle out'.

In the morning, I go and wash my pots from last night's tea at the communal sinks where I'm joined by a short old woman of about 70, also in the buff. It feels quite surreal to be stood chatting to a naked old lady whist doing your chores, yet feels so natural at the same time. I start the packing process, again using my Union Jack to protect the fellow naked people from the sight of my Japanese flag. When I finally get to unpegging the tent, I look over to my left and see the sight of the hairiest man I've ever seen get out of a small tent, he looks like Chewbacca with a perm. Not long after, I look over at just the wrong time and realise his missus is a hairy one too as she's bent over, showing me an unbelievably hairy crevice and undercarriage hanging between wide-spread legs! I wonder, with both being so hairy, if they ever get Velcro-ed together and stuck during more adventurous sex sessions?

Back on the road and It's a lovely morning riding under the thankfully cloudy sky. The road is never far away from the sea and I pass beach after beach of glorious, dusty, white sand, segmented by palm-tree-lined resorts containing whitewashed apartments and every type of eatery imaginable. I trundle along, smirking happily to myself over finding yet another amazing experience yesterday, then grimacing slightly at remembering seeing the lady's growly jowls. Another funny experience on this forever-giving adventure.

I make it to the coastal town of Carboneras by lunch. Hungry, I find a nice little eatery at the other end of the waterfront where, on entering, I'm reminded it's Sunday as the place is packed. There's not one free table, and the waiters and waitresses are frantically running around trying to serve everyone by shouting orders through to the bustling kitchen over the din of the chatting diners. It's a really busy place and they seem to be going for the 'survival of the fittest' approach to food retail as everyone is trying to grab the poor waiting-staff's attention. Speaking to the staff seems to be difficult enough, but with the obvious language barrier, I don't really fancy my chances. I consider turning around and leaving but I don't really have much choice as I'm starving hungry, and I'm sure the other places will be just as busy. And if they're not, then they'll probably be crap.

After waiting around for 15 minutes in the melee of people next to the bar, I manage to grab the attention of a short, athletic-looking waitress carrying a selection of empty glasses on a large, round, bin-lid-sized tray. She jabbers something to me over the din of the place as she walks past me around to the other side of the busy bar.

'Uh?' I state back. I know is not helpful, but remembering the last episode of trying to speak Spanish at volume across a bar, I don't want to take any chances.

She hurriedly jabbers something again, but this time I hear the word 'fritas'.

'Ahh chips, Si, Si!' I shout back.

'OK!' she replies dramatically, before writing something down on her pad, slapping it on the frame of the kitchen serving hatch, then having a brief, shouted conversation with a guy on the other side. I fight my way to a newly-vacated table, tight in the corner of the outside space, plonk myself down, and wait in anticipation as to just what will be arriving.

Eventually it arrived and YES! Pork and chips, get in! She bangs it down unceremoniously and scurries off and I'm happy. It's the first bit of solid, non-processed meat I've eaten for a while and is as succulent as a virgin's thighs. I'm a bit of a fussy eater and so this approach to ordering is a bit of a gamble, but it's paid off and I'm happy. No sooner have I finished than the plate is whisked away and replaced with the bill. €6, no wonder it's so busy, even the Spanish love a bargain.

Refuelled and ready, I pay up and bugger off. I climb back out of the seaside location on a really steep incline, which, in the heat, has me holding on tight to my lunch. I'm not wasting €6. The road carries on through more mountains of wild barren countryside which has me reflecting on just how mountainous Spain really is. Almost everywhere I've been in Spain I've been in, or surrounded by, mountains. I'd kind of expected the resort-filled coasts, teeming with drunk, excited tourists, but the mountains have been a big surprise and they make the land so picturesque, yet very humbling. Once you get off the main roads, you can be out alone, without seeing a single car, for hours at a time. And it's also been either super hilly or super flat. When I was in Scotland, I'd started in the mountains and they had slowly petered off as I went down through the country, continuing into the Lake District in England and then flattened out, more or less, as I got down to the south coast. Into France too, it was slow, gradual changes from hills in the north to flat riding before I hit the Pyrenees. In Spain though it's either been big hellish mountains or almost perfectly flat with not really much in-between. I've also been surprised by the quality of the roads, such is the difficult terrain the Spanish have to deal with. Not only are they silky smooth, they are designed in such a way as to engineer out the more undulating parts using large viaducts, or by blowing large trenches or tunnels out of the rock. Judging by the partying attitude of the Spanish people I've met so far, I can't help thinking they've had just a little bit of foreign help on this.

The road flattens out again and I pass through another vast area of white tents. I ride along, walled on all sides by white tarpaulin. I swear I can hear Ed Sheeran out of one of them, I guess that one was the main stage. After cycling through Glastonbury for a bit, I run out of back-lanes and am faced with the unnerving sight of another motorway. I ask for directions at a petrol station, where the 'Oil Distributor' tells me that the only way to continue on is to use the motorway adding, 'It's OK, you're allowed.' I make my way through the tunnel under the motorway then onto the slip road, where I get to watch truck after truck blasting down the 2-laned highway at terrifyingly high speeds. The noise is deafening and fear wells up from the pit of my stomach. Sod that, I'm not getting on there any time soon.

As I'd turned onto the slip road, I had noticed a narrow track running along the side of the motorway and, after deciding this was worth a punt, I shuffle backwards and proceed down it. The nice, smooth, tarmacked road travels safely down the side of the motorway, past a cement works, before turning into a dusty, rubble track. I stop for a moment to consider going back, but spurred on by the noisy, and the fast running traffic to my left, I decide the track is still the more favourable option. Continuing on, the track gets worse and worse till it turns into dust-like sand. I'm left with no alternative but to get off and push as the wheels are getting bogged down in the soft ground. I heave the heavily laden bike through deepening sand, continually weighing up at what point I need to turn back and face the hell of motorway cycling. A quick look at the speed and volume of the motorway traffic is all I need to decide to carry on.

With panic rising a little as to where this track will end, I see a sign over the motorway signalling the next junction, and therefore road, is on the other side of a 20-metre high, sandy mound ahead. Elated, I try to drag my bike up the steep sandy path over the mound, but it's too steep, and, in the heat, too exhausting. I eventually remove the panniers and carry the bike, feet slipping and sinking in the sand, then each of the panniers in turn, up and over the mound. I get to the top after lots of effort and sweating, but I'm rewarded with the beautiful sight of uninterrupted tarmac. YES, I'm back to the open road, though slightly gutted I needed to push again. I can hear Carlos' grating voice now as he tries to dampen my achievement. 'But you didn't ACTUALLY manage to cycle to Gibraltar, did you? You did well, but you didn't QUITE make it all the way'. But that's ok, he knows I'd do exactly the same to him if he ever got sober enough to try it. That's what mates are for after all.

Happy that I now have tarmac under my wheels, I make it the short way to the outskirts of the golfing resort of Retamar before I realise I've got a flatty. I've not been doing too badly for flat tyres of late, but I think all that off-roading was too much for the now balding tyres.

I proceed towards the coast in search of accommodation. On finding out that the only campsite is about 5 miles in the opposite direction, I continue down to the coast where I find a run of about 4 resort hotels. I go into the first one where I know instantly it's not my type of place as I see gold-plated everything and 5 or 6 staff in the grand looking foyer, all wearing the same uniform of pristinely creased, light brown shorts and white polo neck T-shirts sporting the hotel's logo. I try to get a room but am quickly back out after being told it's €140 a night. The next hotel was the same, albeit at the cut down cost of €115, but thankfully the guy behind the desk did show me directions to a more 'appropriate' place, a pension back near the main road.

After getting setup at a very 'appropriate' place for a mere €25, I go looking for a bite to eat. I stroll down the main street but fail to find anything on account of all the restaurants being decidedly 'inappropriate' in this affluent area, and resign myself to a 3-course, a-la-petrol-station meal. Stocked up on sausage rolls, a Curly-Wurly, and a few beers, I leave the petrol station. As I'm on my way back to the hotel, I spot a nice-looking bar around the corner appearing to be serving tapas. Perfect! I go over and in, passing a couple of drunks smoking at the door. Then enter the small, double-roomed bar decorated in various shades of brown and yellow with a long bar at the end. The place is quiet with a few couples in for a quick drink and I settle myself at the bar and, after failing with my Spanish, I order some tapas and a drink by pointing at the menu. Just as I'm getting through a nice few mini-meals, the drunks come back in. And they are legless. The first one is tall, in his 30's and has greased-back, jet-black hair, and is wearing a leather jacket. The other, also in his 30's, is shorter, and is scruffy-looking in jeans and a striped jumper. I sit quietly at the end of the bar as the big one orders 2 double brandies and 2 beers. He then proceeds to annoy the poor barmaid by holding onto her hand for just longer than she's comfortable with after handing her a €50 note he'd pulled off a large roll from his pocket. He's not exactly aggressive, and everyone seems to be laughing at him, but he's overbearing and definitely appears to be putting people slightly on edge.

After a while, he starts propositioning the barmaids and I can see they are playing along a bit, awkwardly smiling, just to try to keep him in tow. He's also around the room, larger than life, kissing everyone's hand, even the guys, whilst the shorter guy stays quiet at the bar. He's obviously well known in here and boy is he a menace!

I've tried to stay incognito, but it's no good and he comes back to the bar and starts to jabber to me in Spanish. Ok, here goes, 'Habla usted Inglés por favor?' I reply, trying to sit as tall and as confident as possible on the high barstool.

'English?! Ahh, Beatles, Rolling Stones!' he drunkenly shouts whilst air-guitaring, 'Awright me old mucca?' he continues in an attempted cockney accent. He understood me then!

He's very funny, but unnerving at the same time and I weigh up whether to stay here or to do one. This could end up being a very interesting evening, or going horrifically wrong. But given that my other option is sitting in my room with a sausage roll watching Spanish TV, I decide to stay.

We get chatting for a bit and the beer starts flowing big time. My new friends, Pablo, and the other one, whose name I keep forgetting, are smashing down the brandies and we're into tabbed rounds before long. It's a good laugh as we try talking in broken English - it was so broken that I think at a number of points we end up having different conversations. But as we're all legless by now, it's kind of immaterial. Pablo can't stop laughing, real over the top laughter mixed with over-loud talking. He's a real reprobate and the more drunk I get the more the alarm-bells start ringing about this fella and I start to feel uncomfortable. At one point, he asks me if I am gay. And when I reply with a resounding no, he briefly looks a bit gutted. He also gets talking about AC-DC for a while, which I think is a way of saying someone is bisexual. He's such a big youth and, given his overbearing attitude, he looks the type of bloke that if he wants something he'll have it, regardless of anyone else's thoughts. I start sobering up through natural self-preservation, weighing up the situation and what Pablo just might have in mind. Eventually, the unnerving feeling gets the better of me and, with Pablo now gone to the toilet, I ask for the bill, ready to leave - I think he's probably fine but I don't want to take any chances. But when the waitress tells me Pablo has already paid my bill, my survival instinct kicks up to 11 and I grab my plastic bag, and I jump off my bar seat ready to do one. Pablo's little mate tries to stop me, but I complain of needing sleep and calmly walk out of the door. Then, when I get around the corner, I run as fast as my flip-flops will allow back to the sanctuary of my room and bolt the door!

After a night spent worried that the door was going to get smashed through, I pass through the massive city of Almería by mid-morning, where I stop off for breakfast and to update my blog at a McDonald's. I also start scouring the internet for more 'naturist' sites and it appears that there are a few along the coast, though sadly not that many. I get my map out and excitedly mark on the locations of the few that I find. I ride down the Almería port access roads, passing massive yachts and cruise ships. Once through the city, I stop off for a rest from the now blistering heat. It definitely feels like the heat's gone up a notch today. Still sniggering at having possibly been offered man-love last night, I reflect back and realise that at no point, other than last night, have I ever felt really threatened on this trip and even that might have been a misunderstanding. There was the small 'disagreement' with the English boy at the restaurant when he told me I was too loud, but that wasn't really anything. Even though it feels a bit crazy and care-free, not once in Spain have I ever felt in a proper predicament. I'm sure if you go in Madrid or Barcelona, you'll find an El Moss-Side, but out here, on the coast, they seem to be more interested in liberal partying and having fun than causing grief.

Out of the city and the road, a main, single-carriageway carved out from the coastal rocky-mountains, hugs the coastline and gives beautiful flat riding and views over the rich blue sea. The sun is hot and the brightness is lighting up the scenery, showing it off to its best with the sun glistening off the ripples of the sea. As the road takes me in and out of the various nooks and crannies of the coastline, I pass near-deserted beaches and I start looking for opportunities for a skinny-dip. Given that I don't really have anything to use as a cover whilst changing into my swimming shorts, skinny-dipping is going to be my only option for a swim in this soaring heat. And besides, I now realise that being naked outdoors is absolutely brilliant!

I pass a number of secluded resort hotels, all with tiny beaches, and all tucked away with the surrounding rock giving the feeling of uninterrupted privacy. Sadly though, I run out of road before I get a naked-dipping opportunity and I get into the large, bustling, built-up holiday areas of Aguadulce, then onto Roquetas del Mar. I spot another pharmacy thermometer/clock, which states it's 38° and 13:16. Wow, I knew it was getting hot again, but that's a record equalling high. The miles are getting chomped up, in spite of the incessant heat, and I make it to the industrial port-town of Adra by mid-afternoon where I'd put a big fat X on my map. Hoping for some more nakedness, I make into the town and ask a street-vendor selling lottery tickets for directions to the campsite, but am gutted when he signals it's closed. Ah well, 'Hotel, por favor?' I then ask hopefully.

'Errm, no.' He replies after mulling it over, 'Momento'. He then gets up, struggles onto his crutches and over in the direction of a flower seller across the street. I gesture for him to stay put, realising both legs are badly deformed. But he's adamant, and after an awkward and painstaking minute, he makes it over to his mate 10 yards away. Now don't I feel the tight git!? They proceed to natter for a while before the flower seller points me back in the direction I'd just come, and to the Hostal Familia Zapata.

The hotel turns out be a full-on family affair as the name suggests. Granddad is the owner, the grandkid is the porter - who earned himself a shiny 1 euro coin for hauling all my gear up to the room - and dad simply lounges around the foyer playing games on his phone. Another good €25 spent as it got me bed, breakfast, and a tour of the store-cupboard to see dad's fine array of both road and mountain bikes. He was a nice bloke, besides being lazy, and he lent me a foot pump to blow up my tyres after fixing yet more punctures.

After a morning of repairs, I bid them farewell as they tuck into a nice family breakfast cooked by grandpa and served by grandchild, with dad responsible for condiments, and leave. As I cycle along through more breathtaking coastal roads, I note that I was actually quite bored last night, and actually, I've been a bit bored during the riding recently too. I'm seeing some fantastic scenery, particularly in the hills, but now my body is the perfect specimen of a MAMIL, along with the fact I'm proper acclimatised now, the riding is, in general, nice drift-along riding. It is pleasant, with a nice feeling of wellbeing, but it is not bringing anywhere near the same contrasting feelings of euphoria and despair I've had along the way. The views are still breath-taking, as are the beaches and I am still really excited to be doing this, but I guess as with everything, if it's easy, some of the reward is lost. I've also had enough time now to get things straight in my head. I was so disgruntled with my 'normal life' and about who I'd become and for why? I had a great life, good friends, a good job, no money worries, and a wife that loved me even through my grumpier times. I make a mental note to thank her for not punching me in the face, because I must have been a right git to live with sometimes, most of the time probably. I've always been a self-soother and this trip seems to have given me a chance to rehabilitate. I've been through so much that I have confidence in myself again, confidence to stick at something even when it has been at its toughest.

But now that I've found a bit of that guy I was 20 years ago, the riding has sadly turned into a 'Sunday ride', albeit a bloody long one. I think that is why, subconsciously, I've been trying to actively seek out the fun stuff, such as drunkenness and nakedness - my own as well as from female magicians - in an attempt to keep this trip from petering out. I think I've been looking to perk up the adventure, which made sitting in my hotel room last night just a little bit of a drag. I decide I need to get back to my tent. I like it in the tent, even though the stench is now beyond horrific. I need to get back to campsites full of overexcited Spanish. I need to get back to being a drunkard again.

I get to the small coastal resort of Castell de Ferro and decide to stop off for a rest. The beach is quite stony, and therefore rather undesirable for the normal holiday maker, but this also means it's not too busy and is a beautiful scene of tranquillity. There are palm trees right the way down the short waterfront walk, which is bordered from the beach by a 2-foot high wall and is the perfect place for a sunbathe. I get some water and an ice-cream from a small shop on the front before lying back on the wall outside to enjoy an afternoon snooze.

I quickly drop into the no-man's land of not really awake, but not asleep either, and rest peacefully with the sun beating down on my face. I turn a few times, trying to even out the sharp edges of tan lines, and it's bliss.

After about an hour or so I hear a 'pssst, pssst'. Ignoring it, I keep my eyes closed, but it starts again moments later, 'pssst, pssst', only this time louder. I slowly open one eye, shading it from the bright sun with my hand, to see the bespectacled shop keeper standing about 2-metres-away bent over sideways. 'Pssst' he states again, only this time I see he's waving a bottle of water at me! I sit with a smile, take the water and, taken aback by his kind offering, I proceed in thanking him in 4 languages; English, French, Italian for some reason, and then finally finding it in Spanish! What a nice bloke, and another of those small gestures that fills me with joy.

I get to Calahonda where I consider stopping off for a bit but, given my new role is as a drunk Brit, I want to do the miles and get to my anticipated destination of Motril. I plough on back inland and back into farming land again, and through the inevitable fields of large, white, plastic tents. I never stop appreciating the effort that must have been put into creating these massive structures. I guess without them, these flat open spaces would be filled with nothing and probably half the population of Europe would be without oranges. I also note that I've not seen any farm animals that I can remember, which seems rather strange. I wonder if it's the heat that is too much for them, or maybe it's that they've all been killed off by the matadors.

I get to Porto Motril by late afternoon, eagerly anticipating a night of getting drunk. But when I get into town, I'm gutted to find it's almost deserted. I'm further distressed as I cycle up the main street to see a large woman in white leggings with the material thinning as it stretches out over a massive, bulbous behind. And she's had bad bum sweats, leaving a brown sweaty stain down the middle. I ride past her nearly retching, trying desperately to un-see it.

I wake to the unsettling sound of something scratting about inside my tent. When I bring up the courage to pull my head off the pillow of clothes, I find a kitten has made it under the outside skin of the tent and is trying to prise its way into my food-bag! 'Get out you little shit!' I shout, to which he calmly pauses, gives me the death-stare cats have mastered so well, before casually traipsing off back under the side of the tent. I think it'd smelt my weakness, either that or the pâté, although I was surprised it could smell either given the stench of the tent.

Breakfast this morning is more of the tomato and olive oil stuff on baguette, and it's bloody lovely. I never get bored of this and it's a nice refreshing start to the day. After a friendly wave and a 'Hola' from a girl hanging out of the top floor flat above a lap-dancing club, I am back onto the main road heading west. It's a busy, single carriageway road and I'm left to survive by trundling along in the emergency lane, trying to dodge all manner of items discarded along the road. Including my nemesis, broken glass. It's a filthy stretch of road and it heads inland for miles, before I'm back onto the meandering and undulating terrain of the coast.

Spurred on by the fact that I think I've located another naturist campsite at Torre del Mar, about 40 miles from here, I giddily make my way along the coast till I get yet another flatty. The rubber of the tyres is still holding up. But with the knobbly tread long since gone, the main body of the tyres must be getting rather thin, and are no match for the mighty glass. I change the inner tube in a layby next to a rather nice marble cross at the roadside. I wonder how it's not been nicked yet, but I guess even the thieves don't chance messing with the 'big-man'. After fixing the puncture in 35+ degrees, and uttering a few words of divine intervention at the cross, I'm back travelling, and back to the Krypton Factor styled challenge of dodging all manner of items in the emergency lane. I'm starting to get rather worried about getting stuck in the middle of nowhere with a flat tyre in this heat, especially given I find I've left one of my repair kits, which annoyingly also contained my spare lock key, in the hotel in Adra and I'm now getting low on patches.

After asking a few people, I eventually find a bike shop and stock up on 2 new spare tubes and 2 replacement repair kits. On reflection, this is quite an extravagant purchase for someone as financially careful as me, especially given I'm so close to the end. But, the roads are getting really bad and the thought of standing around in the middle of nowhere in this heat, hoping someone will give me a lift, is enough to spur me on. And besides, they were only €3 each.

The road undulates heavily, and the downhill parts give good long sections of fast freewheeling, however the uphill sections bring on the inevitable slow grinds where I'm helped by more beeping cars and their smiling, waving drivers as they pass. There's still no sign of a skinny-dipping opportunity, however this is not through want of trying. On seeing a bunch of women walking from an overflowing carpark down a dirt track in the middle of nowhere, I ask them what was special enough to bring so many people to this remote beach.

'Oh, it's a beach of special nature', one of them replied.

'Oh, nature... Naturist?!' I ask, complete with the double-barrelled whistle and a mime of removing of shorts.

'NO! It is of beautiful nature!'

'Oh, right.' I think I'm getting a bit obsessed.

I stop for lunch at El Morch, then carry on through Mezquitilla where I finally find a skinny-dipping opportunity! After cycling through the town, I notice a spot where the road is almost directly next to the sea, only high up, leaving a steep bank of rocks of about 20 feet in between. I contemplate riding on to the naturist campsite ahead, however I figure why wait till later if you can do it now? I lock my bike up, then climb down the rocks. I give a few furtive glances, both left and right, as well as up, and then quickly strip down and in. Even though I'm on the bend of a really busy road, because it is so high up, I am almost invisible and I relax in the sloshing tidal water laughing my head off at the cheekiness of being naked. It's so relaxing to be out of the sun and cooling in the water, as well as liberating to have your big-fella wafting around in the current of the water. Ahhhhh, bliss!!

With the giddiness of the prospect of another naturist campsite on the other side of Torre del Mar I eventually sneak out, get dressed and then off. I pass through the elongated town, stretched thinly as it hugs the coastline for the best use of the beautiful beach and glorious views of the south Mediterranean Sea. It's quite a lively place with bars and restaurants lined up down the main street. I decide instantly that I'm going to be having a day off tomorrow, maybe this is the place I can let out my inner 'drunkard Brit'.

I get to the campsite via a long lane off the main road and am excited to see it advertised as a 'naturiste' site. But, after leaning my bike against the wall, eventually, I go inside only to be denied by the young, beautiful attendant, who I had hoped was also keen on a bit of naturism. As I walked into the reception, she immediately looks surprised, and verified it is a naturist site. When I confirmed with a big beaming grin though, she asked me for my naturist card which I obviously didn't have. Apparently, naturism has an international association, which issue cards. It's like a naked version of the 'Caravan and Camping Club'. So sadly, I'm denied. However, on the way out I spot a sign for the 'nudist beach'. I'll be back and naked in due course....

I get setup at a campsite almost in the centre of Torre Del Mar, which turns out to be a very close second to being naked. The place is packed, and when I get put on the end of a small triangle of grass, surrounded by nutty drunk Spaniards, I know I'm in the right place. After putting the tent up, I crack a couple of cans and drift off to sleep. I wake after a short powernap, open my eyes and look down to my side to see a plastic see-through beaker containing crushed ice and the minty leaves of a Mojito cocktail! Confused, I slowly look around and find a coolly dressed couple of about 40 sat on camping chairs, saluting me with their own Mojitos raised high. They look like old hippies, the lady wearing a flower dress, and the guy in a cotton shirt and shorts. 'Nice one, errr, merci... ', I reply holding the drink up in their direction, trying to come around after the sleep. They give me a smile and carry on with their conversation. Brilliant, another small offering and another amazing feeling. I am falling in love with Spain, big time. They go on to feed me with pistachio nuts, whilst I lie in the sun drinking bottomless Mojitos. Every time I stop, they come over and offer me more nuts or a top-up of booze from their large jug of the stuff. I wish, not for the first time on this trip, that I could speak bloody Spanish.

So, it turns out that my new hippy mate has the deepest voice known to man. Last night, whilst we were sharing their drinks, he was very quiet, mainly leaving the talking to his missus. But later, when I was trying to get to sleep, he got very drunk and was talking louder and louder, and my god was his voice deep. He made Brian Blessed sound like a pre-pubescent choir boy. It was more comical than annoying and I eventually got to sleep, overcome by exhaustion and alcohol… on my slowly deflating bed.

With today being a day off, I go for a wander into town and after a haircut and shave, I find it's market day and I buy a present for Sue, and a new pair of under-crackers for me on account of the others now being beyond repair. I'm actually thinking I might splash out on a new set of clothes to wear on the plane home for the sake of the other passengers, and to ensure I don't get divorced the instant I walk through the arrivals lounge.

I was looking at the maps last night and I was surprised to find I'm a little over 100 miles away from Gibraltar. I am so close to the end and it's kind of crept up on me. My mind has been drifting towards thoughts of home more and more, but I've just been plodding through the miles and I now realise I'm 2 medium-length cycling days away from the end. At this rate, I'm going to have a nice few days in Gibraltar before my flight, which Sue has booked for me in 6 days' time. And if I don't go home piled high with gifts, I know I'll not be allowed on another trip anytime soon.

I cycle up to the nudist beach just after lunch and, again not knowing the etiquette on nakedness, I stand in the remote carpark and strip off. It feels weird, but really comical to be stood completely naked, save for a pair of flip-flops, in the middle of a carpark.

After smothering my more sensitive areas in suntan lotion, I pay my €2 fee to enter and find a spot high up the beach. The place is quite quiet and I settle in on the unbearably hot volcanic sand. I am shocked, and slightly disappointed to find this is a completely different experience to the liberating, care-free approach of the naturist campsite a few days ago. Instead of a serene setting, at one with nature, the place is full of posers walking up and down the beach in sunglasses, and I actually feel a bit self-conscious, particularly given my strong, 2-tone tan. Most people seem to be in couples and I see a lot of all male pairs, which I can only assume are gay couples after considering that it's highly unlikely I'd go for a naked day at the beach with any of my own mates.

On the plus side though, given the higher calibre of participant, some of the women are absolutely stunning. But it's ok as I needed to concentrate on topping up the tan on my back anyway.

After an hour or so bubbling away on the beach, relieved with regular cool downs in the clear sea, I head back to the tent. I go for a walk late in the afternoon to find a bustling and pleasant seaside town. There are families of holiday makers everywhere, all enjoying the beautiful grey beach and large grassed promenade, complete with palm trees, paved walkways and a large bandstand in the middle. There are loads of street entertainers out too, mainly consisting of singers and bands, and I walk along the front, nonchalantly admiring the surroundings, knowing deep down I've come here with an ulterior motive. I walk for about 20 minutes or so before I choose my moment.... to bring the mighty warrior that is Manion Friday back to life!

Look who I found....

Look who I found hiding out in the Costa del Sol..... And good news, he's coming home!!!

So, it turns out he's not dead!!! He says there was a scam going with the Columbians and something to do with life insurance. He got in too deep with the 'happy dust' and they told him it was his only option. He was whisked over to the Costa del Sol by Ronnie Biggs' old crew and given a (crap) makeover with a pen as it was all they had to work with.

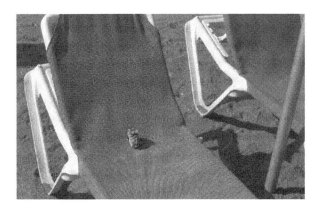

He realises there may be some people who want to 'speak to him' in the UK but he wants to get back to his 'brother from another mother'.

I'd actually decided to resurrect him a few days ago. I know I'll be home at some point soon and, whilst I know Mavo actually doesn't really care about this little plastic toy, I think it would be a nice thing to give him back anyway. Manion has been a valued member of the team and has helped me out no end, even with his scary grin. So, on getting close to the end, I decided he needed to be found alive and, in fitting with being on the Costa del Sol, the home to many absconded British criminals, what better way to come back to life than with a faked death and a makeover!

I wake with the familiar sound of someone regurgitating lungs full of phlegm. It is not a nice sound at all and is made worse this morning by the fact there is actually a chorus of them going on. There are about 3 or so, trying desperately to release the tar filled fat and it's enough for me to decide that I am going to have a day off the fags today. I've only been smoking a few each day, in the evenings, but I don't want to get back to needing to smoke constantly once I get home.

For breakfast, I revisit a place I found last night that was doing 3 tapas for €2, which, even by my standards, is deemed good value. I got dinner and a beer for €3.20, happy days. For breakfast this morning, I get more of those toasted half-baguettes with grated tomato and olive oil I am now addicted to, and a shot of strong, thick coffee, something else I may need to wean myself off once I get back to the UK.

For what seems like the first time since I got into Spain, the temperature this morning is bordering on acceptable for cycling. It's cloudy and there is a slight cold breeze and, on finishing my coffee, I am quickly on my way along the coast again, taking advantage of the favourable conditions. It's amazing what a difference it makes as the miles trickle by without notice. The pleasurable morning's riding is only broken as the road feeds me unknowingly onto a motorway, leaving me to fend for my life as trucks and cars fly past at varying uncomfortable speeds. The roads in Spain are nice and smooth, and I am continually impressed by their structure and ability to handle such undulating terrain, but my god are they confusing. There just doesn't seem to be any order to them, or at least, none that I can understand anyway. There is no description by road names, such M is a motorway and so-on. There are also sections where it is almost impossible to get from one place to another without going on the motorway, like this one, but that's ok, because some of the motorways you can ride a bike on anyway! It seems that the development of the road system went through two, clearly defined, stages. The first, was performed over 100's of years and resulted in a network of small, poor quality roads connecting places with tricky navigation. But then something happened, and they finally found some money to build a smaller, but wider and more impressive network of larger roads and motorways. This large network, which connects most of the country, is impressive but sometimes it seems that they simply couldn't be bothered to connect every town with an alternative to the motorway and so, rather than adding a new road, they simply allow bicycles, and presumably walkers, to go on it. Spanish-style problem solving; simply change the rules to make problems disappear.

With the precarious motorway riding safely negotiated, I continue on the more tranquil single carriageway costal road and eventually into the large city of Malaga. I stop off at the large port and observe what can only be described as a sea of wealth. The port, which seems to have been revamped recently by the clean modern look of the place, is bordered by large apartment blocks, and is filled with massive yachts and cruise ships. The stench of money is nauseating, particularly given the ostentatious manner in which it is being displayed. It's in distinct contrast to the little villages I've been passing all morning. I don't like it here. I move on quickly.

I travel out of the heart of the city and along a massive dual carriageway carrying 3 lanes in each direction. I don't think is a motorway, but who the hell knows. I pass by the airport and the traffic is unreal, the noise in itself is bad, but the speed at which the traffic is travelling is really discomforting. It feels like I've been teleported from a Simon and Garfunkel gig this morning to a happy hard-core rave. I will never get used to the feeling of coming into a busy area after spending hours out in the countryside.

As I approach lunch, my stomach gives me this nod and I start keeping a lookout for a place to eat. I know I'm not going to find some nice little eatery whilst travelling down this massive connection route, so I guess it's going to have to be some fast food place. I have a love/hate relationship with McDonald's, but as I see those golden arches glistening on the horizon, I know the devil today will win-out. Besides, my body is doing that thing again where it is screaming out for required nutrition of sugar and salt, and the thought of a meal with a large coke and fries is making my mouth water. But when I get closer, I am blessed with a sight in the background that makes all junk-food enthusiasts weak at the knees; an Ikea superstore.

To most, Ikea is known for its cheap, but robust, easily constructed home furnishings. However, what is more appealing right now is the fact they do long hotdogs and fries for 60p each, or the Euro equivalent, as well as cups of coke with unlimited refills. The temptation is too great and so, with rather a few strange looks, I go into the store where I am absolutely devastated to find they are out of fries, and the drinks machine is not working. I'm left with a couple of hotdogs and a bottle of diet coke, neither of which quashes my junk food desires. Still, at least lunch for €2 puts a smile on my face. I wonder if Sir Ranulph Fiennes ever ate Ikea hotdogs when out exploring?

After a rather crap lunch, I continue on and am instantly into the huge resorts that bleed into each other along this coast. The road I'm on flirts around the outside of the built-up areas, but a massive road sign stretching right over the 6-

lane highway tells me I'm first into Torremolinos, before cycling past Benalmadena, then Torrequebrada, and Torremuelle. The road climbs a bit and falls a bit but the overriding sense at the moment, apart from the busyness of the road, is just how tacky the places are. I hate this type of resort for their crassness and unimaginative approach to holidaying. I am conscious of the fact I don't have kids and so maybe this is the reason I don't see their appeal. But there is nothing really interesting, or unique about any of them. There is nothing new to experience or to appreciate, it's just full of British people all getting sloshed on British lager and eating British food. Everything seems so plastic, a façade to draw as much of your holiday money out as possible. I guess if you have kids, maybe knowing you're in a place where everyone speaks English is easy and convenient, leaving you to enjoy the simple activity of being with your children. But for me, I want to be in places where I get laughed at for not speaking the language, I want to have to point at my food and to do silly mimes to get what I need. I want to see how other countries live, and to embrace their cultures. I know how the British are and, whilst I like our silly little ways, I don't want to be engulfed in it when I'm on holiday, I want to be able to get out of my comfort zone and to see a country in its true colours. This, I can conclude, is everything travelling by bicycle is, and obviously, a whole lot more beside.

I make it to Fuengirola, and finally to a place in Spain I've been before. I came here for a week when Carlos lived here, but I don't remember anything of the town I have seen so far. It was only about 10 years ago, but it all looks so different. I guess being in February when I was last here it was a lot quieter, and being drunk the whole week, it was also a lot hazier. I give Carlos a call and I instantly regret it as he tries to work out exactly where I am based on what bars and hotels I can see.

'Can you see the Hotel Yamar?'

'No'

'What about Franco's Bar, can you see Franco's Bar?'

'No.'

'It's a massive place near a little ice-cream shop thingy?'

'No.'

'Are you near, oh what's it called. Errm, bloody hell, It's a pub with a red sign.'

'No.'

'It's next to a pizza place.'

'No.'

'Are you even looking?!'

'No.'

'Are you even in Fuengirola?'

'Yes, but it's a big place mate and I can't be arsed with your questioning. Besides, it was years ago that you were here.'

'Guess so. Oh, are you near the port?'

'Shut up and tell me where the campsite is in Fuegurola?'

'Hahahaha! You nazzy shit! Have a drink and calm down!'

He laughed himself stupid at my irritation for a few minutes till he composed himself enough to tell me that the campsite was on the way out of the town. I didn't realise I was getting annoyed but I guess being in such a claustrophobic place is making me itch. I think I've also got the unsettling feeling that my journey is slowly coming to a close. For the last 50 days, all I've had to think about is finding food and water, locating accommodation and, of course cycling. Now I have deadlines to maintain, as well as sorting out having my bike packed for transfer, and ensuring my luggage is not overweight, and that's even before the blag of adjusting to life in the normal world when I get home. I know these would normally seem like simple tasks, but given I've not really needed to think about anything for a while, these things seem to be engulfing my mind. I like to know everything is in order otherwise I feel uncomfortable and, whilst I know deep down everything will be fine, I can't help the feeling that I just want to be in Gibraltar now, knowing everything is organised and I'm ready to fly home. I just don't want any hassles to deal with right now as I'm not sure if I could cope.

I find the campsite at the other side of the town. But after finding it will be €35 for a plot, I decide to move on. and am told by the attendant that the only way along this part of the coast is by using the horrifyingly fast road I crossed over. It looked very much like a motorway, as well as being noticeably void of other cyclists or, more worryingly, any form of emergency lane.

On building up the courage, I'm onto the slow, or more accurately less-fast, lane of a motorway - oh, if the Cycling Oracle could see me now I'm sure he'd wee a little bit with worry. The road continues along the waterline, about 50 feet from the sea, and I pass resort after resort, but this is of little significance as I barrel along as fast as I can with death now more than a little nagging feeling. I am really, really scared.

I safely make it the 5 miles it takes to get to the next town and to 'Camping Los Jarales' at Calahonda. That has got to be the scariest, and fastest bit of riding I have done so far and I'm thankful when one of the Chuckle Brothers behind the desk at the campsite office tells me its €25 for the night. It's worth every penny to not be on that horrific road.

After pitching the tent, I go in search of a beer and am happy to find a bar located on the first floor of a building next door. On entering, I find it is empty except for a guy sat at the end of the bar watching Birmingham City v Derby County on Sky Sports. It's a large place and is dimly lit with low-lit ceiling lights, and by various coloured neon strip-lights behind the bar. As I walk in, both the barman and the lowly punter turn to look at me, before being distracted by an incident on the telly and start shouting at it.

I grab a seat at the bar and order a pint and eventually get into a conversation with the only other customer who introduces himself as Trevor. He's a stocky bloke of little over 5 feet, and looks quite trim for the 64 years old he tells me he is. He's wearing shorts and a T-shirt, which displays the successful completion of the 3-peaks challenge he completed in 2014. When I ask him about it, he informs me it was the 4th time he'd done the race, and that it entails climbing the highest mountains in mainland UK comprising of Ben Nevis in Scotland, Scafell Pike in England, and Snowdon in Wales, and they all must be completed in a 24-hour window. He's got a real broad Geordie accent and I have some trouble understanding him, leaving a short delay after he speaks for my sleepy brain to process his words like we're on a long-distance telephone call. He turns out to be a really interesting guy and he proceeds to tell me how he owns two small businesses, one as a roofer, the other in scaffolding. He's clearly minted as he tells me he's semi-retired and lives 2 weeks in Newcastle and 2 in his apartment down the road. He's the kind of grafter I have utmost respect for as he's worked hard and is driven to succeed in everything he does. He's made his money from blood, sweat and tears. He reminds me a lot of Carlos' dad, Les, who also made money under his own steam, building himself up from nothing. This is not really something I particularly want to do in life, but I totally respect the 'give it your all' approach to doing things. If you're going to do it, give it your best shot. An approach I consider has got me a long way over the last couple of months.

We talk for ages and cover all sorts of conversations including children. He is gutted to find out I don't have any and excitedly insists that I should while I have the chance. When I ask him if he has any, he replies that he does. 'Eye, ah 'as 1 girl of me own, but ah has brought up about 5 on and off'. I decided not to pry any further.

He is an amazing character and, after insisting on buying me a few beers as a celebration for getting this far, I get up to leave. He'd previously asked me how my funds were going, to which I'd told him they were getting drastically low. And so, as I get off my stool, he pulls a massive wad of notes out of his pocket and tries to give me a €50 note. I keep saying no, but he is insistent and it seems like he'll be a bit insulted if I don't accept. I eventually take it, deciding instantly that I'll give it to the Macmillan cancer charity when I return.

What a bloody horrific night's sleep. I have grown to really love the Spanish over the last few weeks, not that I didn't before, but by Christ are they noisy. At 2:00, I was woken by someone revving the nuts off their car. And at 4:00, four youths were having a good old chat right outside my tent till I did the truly British thing of projectile tutting.

I find a small café for some breakfast and take advantage of being in 'Little Britain' with a full English fry-up - I need the hit this morning. Whilst waiting for it to arrive, I get the maps out and workspace I've only got about 50 miles left, well within my abilities for a single day's riding, providing the traffic doesn't kill me first of course. I remember Trevor last night telling me they call this main road 'death road', due to the number of fatalities that occur on it. He also mentioned there were no other options to get west along the coast, other than cycling an extra 200 miles detour through the mountains. I was absolutely going to see the worst of it, which lies between here and Marbella.

With a mere 50 miles to do to get to Gibraltar, I contemplate how best to spend the rest of my days. Sue has booked my flight for the August the 26th, which leaves me 4 days to get there and to get things sorted out ready for flying home. So, I can either do another day off somewhere, or I could keep going and have a more chilled out time at the end in the nice campsite Gerald mentioned back in Aguilas. I feel really exhausted this morning, not least due to being awake a lot in the night, but I think I'm also feeling the exhaustion of my body and mind knowing it's nearly over. I know this feeling from when I've been walking where, whenever you get near to the end, you mentally and physically loose the drive to complete the task. All the aches and pains take over and it becomes a real effort again. It doesn't matter if it's a long or a short distance, when you get to the end, you subconsciously allow yourself to hurt again, and you know you're ready to stop.

So, I think I am going to try to make it Gibraltar today. If I see a nice site or something of interest, such as a spot of naturism for example, then I'll stop, but otherwise, I think I'm going to try to get to the end. Finally, after 53 days, I'm ready to not be doing this anymore.

I head off back onto death road and am instantly into fearful riding again. The traffic is so fast and comes way too close given the lack of an emergency lane for me to use, and it has me involuntarily putting my war face on and shouting like a Banshee. I stop a few times to rest my heart and my twitching bum, as well as to ask a few people for alternative directions in hope that there is any other way of getting west without being on this road. But sadly, nope.

I get to Marbella and it seems a nice place in general, but I'm really not feeling it this morning. It's a big bustling city and is full of interesting displays such as the 'El Piruli de Marbella', a cone shaped, copper covered lantern over 50 metres high; and the 'Avenida del Mar', a pedestrian walkway filled with various sculptures including work by Salvador Dalí. There are structures and pieces of artwork everywhere, and it's an interesting place to be, but it's way too busy for my brain to cope and besides, I now realise I just want to be at Gibraltar. So, after a short chill in the shade of the densely populated trees in the 'Parque de Alameda', I decide I need to leave.

I travel through the city's suburbs and progress is really tough, even though the roads are pretty flat. All morning I've been fighting this lethargy that seems to have taken over me since accepting the end is near, and it's a real strain to keep my lactic-acid-filled legs turning the wheels.

The built-up areas drift almost seamlessly into each other but as I get into the extremely affluent area of Puerto Banús, the surroundings start to change. The road is now flanked with massive houses, all crisply whitewashed and protected by huge gates and 5-metre-high whitewashed boundary walls. The number of expensive motors that pass by increases dramatically as well. I'm passed by Bentleys, top-end Audis and Range Rovers, all pimped up with that extra little bit of bling with bespoke items like strip-style headlights and shiny wheel trims. I feel a little out of place in my salt-stained Lycra, right up till the point I see a Burger King. I guess even the super-rich like a bit of junk food now and again.

I'm back on the horrendous motorway that is not a motorway and then into Estepona, which is actually a really nice version of a tacky-resort. The high-rises seemed to have been limited to 5-stories-high and so it gives the place a less in-your-face feeling of money-driven tourism. It's just a bit more classy when compared to the other resorts in the Costa del Sol. But again, I have an ulterior motive for today and I cycle on with heavy legs in my quest for the end. This really feels like a battle of wills between me and myself, but I know, eventually, I will make it to the end today. As I get out of the town, in the thankful comfort of a cycle lane, I look up across the sea and there it is, for the first time, I can see the 'Rock of Gibraltar' rising out of the water in the far distance down the coast. I wasn't expecting to see it so soon, but it's so massive that it's clearly visible over the flat water even though I'm still over 20 miles away. I stop for a moment, hoping to feel some excited emotion of triumph. But nothing. I guess this will come later.

The road continues on along the coast through golfing resorts and gated estates complete with security guards which, by the look of them, are more for decadence than for safety. The area seems to be getting richer and richer as I head further south and I feel slightly uncomfortable in the pomposity of the few people I meet. Although I guess I'm not looking – or smelling - my best at the moment.

I head ever deeper into the cul-de-sac at the foot of Spain. I climb away from the coast and into the countryside where I see my first road sign for

Gibraltar. Wow! I'm getting really close now! The road takes me up and over the hill and through farmland till eventually I get to see it again, the massive 'Rock of Gibraltar' sticking out of the flat expanse of land and sea all around. Gibraltar is a small peninsular sticking out from the bottom of Spain, and is a little over 2.5 square miles in size. It is absolutely dominated by the 400-metre-high Gibraltar Rock which takes up most of its footprint of the land, leaving the Gibraltarians to continually reclaim the sea for building on. On the Spanish side of the border, there is the large town of La Línea de la Concepción whose population of 65,000 is predominantly made up of people who work in Gibraltar but live in Spain, taking advantage of the significantly lower cost of housing.

I take a break at a large layby high up the mountain where I can see the mass of buildings of La Linear sprouting out from the acute angle of land adjoining the border. It feels strange to be here, and not quite the excitement filled moment I'd thought it was going to be. I was expecting a buzz from head to toe from the feeling of accomplishment, having cycled close to 3,000 miles in 53 days. I was expecting to be excitedly jumping in the air, trying to kiss the closest person I can, wanting to tell anyone how amazing it's been and what I have been through to get here. But I don't. I know in my head that this was an amazing accomplishment for me, but I don't want to jump in the air, and I don't feel like kissing the closest person - which is lucky because the car next to me has two weed-smoking teenagers in it - and I don't want to shout about my achievement. I just want to go home.

I'm kind of disappointed in myself and my attitude to what should be a very special moment. I should be happier about being here but I'm not, and I suddenly realise that this moment was only ever going to be a disappointment. After all, this moment is the start of the end. This is the closedown of a very special and amazing experience and, whilst not finished yet, it is only a matter of time till it is all over. This trip was always about the journey and not really about the end. I made Gibraltar a target because I like to have things to aim for, things to achieve. But that was just a small part of this amazing adventure. The main part, the most important part by far, is what I've been through to get here. It was the places I've been, the things I've seen and the people I've met. It was about seeing wild deer and an eagle, and about seeing Knight Rider. It was about meeting travelling unicyclists and partying campers as well as ladies awkwardly hiding objects about their person, as well as people wanting man-love.

But more important than any of that, it was about me. It was about testing myself, testing my guile and my ability to survive when things got tough. It was me reaffirming who I am and what I can do when I set my mind to it. It was about getting off my ever-fattening backside and about getting out there and to challenge myself. I needed time to think without the complexities of life getting in the way. I needed to break myself out of the grumpy downward spiral I had created. I needed time to look back and be proud of who I am, to realise how lucky I am. I needed to think of the past, but to look to the future and to get excited again about where my life might take me next. And now I'm here, I can be happy in the fact I've achieved all that. And if I can make it the last couple of miles down this hill without falling off, I can proudly add to the achievement of cycling from John O'Groats to Gibraltar... with Manion Friday's help of course.

Chapter 13: ...To Home

So, after finding the campsite on the outskirts of La Linea last night I went for a few beers and some tapas. Before giving into temptation and cycling across to Gibraltar....

.... The campsite is run by a children's mental hospital located right next to it and it employs some of the patients to perform some of the basic maintenance tasks. And the place is spotless because of it. All the paths and facilities are completely clean of everything as the workers busied themselves late into the evening. No sooner has one of the leaves of the many bushes and trees hit the deck then there was a steward to clean it up. It's a very surreal setup, but after a while I realised it makes perfect sense; cheap labour for the owners, a sense of worth for the workers, and a clean environment for the customers. Everyone's a winner!

The site was very quiet, but I did meet a very strange, gaunt looking man of about 60 who was doing a tour in a little, 3-wheeler Piaggio van. He was from Switzerland and was quite annoying, although that may have been to do with the fact he was convinced he'd beaten me in a game of traveller top-trumps. He'd travelled further than me at 7000km to my 4500km, had been travelling for 4 more days than me at 57 to my 53, and had 1 more wheel. But everyone knows that power supersedes all other statistics, and that leg power is the Lamborghini Countach of the cycling-top-trumps cards. Leg power beats petrol power every day of the week!

I went for some tapas and a beer, before temptation got the better of me and I went back to my tent, dug out my passport for the first time since the UK, and headed the 1 mile it took to get to the border. I had originally decided to wait till today to get over the line, but I couldn't resist it and so I went through the border, across the airport runway that crosses the border access road, did a U-turn, and came straight back.

As I sit here at a beach bar, chewing on yet another tasty breakfast of grated tomato and olive oil topped baguettes, I can proudly state that I am a man that has cycled from John O'Groats to Gibraltar. Ok, so I walked about 50 yards but the rest was ridden. And proudly, I can state I only fell off once, even though it was quite a spectacular one in the awkward setting of a nudist camp. I guess I'm an average type of bloke, but I got out of my comfortable life and I did it. And it feels good, really bloody good. I feel a pride I hope will last me a long time. Of course, I don't really know what will happen in the future, but I definitely feel a cleaner, purer person than the one I left behind nearly 2 months ago. My head was a mush of anger and dejection and I didn't really know what to do. But this journey has given me the opportunity to declutter my overflowing mind and now I feel focused and more relaxed with the world. I hope that I can keep this going because I'm happy with myself for the first time in a long time and with it, I'm once again happy with my life.

With breakfast now devoured and the bill paid, I complete one last blog before I go back to Gibraltar and perform some necessary tasks like throwing the stone I carried from Scotland into the sea, sorting out my travel home, and of course, going to see the Gibraltar Apes....

... So, with the trip now finished, I wait it out for my flight home, I guess the number one question is would I do it all over again? Well.... would you?

MISSION ACCOMPLISHED!!

So, it's all done! After 54 days (I think!) and over 2500 miles I have reached the end of the greatest journey of my life! And how does it feel? Well a bit shit to be honest! But I guess it was always going to be an anti-climax given this thing was all about the adventure rather than the end point. I am a bit gutted that it's over and at one point considered the option of riding back!! Although, I am looking forward to seeing Sue more than I can describe, and to eating one of her Sunday roasts!

I guess it goes without saying that you don't pursue a challenge like this without necessity, and I've achieved what I wanted out of this, and more. I've seen some great places, eaten some great foods and remembered that I can be a resourceful mother fucker with the heart of an ox when I need to!!

So, I've been thinking about which country I enjoyed the best and I have to say I like them all for different reasons. To expand, if the countries were women:

Scotland would be a fitness freak, very angular and ripped. She'd be a triathlete who does a power shake for breakfast and can tell how well you are from the colour of your piss. But sadly, she has no boobs....

England would be very beautiful and soft. She'd be all mother. She'd wear a flowery dress and be comforting and nurturing. Though don't forget she can still smash down the Pimms and do a donor kebab when she decides to.....

France, now France is a high-end escort girl. She's elegant, classy and spends more on lingerie than she spends on fags – which is a lot! You know she'd give you the night of your life, however you can't see it lasting past breakfast....

Spain is a big hipped, characterful mental case! She's got massive norks and likes nothing better than getting your face and burying it in them. She's a party girl who loves a laugh and is hot as hell!!

So, I like them all, but my god, I really love Spain....

Thanks for the support and helpful advice, it was a real pick me up to see so many had read the blogs.

Peace out (till the next one!!)

If you liked my story, please drop me a message or post a review on Amazon.

There are pictures available at:
https://offtoseetheapes.travellerspoint.com/

Thank you for reading… now go find your own adventure!

23924419R00157

Printed in Poland
by Amazon Fulfillment
Poland Sp. z o.o., Wrocław